D1570093

RESIDUES OF JUSTICE

RESIDUES
OF JUSTICE

LITERATURE, LAW, PHILOSOPHY

WAI CHEE DIMOCK

University of California Press

Berkeley · Los Angeles · London

The use of previously published portions of this book is
gratefully acknowledged:
"Class, Gender, and a History of Metonomy," from *Rethinking Class: Literary Studies and Social Formations*, edited by
Wai Chee Dimock and Michael T. Gilmore. Copyright ©
1994 by Columbia University Press. Reprinted with permission of the publisher.

"Criminal Law, Female Virtue, and the Rise of Liberalism,"
reprinted by permission from *Yale Journal of Law and the
Humanities* 4 (Summer 1992).

"The Economy of Pain," reprinted by permission from
Raritan: A Quarterly Review, Vol. IX, No. 4 (Spring 1990).
Copyright © 1990 by *Raritan*, 31 Mine St., New Brunswick,
N.J., 08903.

"Rightful Subjectivity," reprinted by permission from *Yale
Journal of Criticism* 4 (Fall 1990).

University of California Press
Berkeley and Los Angeles, California

University of California Press, Ltd.
London, England

Library of Congress Cataloging-in-Publication Data

Dimock, Wai Chee, 1953–
    Residues of justice : literature, law, philosophy / Wai
Chee Dimock.
        p.   cm.
    Includes bibliographical references and index.
    ISBN 0–520–20243–0 (alk. paper)
    1. Justice in literature.   2. Justice.   3. Justice
(Philosophy)   I. Title.
PN56.J87D56   1996
809'.93353—dc20   95-39867
                                                  CIP

Printed in the United States of America
9 8 7 6 5 4 3 2 1

The paper used in this publication meets the minimum requirements of American National Standard for Information
Sciences—Permanence of Paper for Printed Library Mate-
rials, ANSI Z39.48-1984.

To the memory of my father

The very mercy of the law cries out
Most audible, even from his proper tongue,
"An Angelo for Claudio, death for death!"
Haste still pays haste, and leisure answers leisure;
Like doth quit like, and measure still for measure.

William Shakespeare, 1604

Contents

Acknowledgments

This book took some unexpected turns in the years that I spent writing and rewriting it; it would never have ventured upon its present path without the help of my colleagues at Brandeis. I especially thank John Burt, Mary Campbell, Billy Flesch, Timo Gilmore, and Susan Staves for their wackiness, their erudition, their habit of argument, and their forbearance. At an earlier stage, Walter Benn Michaels, Toni Morrison, and Richard Poirier made this book possible in ways they might not have suspected. Laura Kendrick kept me going, often from hundreds and sometimes from thousands of miles away. Sacvan Bercovitch, Richard Brodhead, Morton Horwitz, Mary Poovey, Carroll Smith-Rosenberg, and Alan Trachtenberg not only read various chapters, they are also vital presences throughout, offering inspiration, provocation, admonition. My dog Ishi, a vital presence as well, has done much to sharpen my thinking about luck and desert. My heartfelt gratitude goes also to the editorial staff at the University of California Press, especially Doris Kretschmer, who began supporting this book many years ago, and Alice Falk, who went over the manuscript with meticulous care. To Paul Schechter, for the pleasure of his conversations, and for his example that justice is not all, my deep thanks.

In the last letter that he wrote me, before his sudden death in 1993, my father asked about this project, reassuring me that books must sometimes take precedence over parents. I only hope that some of his wisdom and great good humor have found their way into this particular book. It is, in any case, dedicated to his memory, and will always miss having him for a reader.

Introduction:
Justice and Commensurability

A bitter dispute has broken out between Aeschylus and Euripides, for dead poets, it appears, are not immune from those jealousies and rivalries that plague their living counterparts. As Aristophanes recounts this episode in his farcical play *The Frogs*, what occasions the dispute is a certain dining privilege—a chair by Pluto's side—a privilege long enjoyed by Aeschylus, but which Euripides, new arrival in the underworld, now fancies his due. And so the battle lines are drawn and the poets stand before Dionysus, taunting each other and hacking away at each other's poetry until, after some lapse of time, an enormous pair of scales is brought out to settle the dispute. "Poetry will be measured by the pound, . . . weighed in scales like so much butcher's meat,"[1] Aristophanes tells us, and the heavier one will be declared the winner. Three times the poets go to the scales, throwing in their respective lines, and each time Aeschylus wins hands down, for, unlike Euripides, who speaks only of "light and feather-brained" things (such as persuasion), Aeschylus has wisely gone in for the heavy topics. In one line, for instance, "Two chariots and two corpses he heaved in. / A hundred gypsies couldn't hoist them."[2] It is not much of a contest, after all.

The Frogs is, of course, a parody of justice, a parody of the way disputes are settled, conflicting claims resolved, a binding verdict arrived at. And yet the object of its parody, or at least the material emblem of it, is perhaps more organic than we might think to a conception of justice that is not meant to be parodic, a conception that takes itself, in all seriousness, as a normative ideal, the transcendent end of an adjudicative process. The conceit of the scales, I suggest, is central to our idea of justice, central to it in a rather fundamental sense, not only as a figure of speech but also as a figure of thought. For it is this conceit, with its attendant assumptions about the generalizability, proportionality, and commensurability of the world, that under-

1

writes the self-image of justice as a supreme instance of adequation, a "fitness" at once immanent and without residue, one that perfectly matches burdens and benefits, action and reaction, resolving all conflicting terms into a weighable equivalence. The language of justice, I want to argue, is first and foremost a set of cognitive postulates, a set of grammatical propositions describing the world and, not infrequently, dissolving the world in the very act of describing it, converting it into a common measure, a common evaluative currency, grounding the very possibility for adjudication on the possibility of such a currency. The language of justice is thus a language of formal universals, one that translates warring particulars into commensurate ratios, that takes stock of the world and assigns due weight to disparate things. Such a language, I argue, is most graphically expressed by that adjudicative instrument long taken to be its emblem: the scales.

Aristophanes, then, was both more and less parodic than he might first appear. Less, because the scales of justice are actually serious business, and more, because what is being ridiculed here is not so much a particularly absurd instance of judgment (though this one is certainly memorable) as the ground of judgment itself. That ground, I have tried to suggest, is something like a premise of commensurability, a premise about the weighable equivalences of the world and about the solvability of conflict on that basis. The search for justice, in that sense, is very much an exercise in abstraction, and perhaps an exercise in reduction as well, stripping away apparent differences to reveal an underlying order, an order intelligible, in the long run, perhaps only in quantitative terms. Aristophanes was, in any case, not the only one to wonder about the reductive grounding of justice. This was the uneasy sense as well of none other than Aristotle, who, in the much-discussed Book 5 of the *Nicomachean Ethics*, would give an eminently unparodic (though hardly untroubled) account of the numerical equivalences underwriting the idea of justice:

> The just, then, is a species of the proportionate (proportion being not a property only of the kind of number which consists of abstract units, but of number in general). For proportion is equality of ratios, . . . and the unjust is what violates the proportion.[3]

Distinguishing between different forms of justice, Aristotle goes on to relate them to different forms of proportionality. Distributive justice, for example, should be conceived "in accordance with geometrical proportion" (for the just here "involves at least four terms," that is, at least two recipients of distribution in respective proportion to two distributive shares). Rectificatory justice, by contrast, should be conceived "in accordance with arithmetical proportion" (for here, "injustice being an inequality" arising from the fact that "one has received and the other has inflicted a wound," the task of the judge is simply "to equalize things by means of the penalty, . . . subtracting from that which has more, and add[ing] to that which has less"). And, finally, when it comes to justice in exchange, where "all things that are exchanged must be somehow comparable," Aristotle points to money as a necessary (if regrettable) instrument, for "money, acting as a measure, makes goods commensurate and equates them."[4]

As an epistemology which subjects disparate terms to a uniform reckoning—an epistemology which translates the tongues of Babel into a common language of ratios and equivalences—justice would seem to be the most elementary as well as most encompassing of virtues, one whose jurisdiction is not only coextensive with the world but in some sense constitutive of the world, one that not only covers all agents and all events but "weighs" each in turn, resolving each of them into a common measure of right and wrong, merit and desert, obligation and entitlement. Justice is thus often thought of as "complete virtue," "virtue entire," and "proverbially 'in justice is every virtue comprehended.' "[5] Still—and the point is worth emphasizing—that comprehensive justice does not seem to be Aristotle's own working definition. Indeed, in marked contrast to the breadth of the proverbial claim, his own understanding of justice turns out to be surprisingly modest, carrying with it always a definitional disclaimer, a conscious shying away from any presumed totality. "But at all events what we are investigating is the justice which is a *part* of virtue," he says, and "the justice, then, which answers to the whole of virtue . . . we may leave on one side."[6] The justice that concerns Aristotle is neither equatable with nor exhaustive of all imaginable human goodness; its operative limit—its inability to encompass the full range of experience, the full range of the ethically desirable—suggests that its domain is to be imagined not as one of adequacy but as one of necessary supplementarity: a domain by definition nonabsolute, incomplete.[7]

It is this scrupulous restraint on Aristotle's part—his refusal to "cover" the field, as it were—that is progressively eroded in the ascendancy of justice as a philosophical concept,[8] an ascendancy most powerfully shaped by Kant and most powerfully exemplified, in our own time, by John Rawls. "Justice is the first virtue of social institutions, as truth is of systems of thought," Rawls writes in the opening paragraphs of *A Theory of Justice* (1971), a book regarded by many as a twentieth-century counterpart to the *Nicomachean Ethics.* Justice, for Rawls, is analogous to truth not only because it presides as an absolute ideal but also because it exists as an ontological given. Whether or not it is actually achieved, it will always be imagined as having an objective reality, a reality coincidental with the immanent relations among things and discoverable through a rational process of deliberation. Indeed, Rawls sees justice as nothing less than the axiomatic expression of human reason itself: it is "the choice which rational men would make" when their reason is given free rein, uncompromised by particular interests. Understood as the ideal endpoint of reason, justice is thus the first virtue not only of all social institutions but of all "human activities," embraced by all "free and rational persons," and underwriting "the fundamental terms of their association."[9]

This expansive claim made on behalf of justice is not unique to philosophers. In our commonsensical understanding as well we tend to see justice as a virtue at once transcendent and intrinsic, foundational and all-encompassing, a virtue descriptively answering to the shape of the world and expressively answering to the scope of human reason. We worry, perhaps, about the local implementations of justice; but the idea itself—its ethical primacy and its descriptive adequacy—is almost never questioned.[10] Justice, as our admiring idiom attests, is something that will eventually (and sometimes instantly) "prevail," not as a construct but as a kind of indwelling truth: an ethical order objectively immanent in, and therefore objectively deducible from, any given conflictual situation and adjudicative context. As John Stuart Mill says, "the powerful sentiment" of justice and the "apparently clear perception which that word recalls" are such as to make it "resembl[e] an instinct." At once reflexive of the world and incarnate in what it reflects, the concept carries with it an aura of the axiomatic, a kind of ontological coincidence with the world, so much so that "to the majority of thinkers" it seems almost to be "an inherent quality in things," as if "the Just must have an existence in Nature as something absolute."[11]

The broad ambition of this book is to unsettle this axiomatic conception of justice: to make it less immanent, less exhaustive, less self-evident both in its ethical primacy and in its jurisdictional scope. Justice, I want to argue, is one particular virtue, one virtue among others. And, rather than invoking it as a sovereign ideal, we should perhaps grant it no more than a particular claim, a conditional claim, on our allegiance. This nonfoundational character of justice is worth emphasizing, for its language—a language whose charge is to disentangle the world, to resolve its conflicts into a commensurate order—is a language that abstracts as much as it translates and omits as much as it abstracts. Focusing, then, on "commensurability" as a central premise (and a central embarrassment) within the language of justice, I call attention to the porousness of that language, a porousness especially noticeable and especially worrisome when seen against the stubborn densities of human experience. What issues from that linguistic porousness, I would also argue, is a category of "residues": residues unsubsumed and unresolved by any order of the commensurate, residues that introduce a lingering question, if nothing else, into any program of justice, whether corrective, distributive, compensatory, or revolutionary.

I am encouraged in this immodest undertaking by Mill's suggestion that "the feeling of justice might be a peculiar instinct, and might yet require, like our other instincts, to be controlled and enlightened by a higher reason."[12] For Mill, that "higher reason" answers to a very definite name, the name of social utility. But without embracing his particular advocacies, we might benefit, nonetheless, both from his skepticism about the absolute claims of justice and from his attempt to circumscribe its domain, to emphasize its incomplete summation of human goodness. In this context, it is especially helpful to be reminded that, etymologically as well as historically, justice is a derivative concept, given primacy only under the rule of law, only with the legal mediation of human relations. It is the "most legal of the virtues."[13] "*Justum*," Mill tells us, "is a form of *jussum*, that which has been ordered. Δίκαιον comes directly from δίκη, a suit at law. *Recht*, from which came *right* and *righteous*, is synonymous with law," and "*la justice*, in French, is the established term for judicature," so that there can "be no doubt that the *idée mère*, the primitive element, in the formation of the notion of justice, was conformity to law."[14] Given this genetic history, justice is thus centrally predicated on the notions of rewardability and punishability, the twin operative tenets of the law. And it is predicated, above all, on the notion of "adequate repayment," which in practice (and perhaps in spirit as well) is how the law dispenses both punishment and reward:

> No rule on the subject recommends itself so strongly to the primitive and spontaneous sentiment of justice as the *lex talionis*, an eye for an eye and a tooth for a tooth, ... and when retribution accidentally falls on an offender in that precise shape, the general feeling of satisfaction evinced, bears witness how natural is the sentiment to which this re-payment in kind is acceptable. ... The principle, therefore, of giving to each what they deserve, that is, good for good as well as evil for evil, is not only included within the idea of Justice as we have defined it, but is a proper object of that intensity of sentiment, which places the Just, in human estimation, above the simply Expedient.[15]

Extrapolating further from Mill, we might say that justice is ultimately a form of reification: the reification of commensurability itself. The commensurate order—good for good and evil for evil—is taken, that is, to be something of a natural order, an objective relation between the two terms in question, as if one good could equal another good in the way that one eye equals another eye, or one evil could equal another evil in the way that one tooth equals another tooth. It is this dream of objective adequation which makes the concept of justice intelligible in the first place: intelligible not only in retributive justice, where we yearn for a punishment equal to the crime, and not only in compensatory justice, where we yearn for a redress equal to the injury, but also, I might add, in distributive justice, where we yearn for a benefit equal to the desert.

Against this dream of objective adequation—this dream that the world can be resolved into matching terms, fully recuperative of each other or fully corrective to each other—I want to make a contrary claim on behalf of the incommensurate, understood both as the operative conditions and possibly as the operative limits of justice. What concerns me is the abiding presence—the desolation as well as the consolation—of what remains unredressed, unrecovered, noncorresponding. The phenomenon I have in mind is something like that of being "lost in translation," a phenomenon at work in any adjudicative process, any attempt to unify two disparate terms, to make them conform to a principle of equivalence. This skepticism about the adequacy of any commensurate order has been argued most lucidly by

Isaiah Berlin and Bernard Williams, among others.[16] There is no translation without loss, they suggest, nor conflict-resolution without residue. Beginning with this crucial insight, this book takes as its subject
the losses as well as the residues occasioned by the exercise of justice,
surely the oldest, most ambitious, and most comprehensive translation project in human history and one that, like human history itself,
perhaps derives its intelligibility as much from what it fails to register
as from what it does register. I want to foreground the epistemological violence entailed in this process as well as those moments when
this process is palpably tangential to the world, palpably impoverish-
ing of the world, moments when its descriptive thinness and experiential harshness cry out for supplements.

This critique of justice is not, I am happy to say, solely or idio-
syncratically my own. Here I want to acknowledge two domains of
discourse in which this critique has been most energetically argued:
political philosophy and feminist theory. I have in mind Michael Sandel's *Liberalism and the Limits of Justice* and Carol Gilligan's *In a Different Voice*, both published in 1982 and both (emphatically in the case of
Sandel and obliquely in the case of Gilligan) issuing in a challenge to
the image of justice as a virtue sufficient unto itself. Sandel argues that
justice, absolute and underived as it might seem, is actually predicated on two prior constructs—about the subject of justice, and about
the circumstances of justice—neither of which can be said to be empirically exhaustive or epistemologically foundational. And so, against
the dream of rational adequation in Rawls, and against the dream of
rational adequation within the entire Kantian tradition, Sandel argues that justice is a necessarily limited concept, not because it can
never be fully realized in practice but because "the limits reside in the
ideal itself."[17] Gilligan, meanwhile, from the perspective of feminist
developmental theory, posits two contrasting ethics—what she calls
an ethic of justice and an ethic of care—the former characteristic of
men and espousing a "formal logic of fairness," the latter characteristic of women and embracing a "cumulative knowledge of human
relationships." Justice, for Gilligan, is literally an incomplete virtue,
occupying no more than one-half of the ethical field. Its abstract impulse toward "balancing claims," she argues, must be tempered by a
contextual awareness of responsibility "as given rather than as freely
contracted."[18]

Indebted to both Sandel and Gilligan, my study also represents, I

justice is limited

— INCOMPLETE

hope, a historicized departure from both. Unlike Gilligan, I am reluctant to see justice as a rigidly gendered phenomenon, a rigidly locatable axis of differentiation between men and women. I am reluctant, in particular, to accept her model of causality, one elaborated strictly within the domain of object relations and glossing the concept of justice as, in effect, a function of male ego psychology. Against this unduly restricted (and unduly polarized) account, I want to experiment with an analytic frame of somewhat broader scope and perhaps less determinate boundaries. The concept of justice is historically interesting, I want to suggest, not because it crystallizes the psychic opposition between men and women but because the concept itself has never been without a zone of problematic residuum, a zone marked above all by the nontransparent relation between the various descriptive languages enlisted on its behalf. What especially intrigues me, then, is the "uneven primacy" of justice—the varying breadth of its claims and the varying fitness of its resolutions—a phenomenon analyzable not only across time but also across the cultural landscape at any given moment; for the differentiation among cultural domains must bring into play, I think, a significant unevenness among their languages of justice.[19] This book is a history of that unevenness. It is a history of two primary languages of justice, law and philosophy (as instanced by the changing jurisdiction of criminal law, or the changing definitions of torts, or the ascendancy of rights as an ethical norm). And it is a history, as well, of an alternative language, the language of literature: one that dispenses justice almost as a generic requisite and brings to that dispensation almost a generic question mark.

And here, departing not only from Gilligan but also from Sandel, I examine the concept of justice not as a unitary given (not as the settled expression of male psychology, in the case of Gilligan, or as the settled foundation of Western philosophy, in the case of Sandel), but as a concept more or less migratory and more or less mercurial in its migrations. Absolute and categoric in philosophy, negotiable and assignable in law, wayward and unsatisfactory in literature, justice, dispensed in different operative theaters, seems to carry different causal circumferences, different modes of evidence, and to yield up different styles of knowledge as well as different descriptive textures of the world. These conflicting images of justice call into question the self-evidence of that concept as well as its claim to being the axiomatic expression of human reason.

Indeed, it is the axiomatic nature of "reason" itself, its transcendent unity and its categorical imperative, that this book hopes in part to complicate, in part to contest. Putting aside its received image—as an objective given, unwavering in its trajectory and unvarious in its expression—I want to experiment with a *nonintegral* conception of reason, theorizing it, that is, as a field of uneven definition: more heterogeneous, more responsive to contrary plausibilities, and therefore less harmonizing, less effective as a foundational guarantee. Imagined as the ground for disagreement rather than the ground of commensurability,[20] human reason might turn out to underwrite not a unified propositional universe but many domains of thought, many styles of reasoning—overlapping to some degree, but not necessarily reconcilable with one another and certainly not collapsible into one another. These cognitive domains make up so many languages, so many inflecting media, for the idea of justice. This book is a tribute to their multiple inflections. Almost by necessity, then, this is a synthetic project, ranging incautiously but perhaps unavoidably from political theory to legal history, cognitive linguistics, even theology, and shuttling back and forth between Aristotle and Augustine, Kant and Marx, Locke and Luther, Noam Chomsky and John Rawls.

Alongside these figures, and in emphatic challenge to some of them, I will also be looking at a rather diverse group of nineteenth-century American authors—Herman Melville and Rebecca Harding Davis, Jonathan Edwards and Susan Warner, Walt Whitman, James Fenimore Cooper, William Dean Howells, Kate Chopin—although this is not, strictly speaking, an attempt to redesign the shape of American literary history. It is, rather, a series of intense (and sometimes counterintuitive) engagements with a group of texts that, to my mind, offer some of the most vivid demonstrations not only of the historical meanings of justice but also of its historically problematic relation to the densities and textures of human lives. It is among these literary texts, I argue, that we can encounter the idea of justice not as a formal universal, and not as an objective relation among things, but as a provisional dictate, an *incomplete* dictate, haunted always by what it fails to encompass. Literary justice is a point of commensurability rationally arrived at, but it is simultaneously registered as a loss, a strain, a necessary abstraction that necessarily does violence to what it abstracts. Such an image of justice, sedimented out of the cognitive conundrums of a different tradition and carrying with it a different vocabulary, a different language with which to describe the world and what matters in that world, must stand as a supplement and a corrective to any legal or philosophical propositions.

Rather than being a formal logic, justice in these literary texts is a phenomenon whose lineaments are traceable in the fate of some specific characters, generating not only an ever-widening horizon of meaning but also an ever-widening spectrum of queries. From the democratic personhood in "Song of Myself" to the economic personhood in *Life in the Iron Mills*, from the punitive fervor of *The Deerslayer* to the compensatory fervor of *The Rise of Silas Lapham*, from the luck-driven universe of *The Wide, Wide World* to the rights-driven universe of *The Awakening*, the problem of justice is given a face and a voice, a density of feature that plays havoc with any uniform scale of measurement and brings to every act of judicial weighing the shadow of an unweighable residue. In the persistence of that residue, in the sense of mismatch, the sense of shortfall, that burdens the endings of these texts, we have the most eloquent dissent from that canon of rational adequation so blandly maintained in philosophy and law. Overlapping with both but reducible to neither, justice as a literary dream (and often as a literary nightmare) remains a live issue not for what it manages to put to rest, but for what it fails to.

We might think of literature, then, as the textualization of justice, the transposition of its clean abstractions into the messiness of representation. We might think of it, as well, as the historicization of justice, the transposition of a universal language into a historical semantics: a language given meaning by many particular contexts, saturated with the nuances and inflections of its many usages. Such a semantics of justice can serve no single purpose, even as it can tend toward no unified end. Literature, in this sense, might be said to be the very domain of the incommensurate, the very domain of the nonintegral. In its signal failure to make good its logic, to affirm the adequacy of any rational order, it denies us the promise extended by law and philosophy both. But for that very reason it is a testing ground no jurist or philosopher can afford to ignore. For if the image of justice is here rendered back to us, most often with a shock of recognition, at some rare moments, moments miraculous but not necessarily dismissible, it might also come back to us with a difference, a difference that is both less and more than the dream of objective adequation which justice is: less out of forbearance, and more out of hope.

lit textualizes justice

1

Crime and Punishment

In an unusually striking and indeed unusually chilling moment in *The Philosophy of Law* (1796), Kant takes it upon himself to defend the death penalty. He defends it not on the ground that it is socially efficacious but on the ground that it is philosophically coherent. The death penalty represents the workings of justice at its most absolute and most complete, Kant argues, for what it embodies, what it executes as law, is nothing other than the principle of commensurability, the fitness that comes from matching "Like with Like." And likeness, in this case, can only mean the "Equalization of Punishment with Crime":

> It is just the Principle of Equality, by which the pointer of the Scale of Justice is made to incline no more to the one side than the other. . . . This is the Right of Retaliation (*jus talionis*); and properly understood, it is the only Principle which . . . can definitely assign both the quality and the quantity of a just penalty. All other standards are wavering and uncertain; and on account of other considerations involved in them, they contain no principle conformable to the sentence of pure and strict Justice. . . . [For this reason] whoever has committed Murder, must *die*. . . . There is no *Likeness* or proportion between Life, however painful, and Death; and therefore there is no Equality between the crime of Murder and the retaliation of it but what is judicially accomplished by the execution of the Criminal. . . . This ought to be done in order that every one may realize the desert of his deeds, and that bloodguiltiness may not remain upon the people. . . . The Equalization of Punishment with Crime is therefore only possible by the cognition of the Judge extending even to the penalty of Death.[1]

Kant begins, uneventfully enough, with the familiar image of the Scale of Justice, invoked here to dramatize equality under the law, an equality distributed among all its juridical subjects. Almost immediately, however, this distributive equality is transposed onto a different axis, transposed, that is, into a retributive equality, a relation of "likeness or proportion" between "deed" and "desert," between what one does and what is done to one in return. Retributive equality dictates that punishment must be commensurate with the crime—must be fully answerable to it, or, more to the point, fully exhaustive of it—for it is only with this full correspondence that there can be full annulment, so that everything will be resolved, leaving behind no residue, no "bloodguiltiness . . . remain[ing] upon the people." The death penalty, a closed circuit of act and consequence, thus stands for Kant not only as a specific instance of "an adequate Retaliation after the principle of 'Like with Like' "[2] but also as a supreme instance, perhaps *the* supreme instance, of a rationality adequate unto itself. As such, it is the highest form of justice, justice "pure and strict," imaging forth in its very transcendence and conclusiveness the ideal shape of Reason itself.[3]

KANT, NIETZSCHE, BECCARIA

Far from being an anomaly or an embarrassment, Kant's penal theory, I want to suggest, actually dramatizes and literalizes his philosophy, bringing into the foreground the presumptive equivalence which underwrites his image of Reason as integral and self-adequating, a point too little acknowledged by philosophers who call themselves Kantians.[4] This presumptive equivalence, in any case, is what intrigues and appalls Nietzsche when he observes that "ethics has never lost its reek of blood and torture—not even in Kant." Why is it that in our thinking about justice there is always this "sinister knitting together of the two ideas, guilt and pain," not only in the sense that guilt is imagined to have brought pain into the world but also in the sense that pain is imagined to be the proper answer, the proper sequel and remedy, to guilt, as if its dispensation could somehow obliterate guilt by a kind of corrective equivalence? Why is it that "the infliction of pain provide[s] satisfaction"?

These are the questions that Nietzsche asks, gleefully, importunely, and maniacally, in *The Genealogy of Morals* (1887). By way of answer, he points to the cognitive style of "primitive thought," which, according to him, had always been a barter mentality, dominated by the idea of the commensurate, the idea "that everything has its price, everything can be paid for." That barter mentality gave rise to the "oldest and naivest moral canon of justice." "The mind of early man," Nietzsche says, "was preoccupied to such an extent with price making, assessment of values, the devising and exchange of equivalents, that, in a certain sense, this may be said to have constituted his thinking."[5] Given this history of human cognition—given its genesis under the auspices of trade—it is not surprising that there should arise

> the notion that for every damage there could somehow be found an equivalent, by which that damage might be compensated—if necessary in the pain of the doer. To the question how did that ancient, deep-rooted, still firmly established notion of an equivalency between damage and pain arise, the answer is, briefly: it arose in the contractual relation between creditor and debtor, which is as old as the notion of "legal subjects" itself and which in its turn points back to the basic practices of purchase, sale, barter, and trade.[6]

Nietzsche's genealogy of morals offers one way to historicize the transcendent claims of justice in Kant, a historicization which suggests that the concept of justice, far from being a categorical imperative, might turn out itself to be a categorical derivation: derived, that is, from the lowly habit of commerce—the habit of purchase, sale, barter, and trade.

In my own attempt to explore the limits of justice and to give voice to what is not encompassed or resolved by that concept, this chapter is clearly indebted to *The Genealogy of Morals*. At the same time, the Nietzschean genealogy itself, in making justice a cognitive effect of barter—and thus primordial, universal, and instinctual—would seem to be conceding away too much analytic space, and so strikes me as being, in turn, in need of historicization, if it is to retain any degree of explanatory (or perhaps even descriptive) specificity. It is that historicized genealogy, a more nuanced and more densely elaborated supplement to the Nietzschean thesis, that I want to develop here. More specifically, I want to examine punitive justice not as a relic from times immemorial but as a cognitive mode that has continued to evolve, its scope, purpose, and rationale being shaped and reshaped by its many contexts of action. In this chapter, I will focus on one particular context, the transition from classical republicanism to modern liberalism in early-nineteenth-century America, a development which, to my mind, not only had direct bearings on the boundaries of the punitive but also opened up a new set of expressive venues (and a new set of conceptual conundrums) for that most enduring and most problematic of ideas, the idea of the "commensurate."

Beginning, then, with punitive justice as one attempt at the com-

mensurate, one among others, I will try to map out some of its operative features, its imperatives and embarrassments as it evolves, taking
on new guises and new meanings. And in the end, I want to suggest
that its trajectory is an uneven one: unevenly articulated in different cultural domains, marked by different jurisdictional scopes, different signifying radii, different degrees of resolution, and engender-
ing along the way different orders of perplexities as well as different
kinds of residues. These uneven developments are the subject of this
book as I try to sort out the many faces of the commensurate, not only
in punitive justice but also in distributive justice, not only in matters of
morality but also in matters of polity, and not only within the precincts of criminal law but also under the rubric of novelistic justice.

Toward that end, the conversation here between Kant and Nietzsche might well be imagined as a two-way conversation: an intended
critique of Kant by Nietzsche, to be sure, and—not intended, not ordinarily argued, but entertainable nonetheless—a historicization of
Nietzsche by Kant. For *The Philosophy of Law* had a genealogy that
was, after all, less primordial than the one imagined by Nietzsche as
dating back to the "primitive thought" of "early man." Primitive or
not, Kant was writing in the late eighteenth century and was, moreover, goaded into doing so, goaded most especially by the penal reforms just then sweeping across Europe. If there was a note of hys-
teria in his defense of the death penalty, that was no doubt because he
had been witnessing for some time the phenomenal success of his adversary, Cesare Beccaria, whose treatise on penal reform, *On Crimes
and Punishments*, first published in Tuscany in 1764, was translated
into French in 1766: translated by Morellet, annotated by Diderot,
prefaced by Voltaire, and enshrined instantly as one of the supreme
credos of the Enlightenment. Beccaria was hailed as the "Socrates of
our epoch,"[7] winning the rapt attention not only of the Paris intelli-
gentsia but also of a number of monarchs, including Frederick II of
Prussia, Maria Teresa of Austria, Grand Duke Leopold of Tuscany,
and Catherine the Great of Russia, who called upon the author to
reside at her court and supervise the necessary reforms in person.[8] In
less exalted circles, Blackstone also featured Beccaria in his *Commentaries on the Laws of England*, while Bentham was moved to call him
"my master, first evangelist of Reason."[9] Meanwhile, in the American
colonies, John Adams, as a young lawyer in 1770, saw fit to invoke
"the words of the marquis Beccaria" to defend the British soldiers

implicated in the Boston Massacre—to such effect that none of them was found guilty of murder.[10] Jefferson, too, copied into his *Commonplace Book* long passages from Beccaria, to guide future legal reform in Virginia.[11]

In the name of Reason, Enlightenment Reason, Beccaria rejected the death penalty in no uncertain terms. If "I can show that death is neither useful nor necessary I shall have gained the cause of humanity," he announced conspicuously in the chapter devoted to that subject. The crucial word here was "useful," a supreme criterion for Beccaria, for it was "the idea of *common utility* which is the foundation of human justice." And upon this foundation, Beccaria argued that a "just" punishment should be no more than what would "suffice to deter men from committing crimes."[12] The purpose of punishment, in other words, was not to exact atonement for the crime already committed but to prevent crimes from being committed afresh. And it was because of its inadequacy as a preventive measure that Beccaria would come to reject the death penalty in favor of something more efficient, namely, life imprisonment:

> It is not the terrible yet momentary spectacle of the death of a wretch, but the long and painful example of a man deprived of liberty, who, having become a beast of burden, recompenses with his labors the society he has offended, which is the strongest curb against crimes. That efficacious idea—efficacious, because very often repeated to ourselves—"I myself shall be reduced to so long and miserable a condition if I commit a similar misdeed" is far more potent than the idea of death, which men envision always at an obscure distance.[13]

In short, for Beccaria what was wrong with the death penalty was that it was not efficient enough. Even though it managed to kill off the actual criminal, it had no effect on potential offenders. Life imprisonment, by contrast, worked much better, since its penalty would be felt by all "those who are the witnesses of punishment, inflicted for their sake rather than the criminal's."[14] Sentenced to jail, the criminal would be made into an object lesson, a "long and painful example" to "inspire terror in the spectator." And, to maximize that object lesson, Beccaria insisted that the prison should be made into a place of utter misery and that the jail sentence should be carried out "among fetters or chains, under the rod, under the yoke, in a cage of iron."[15] For Kant, however, even this severity would not suffice, for the very talk of an "efficacious" punishment was anathema to his nonutilitarian philosophy. And so he set out, in *The Philosophy of Law*, to attack the argument of "the Marquis Beccaria" and to expose his "sophistry" and "compassionate sentimentality."[16]

Of course, in the next century it was Beccaria's philosophy rather than Kant's that would come to dominate the field of penal justice.[17] The early nineteenth century was the age of the penitentiary, with its environmental view of crime, its rehabilitative zeal toward the criminal, and its grand ambition to achieve the twin goals of reform and deterrence through the agency of the prison sentence.[18] The United States in particular spearheaded the movement, and new-style prisons soon sprang up: in Auburn, New York, between 1819 and 1823, in Ossining (familiarly known as Sing-Sing) in 1825, in Pittsburgh in 1826, and in Philadelphia in 1829. By the 1830s, the American penitentiary had become world famous, attracting visitors such as Alexis de Tocqueville, Gustave Auguste de Beaumont, Harriet Martineau, and Charles Dickens.

In one obvious sense, Kant and Beccaria stood at the opposite ends of an intellectual spectrum, not only in their rival championship of retribution versus deterrence but also in their rival claims to the august title of Reason. And yet in a different sense, Kant and Beccaria might also be seen not as antitheses but as kindred to each other. The axis of kinship, I would argue, was nothing less than the principle of commensurability itself, a principle embraced by both: embraced by Kant as the reflexive parity achieved by the "Equalization of Punishment with Crime," and embraced by Beccaria as the consequential parity achieved by equating crime with the sum of "harm done to society."[19] And so, no less than Kant, Beccaria also believed in justice as a principle of equivalence. The magnitude of a crime, in his case, was to be equated with the magnitude of its adverse social effect, and the magnitude of the punishment was to be calibrated in equal measure.

Indeed, it was the lack of such a system of equivalences that for Beccaria signaled the malfunction of a penal system. In that eventuality, "an equal punishment [is] ordained for two crimes that do not equally injure society." Such a lapse was not so much inhumane as inefficient, Beccaria argued, for the lack of parity between crime and punishment meant that "men will not be any more deterred from committing the greater crime." The challenge facing the penal

Poe + monomania - absolutely
defeating of the notion of equivalence.

reformer, then, was to devise a principle of equivalence that would
have the maximum deterring effect, namely, "an exact and universal
scale" that would match every crime to its exact punishment. This, to
Beccaria, was not at all idle talk but was a feasible undertaking, for
crime and punishment were both eminently calculable for him, calculable, that is, by using "societal harm" as the common yardstick,
the common measure for both the offense and the sanction. And so
Beccaria's penal universe turned out to be very much a commensurate universe, horizontally organized by the principle of equivalence
and vertically organized by the image of the scale. This was an article
of faith for him, or perhaps I should say an article of Reason, for he
insisted over and over again that what was needed in penal reform
was "geometric precision" and "mathematical exactitude." "If geometry were applicable to the infinite and obscure combinations of
human actions," he said, "there ought to be a corresponding scale
of punishments, descending from the greatest to the least" and en-
suring, in all instances, "a proper proportion between crimes and
punishments."[20]

Crime and punishment, properly calibrated and properly correlated, turn out to embody a principle of "Like with Like" for Beccaria,
much as they do for Kant. The surprising convergence here between
these two thinkers—their shared commitment to a principle of equivalence, over and against their substantive disagreements—says something about the expressive range of Enlightenment Reason as well as
about its cognitive tenacity. What was clear, in any case, was that the
principle of commensurability was neither dismantled nor jettisoned
in the penal reform inspired by Beccaria but was reoriented, rehabili-
tated, assigned a new instrumental function, and assigned a new operative site. Given the versatility as well as the ubiquity of this cognitive principle, it is tempting to study the late eighteenth and the early
nineteenth centuries in just that light: as a field complexly and unevenly marked by the dictates of equivalence and complexly and unevenly institutionalizing those dictates. The history of criminal law,
from this perspective, would seem to be only one strand of development within an interlocking cultural field, and any attempt to address
it must address a much broader set of questions: questions about the
various institutional forms of the commensurate, about the alignment
of those institutions within a cultural order, about the evolving boundaries between adjacent domains, and about the possibility of re-

sidual formations, sometimes in tandem with and sometimes at odds with formations that are emerging.

In what follows, I want to look at the evolution of criminal law within this cultural field, against two related (though admittedly conjectural) phenomena. On the one hand, the shift from retribution to deterrence would seem to have coincided with a broader shift in jurisdictional boundaries, brought about by the much-discussed separation of law and morals in the late eighteenth century. On the other hand, this shift, however pronounced, was nonetheless far from uniform, which would suggest that there might be a transitional residue here: a domain imperfectly "covered," imperfectly rationalized, and therefore imperfectly registering the ascendancy of deterrence over retribution. In this context, it is helpful to remember that for all its public glamor, the penitentiary in America was actually only a minor ornament in a legal system whose center of gravity was rapidly moving in a different direction. Nineteenth-century American law was overwhelmingly economic in focus, the bulk of it occasioned by the needs of an expanding and industrializing nation, and preoccupied with the regulation and enforcement of contract, the sale and transfer of land, the granting of corporate charters, and the authorization of turnpikes, canals, bridges, and railroads. Distribution—not punishment—was the law's business in the nineteenth century, and in the complex reshuffling of institutional filiations, it was toward the economy that the law would now gravitate, honoring the dictates of a thoroughgoing instrumental rationality.[21] As Lawrence Friedman says, nineteenth-century law emphasized "the protection of property rather than morality," and for that reason "criminal justice and civil justice alike ceased to be concerned with the individual."[22]

The triumph of deterrence over retribution must be seen in this context. And to the extent that this "triumph" was itself a complex effect, itself sedimented out of some wide-ranging jurisdictional evolutions, we might speculate as well about its nonintegral character, which is to say, its incomplete summation by a discretely periodizing model. Beccaria's ascendancy, in other words, neither completely displaced Kant nor completely dissolved his claims. And so the language of retribution would end up persisting well into the nineteenth century, becoming more and more marginal perhaps, but retaining, in that marginality, not only a residual resonance but also a residual obliqueness to the normative order.

That resonance and that obliqueness are most richly played out in the novel, I want to suggest, for it is here, within this most sedimented of genres, that we would witness the continuing vitality of an older form of punishment: punishment as retribution, punishment as the Kantian equation of "Like with Like," an equation reflexively executed within a single individual. If this anachronism grants the novel a certain distance from its adjacent institutions, it also induces in it something like a cognitive overload, a justificatory crisis, one that ultimately unsettles the very intelligibility of "punishment" as a concept. And so the justice that the novel dispenses ends up being injudicious and unsatisfactory in almost every way, bringing with it not full coverage, not full resolution, but a generic sense of deficit or excess, a sense that its verdict can never be fully "equal" to its object. If there is in Kant (and in most of us) a "sinister knitting together of the two ideas, guilt and pain," as Nietzsche charges, what the novel achieves, fitfully but also quite faithfully, is the obverse of that phenomenon: a *sundering* of that fated couple, guilt and pain. That sundering removes pain from its causative as well as corrective partner, leaving it dangerously afloat, a phenomenon to be reckoned with entirely on its own. Unreflexive of guilt, unpunitive of guilt, and, most troubling of all, unexhausted by guilt, pain will henceforth occupy a special place in the novel as an ever-stubborn challenge to its rational order. What occasions that challenge and what that challenge means for the concept of justice are the subjects for the rest of the chapter and indeed the entire book.

TAXONOMY AND JURISDICTION

In 1703, Adam Latham, a laborer, and Joan Mills, wife to another laborer, were brought before the county court in Kent County, Delaware, charged with fornication and adultery. For punishment, Joan Mills was publicly whipped, twenty-one lashes on her bare back well applied, and sentenced to one year in prison at hard labor. Adam Latham was sentenced to twenty lashes. This was not the first time the two had gotten into trouble. Adam, indeed, had been charged once before with the same crime, "the Sin of Incontinency and fornication," but he had been acquitted then, the court having ordered him only to post bond guaranteeing good behavior. Now that he had broken his word, he had to endure not only physical punishment but also the public disgrace of "wear[ing] a Roman T on his left arme on the Outside of his uppermost garment . . . for the space of six months next."[23]

As a forerunner of Hester Prynne, and a male one to boot, Adam Latham perhaps has some claim to our attention, although we should also note that his ordeal was in no way out of the ordinary. Indeed, for all its colorful pathos, the trial of this unfortunate but apparently unpenitent couple turned out to be common enough, quite unremarkable really, as trials of this type were very familiar sights in the colonial courtroom. In the seventeenth and eighteenth centuries, offenses against morality (which meant sexual offenses, for the most part) were classified as criminal offenses; they came under the jurisdiction of penal statutes and were routinely prosecuted. In eighteenth-century Pennsylvania, the penalty for the third adultery conviction was twenty-one lashes, seven years in jail, and marking with an "A" on the forehead.[24] Even harsher measures prevailed elsewhere. The Massachusetts Code of 1648 made adultery a capital offense.[25] The Duke's Laws of 1665 in New York had a similar provision.[26] The death sentence was in fact rarely invoked—the harsh penalty being a matter of some dispute—but lesser punishments such as whipping, forfeiture, fines, and imprisonment were standard measures, because according to the legal thinking of the seventeenth and eighteenth centuries, sexual offenses were not only morally transgressive but also criminally sanctionable.[27] William Nelson, studying court records in colonial Massachusetts, reports that between 1760 and 1774, a total of 2,784 prosecutions came before the Superior and General Sessions Courts and that, among these, 1074 were for sexual misconduct (the bulk of which being fornication). In other words, offenses against morality accounted for as much as 38 percent of all prosecutions and made up the single largest category of crime.[28] This astonishing fact had something to do no doubt with the proverbial zealotry of the Massachusetts Bay Colony, but as we can see in the trial and tribulation of Adam Latham and Joan Mills, even in Delaware (as well as in New York, Pennsylvania, Maryland, and Virginia), crimes against morality were arraigned in the courtroom no less than in the pulpit. At once reprehensible and indictable, they were subject not only to divine retribution but also to criminal prosecution.[29]

The lack of separation here between morality and legality, or, as was more often the case, between immorality and criminality, points to a judicial universe recognizably different from our own. What has transpired, in the three hundred and fifty years separating us from colonial America, is nothing less than a transformation of the criminal law, a transformation reflected not merely in its stipulated contents but more fundamentally in its range of enforceable meanings, in its designated sphere of operation, and in its infrastructural relation to other vehicles of justice. That transformation changes the way "crime" itself is defined. What counts as a crime, what suffices as punishment, who is charged with its administration, and how that specific penalty must accord with the general prohibition—these taxonomic and jurisdictional changes are the very ground upon which the criminal law might be said to have a history.

Writing about a comparable shift in taxonomy and jurisdiction in seventeenth-century English law, Christopher Hill has described the abolition of church courts as an "intellectual and moral revolution." What ensued, according to him, was a growing wariness about the question of boundaries: a growing separation between legal and ecclesiastical discipline and a growing distinction between sin and crime.[30] Hill's focus here on the question of boundaries—on the shifting lines of demarcation between adjacent jurisdictions and between categories of offense—seems to me crucial in any historical theorizations about the law: about the shape it comes to take, the sphere it comes to occupy, and the neighboring institutions it comes to adjoin within a social order. Following his lead, we too might want to direct our focus not on the legal domain as it is presently composed but on the shifting contours of its composition: on the fit (or the lack of fit) between categories of the law and categories of ethical judgment. Between the reprehensible and the prosecutable, between what is condemned as sin and what is punished as crime, there is a margin of discrepancy, historically variable and historically significant.[31] The history of such variations casts light not only on the law itself, on its functions and limits at any particular moment, but also on the particular social structure which gives rise to such functions and such limits.

Indeed, what we witness in the colonial courtroom is precisely the absence (or at least the minimal presence) of such a margin of discrepancy. Sin and crime were more or less synonymous in colonial America, synonymous and coextensive. Because sin was readily translatable into and enforceable as crime, the problem of jurisdictional boundaries was neither very acute nor even very meaningful. Thus,

when the Massachusetts law of 1665 referred to fornication as "a particular Crime, a shameful Sin, much increasing amongst us,"[32] the
apposition of the two words—"Sin" and "Crime"—revealed no un-
easiness, no sense of possible disharmony, but rather the assurance of
a clear connection, so clear that it seemed not a connection at all, but
simply the reiteration of the selfsame term.

By contrast, the modernity and liberalness of our own legal culture
would seem to reside in the collapse of that assurance. The identity
of sin and crime, so calmly assumed by the Massachusetts lawmakers
of 1665, is now a subject that inspires anything but calmness. Especially in the context of homosexual practices, tempers have flared up
on just this point. "What is the connexion between crime and sin and
to what extent, if at all, should the criminal law of England concern
itself with the enforcement of morals and punish sin or immorality as
such?"[33] This was the question put forth by Lord Devlin, a distinguished writer on criminal law and a leading protagonist in the contemporary debate about law and morals. The question was loaded,
for its occasion was the controversial appearance of the 1957 *Report
by the Committee on Homosexual Offenses and Prostitution* (commonly
known as the *Wolfenden Report*), which in no uncertain language had
denounced any attempt "to equate the sphere of crime with that of
sin." "There must be a realm of morality and immorality," the report
said, a realm "which is, in brief and crude terms, not the law's business."[34] Lord Devlin disagreed. He strongly objected to the report's
separation of "crime and sin, the divine law from the secular, and the
moral from the criminal." For him, "the criminal law [must] overlap
the moral law," because the two "happen to cover the same area."[35]

Devlin's legal and moral geography has not gone unchallenged.
Indeed, on this point he has come under fire from some formidable
critics, including H. L. A. Hart and Ronald Dworkin.[36] Behind these
critics stands the venerable tradition of analytical jurisprudence—
from Jeremy Bentham to John Stuart Mill to John Austin—a tradition
whose central tenet (in the words of Austin) is that "the tendency to
confound law and morals is one of the most prolific sources of jargon,
darkness and perplexity."[37] The determination not to succumb to
such jargon, darkness, and perplexity was one of the impulses behind
legal change in the nineteenth century, and by and large it was an
impulse that prevailed. By the time Oliver Wendell Holmes set out,
in his celebrated 1897 essay "The Path of the Law," to "dispel a con-

fusion between morality and law," he was speaking from a mainstream position. "The law is full of phraseology drawn from morals," Holmes said, and "continually invites us to pass from one domain to the other." He wished that "every word of moral significance could be banished from the law altogether," so that we might "rid ourselves of an unnecessary confusion." Conceding that there might be "some plausibility to the proposition that the law, if not a part of morality , is limited by it," he insisted nonetheless that "this limit of power is not coextensive with any system of morals."[38]

And indeed, in the course of the nineteenth century, the coextension of law and morality—and the coincidence of sin and crime—was effectively brought to an end. Criminal prosecutions for moral offenses declined sharply after the Revolution—to an average of eleven cases per year between 1786 and 1790 and to fewer than five cases per year in the four decades thereafter.[39] The moral domain, it would seem, was quietly slipping out from under the law's jurisdiction, now increasingly construed as a limited arena. It is a telling sign that during this period the law was frequently described as a bounded enclosure, as a "sphere," a "realm," an "area," or a "province," the last word figuring conspicuously, for example, in the title of John Austin's influential lectures, *The Province of Jurisdiction Determined* (1832). The law was spatialized in the nineteenth century; it had a specific locale and a specific set of boundaries. Henceforth its sphere of operation was to be narrow, precise, sharply delimited. Its enforceable meanings were to be "compressed to the smallest possible compass [its] language would bear."[40] Against this background—against this contraction in semantics as well as in applicability—it is not surprising that in his celebrated essay Oliver Wendell Holmes should choose the word "path" to characterize the legal domain, for narrowness and linearity were indeed the defining attributes of "the law [taken] as a business with well understood limits, a body of dogma enclosed within definite lines."[41]

UNEVEN DEVELOPMENT

The contracting boundaries of the law gave rise to an interesting gray area, no longer covered by the rigor of penal statutes but perhaps not without an alternative form of sanction. If penal law would henceforth limit itself to the specifically criminal, rather than to the generally immoral, how was the latter to be maintained as an intelligible category? What persuasive or corrective instruments must it summon forth? And if sin no longer provided the legal basis for criminalization, what other functions might it continue to perform? In what context and with what resonances would such a concept continue to have meaning?

After all, living as we do in the late twentieth century, we are all familiar with the boldly advertised "sinfulness" of rich desserts, a usage that points to yet another semantic shift—at once a spreading and a thinning out of meaning—which completely transforms a word whose referential contents had once been narrow, literal, and unambiguous. This semantic transformation had its roots in the nineteenth century, I argue, in the growing separation between judicial and nonjudicial categories, especially the growing separation between sin and crime. This, together with the relaxation of religious discipline, effectively dislodged sin from its customary moorings. No longer anchored to a formal system of punishment, it became instead something like a floating signifier, opening itself to an extralegal set of meanings and lending its weight to an extralegal structure of justice.

This extralegal area—newly removed from the purview of the law but residually connected to it and possibly at odds with it—is of special interest to literary critics. For it is in this gray area, this alternative realm of justice, partly overdetermined but also partly indeterminate, that we might be able to observe some of the cultural specificities of the novel. Here I have in mind the recent hypothesis (advanced by D. A. Miller, John Bender, and Richard Brodhead, among others) about the possibility, amenability, and efficacy of the novel as an instrument of social discipline.[42] I want to reorient this hypothesis, taking as my point of departure not the perfected discipline of the novel but its precarious maintenance. What interests me is the uncertain primacy (and indeed the uncertain profile) of justice as it is textualized in the novel, as it takes the form of something other than a purely logical proposition. Unlike criminal justice, whose operative terms are to become specific and explicit, without nuance or ambiguity, novelistic justice remains allusive, elastic, circuitous. And unlike the canon of strict construction in criminal law, which now limits the "punishable" to its narrowest possible meaning, novelistic justice continues to operate under a canon of the broadest construction, pun-

- the narrowing sphere of the law emerged
at the same time as the expansion of
the novelistic

ishing sins no longer deemed actionable by jurists and, out of that residual latitude, also stretching the concept of "punishment" to its breaking point.

The relation between law and literature that I am suggesting, then, is tangential (and perhaps even antithetical) to the ones more customarily proposed, including those offered by the early commentators on the novel. When Hazlitt said of Richardson that "he sets about describing every object and transaction, as if the whole had been given in on evidence by an eye-witness," and when Charles Lamb said that reading Defoe "is like reading evidence in a court of Justice,"[43] what they had in mind was the palpable affinity between two descriptive surfaces: the minute details of legal evidence and the minute details of novelistic portraiture. What concerns me, however, is not so much the affinity between the two surfaces as a discrepancy between what is inscribed or intimated in each. It is this discrepancy—between their figurative widths or densities, between the self-imposed singularity of reference in criminal law and the self-flaunting multiplicity of reference in the novel—that makes law and literature two different signifying theaters, two different punitive environments, generating different meanings for what counts as a crime and granting different degrees of completeness to its proposed resolution.

To put this another way, we might say that by the early nineteenth century, criminal law had become (or was trying to become) a nonsymbolic field, the action of the law being restricted to "the unvarnished meaning of its words," so that "only those acts ought to be crimes which were plainly so labeled."[44] The desymbolization of the law—and the new, invisible forms of discipline that it occasioned—is the subject of Foucault's *Discipline and Punish*, a work that has inspired literary critics to see narrative fiction as one such form of discipline, functionally homologous to that of the school, the prison, and the police. This approach, which assumes a functional correspondence, a functional complementarity, between various social domains, is certainly one way to imagine the novel's historicity. And yet there is no reason why "complementarity" should be a privileged category of analysis and no reason why "society" itself should be thought of as a seamlessly functioning unit, a seamlessly integrated totality.[45] It is equally plausible to assume the opposite, I think, locating the novel's historical resonances not in its *full* complementarity to other social forms, but in its *incomplete* alignment. What is especially worth investigating, from this perspective, is the possibility of an alternative form of justice in the novel: a different order of signification flowing from an actual offense to its intimated prohibitions and a different order of satisfaction (or lack of satisfaction) flowing from the act of punishment itself.

In short, what I want to elaborate here is something like a theory of "uneven development," a theory about law and literature as institutions historically oblique to each other, marked by a historical noncoincidence of boundaries, boundaries of signification as well as boundaries of satisfaction. Because "crime" retains a signifying fluidity in the novel, what prevails here is definitely not the path of the law but something more like a semantic "field": a field of the reprehensible, specified as well as adumbrated, encompassing and interconnecting a range of signifying registers. As in an echo chamber, crime here sets into motion a far more complex series of resonances than in criminal law. It bodies forth an entire spectrum of prescriptions and proscriptions, some having to do with the law and others not. It speaks to anxieties explicit and implicit. Given this signifying latitude, the justice that the novel dispenses is also "justice" stretched almost to its breaking point: stretched not only to accommodate retributive justice, an order of justice affecting one particular offender, but also to accommodate distributive justice, an order of justice affecting many diverse persons and assigning to each a due share of burden and benefit. Indeed, not the least interesting feature of the novel is the slippage that it effects between these two senses of justice—between a general problem of commensurability in collective life and a specific problem of commensurability in personal conduct—a slippage that, in making an issue out of the very meanings of the commensurate, in calling attention to its very ground of being, would also end up making it the most precarious of concepts: most fantasized and most fantastical.

Nowhere is the expansive scope (and problematic commensurability) of the novel more striking than in the "justice" it metes out to its female characters, which, in its punitive zeal no less than in its signifying instability, might be thought of as a distinctly novelistic effect, an effect growing out of its language of gender. That language, Nancy Armstrong has argued, is very much the novel's invention, at once its normative voice and its regulatory instrument.[46] Certainly, among its punitive conventions we find a language not only explicitly sexualized, but sexualized in such a way as to dramatize the bounds of propriety and to penalize any overt or covert infractions. The language of gender carries not just the usual symbolic freight but symbolic freight of a particularly incriminating nature. In fact, we need only look at the harsh fate visited upon the heroines of the nineteenth-century novel, from Hester Prynne to Hetty Sorrel, to be impressed not only by the punitive zeal at work but also by the extent to which that zeal is sexually predicated, the extent to which novelistic justice is gendered justice.

GENDERED JUSTICE: *THE DEERSLAYER*

Within this punitive tradition, James Fenimore Cooper's *The Deerslayer* (1841) must stand as an exceptionally salient example. "We live in a world of transgressions," the novel concludes, "and no pictures that represent us otherwise can be true," even though we do sometimes catch "gleamings of that pure spirit" among corrupt humanity, "mitigating if not excusing its crimes."[47] "Crimes" are definitely a key issue in the novel, and if the fate of its chief criminal, Judith Hutter, is any indication, so too is punishment. For Judith is emphatically punished, emphatically rejected by Natty Bumppo, the man she shamelessly hankers for and shamefully fails to get. As Cooper's many authorial comments make clear, that punishment is not at all an afterthought, a mechanical contrivance, or a random occurrence, but the central burden of the novel. In the preface, he characterizes his heroine as one "filled with the pride of beauty, erring, and fallen." His hero, Natty Bumppo, on the other hand, is known "principally for his sincerity, his modesty, and his unerring truth and probity." Between the "erring" woman and the "unerring" man, one manifestly "fallen" and the other manifestly not, the outcome seems predictable enough. Here, "beauty, delirious passion, and sin" will all come to nought, and the retribution visited upon them, the author assures us, will "be sufficiently distinct to convey its moral" (v).

The unabashed presence of the word "sin" (and its conspicuous placement in the preface) gives a hint of the novel's punitive flavor. That hint is more than confirmed by the end of the book, as Cooper issues a clear verdict, a clear indictment of the Hutters and their "history of crime":

> Time and circumstances have drawn an impenetrable mystery around
> all else connected with the Hutters. They lived, erred, died, and are
> forgotten. . . . The history of crime is ever revolting, and it is fortunate
> that few love to dwell on its incidents. The sins of the family have
> long since been arraigned at the judgment seat of God, or are regis-
> tered for the terrible settlement of the last great day. (533)

With a semantic latitude strikingly reminiscent of colonial usage,
Cooper puts on trial not only "crimes" but also "sins," as if the two
were synonymous (throwing in, for good measure, the word "err,"
clearly a favorite of his and apparently to be equated with the others
as well). The imprecision here is telling, and tellingly evocative of a
punitive universe in which the boundaries between the moral and
the legal, between "sin" and "crime," remain as yet undemarcated,
as yet elastic and commingling. Crime is a hospitable category here.
Within its precincts we find not a single individual (as Cooper's account of his "fallen" heroine might have led us to believe) but the
Hutters as a unit, the whole family apparently qualifying for that
label. Not just Thomas Hutter, a former pirate, but also his wife, a
fallen woman like her daughter Judith, and not just Judith herself,
but also her half-witted sister, Hetty—these four figures, otherwise
quite different, nonetheless seem united in their joint culpability, in
what Cooper generically calls "the sins of the family."

In what sense might the Hutters be understood as a culpable unit,
as a family of sinners? Since it is their common guilt that the novel emphasizes, we might do well to ponder their crimes in generic terms. To
be sure, Thomas Hutter was once a pirate, and his sins might have
been crimes even in a legal sense; and Judith, a fallen woman, has of
course sinned in the most time-honored fashion. Still, beyond these
discrete categories of offense, something more encompassing and
perhaps more deep-seated remains. Indeed, given the Hutters' kinship in crime (not to say kinship in punishment), we should perhaps
be alert to a curious coincidence here between the kinds of "sins" the
Hutters are said to have committed and the kind of family they represent: a coincidence between their profile as sinners and their profile as
a familial unit.

What kind of family are the Hutters? Once we put the question
that way, it becomes immediately clear that something is wrong not
just with the Hutter family but with them *as a family*. This is a family
that turns out not to be a family after all, as Thomas Hutter is revealed

to be quite a stranger to his putative daughters. Judith, one of those daughters, is overjoyed at this turn of events. "I scarce know by what name to call myself now!" she exclaims with some delight. "I am Judith, and Judith only, until the law gives me a right to another name. Never will I use that of Thomas Hutter again" (403). Judith's name and, by extension, her family are now matters of her own choosing. As she explains to Hetty: "*You* and you only are my sister . . . and Mother was my mother—of that, too, am I glad and proud, for she was a mother to be proud of—but Father was not father!" (361)

For Judith, the unfathering of Thomas Hutter brings only elation. Hetty, in contrast, is quite distressed. If fathers can stop being fathers—if one familial identity can dissolve so completely into thin air—what is there to prevent other identities from following suit? What is there to prevent sisters, for example, from being turned into total strangers?

> "How do I know, Judith, that you wouldn't be as glad to find that I am not your sister as you are in finding that Thomas Hutter, as you call him, was not your father? I am only half-witted, and few people like to have half-witted relations; and then I'm not handsome—at least, not as handsome as you—and you may wish a handsomer sister." (361)

Hetty's worries here are local and personal, but they give voice as well to a more general anxiety, general to the modern form of life, with its emphasis on elective identities and voluntary attachments. Based not on inherited lineage but on individual choice, not on blood but on "wishes," this modern form of life challenges the very taxonomy of the traditional order, its grounds for classification as well as for association. In the Hutter family that ceases to be a family, we see, dramatized in caricature, the historical shift from parental control to filial autonomy, from a classical world of organic kinship to a liberal society of self-making.[48] What Cooper collectively condemns in the Hutters—what he denounces as the "sins of the family"—might also be understood, then, as their sin against the sanctity of hereditary estates, which is also to say, their sin against an ascriptive social order.

Sins of this sort do not go unpunished, and, in this case, the wages of sin suitably mirror the sins themselves. Having disowned one parent, however undesirable, and repudiated one identity, however inauthentic, Judith is now in danger of being left with no father at

all and no identity to speak of. Nor is she unforewarned. Her lack
of filial regard has shocked even Hurry Harry, the most mindless
of characters, into a kind of blind prophecy: "Not Thomas Hutter's
darter! Don't disown the old fellow in his last moments, Judith, for
that's a sin the Lord will never overlook. If you're not Thomas Hutter's darter, whose darter be you?" (349).

The question is ominously put. And lest we miss the point, Cooper
hastens to tell us, even more ominously, that "in getting rid of a parent whom she felt it was a relief to find she might own she had never
loved, [Judith] overlooked the important circumstance that no substitute was ready to supply his place" (349–350). One might point
out, of course, that it is not really Judith's fault not to have found a
substitute for Thomas Hutter; she certainly tries hard enough. Her
mother has made it impossible for her, having made sure that "all the
dates, signatures, and addresses had been cut from the letters. . . .
Thus Judith found all her hopes of ascertaining who her parents were
defeated" (400).

But the mother has "defeated" the daughter in a less tangible way
as well. Judith's problem, after all, is not so much that she has failed
to *find* a father as that she has never had one she can *claim*. Her problem is not unverifiable genealogy but all too verifiable bastardy. Still,
this handicap notwithstanding, it is not inconceivable that Judith
could have found a substitute for Hutter, not by discovering a true
father but by acquiring a true husband, who, in giving her his name,
would have bestowed upon her what her own father had withheld.
But, as we know, this "substitute" too is not Judith's to have. In the
last paragraph of the book, we are treated to a curious bit of rumor
about Sir Robert Warley, Judith's paramour: that he now "lived on
his paternal estates and that there was a lady of rare beauty in the
lodge who had great influence over him, though she did not bear his
name" (534).

Judith's crime is the crime of anonymity, we might say. She is the
leading offender, but she is not alone. Indeed, her crime is such that
we can safely assume a host of accomplices and a host of precursors.
The illegitimate daughter of one man, Judith will in time become the
illegitimate consort of another man. She is the daughter of a sinning
mother, and she will grow up to sin in exactly the same fashion. Sin
here is generic and periodic, a family romance, a phenomenon hereditary and repeatable. Such a criminal sequence rests on a kind of gener-

ational fungibility, equating father and husband, givers of names who withhold what they have to give, and mother and daughter, bearers of names who fail to receive what they are obligated to bear. It is surely appropriate (if not downright heavy-handed) that Judith should be named after her mother: she is a *second* Judith, a replication of the first.

Judith's sin, then, is neither local nor unique. It is exemplary and synecdochic, it beckons backward and outward, compounding and compressing into its orbit the sins of others. Nor is the transgression here purely sexual, however convenient a label that might afford. Indeed, just as Judith might be said to stand in for a family of sinners, so her misdeed would also seem to encompass a spectrum of the reprehensible. No longer a maiden but not yet a wife, she has forfeited not just a proper sexual identity but any identity at all. And as the novel administers to her a suitable dose of punishment, it also chastises, through her example, a cluster of offenses having generally to do with the problem of identity: not just the misadventures of the sexual persona but also the vicissitudes of the social persona, not just deviation from sexual purity but also ambition in social mobility.

CRIME AS A SIGNIFYING FIELD

Judith's sexual failing is a figure of speech, then, a kind of punitive shorthand, where novelistic sanction is meted out both literally and vicariously, both to a specific crime plainly so labeled and to an unspecified range of guilty cognates. We might think of it as a point of metaphoric inscription, and it is helpful to remind ourselves of its adumbrative and substitutive relation to other signifying categories. Eve Kosofsky Sedgwick has observed that "the subject of sex [is] an especially charged leverage-point, or point for the exchange of meanings, between gender and class."[49] Eva Kittay, writing more generally about metaphor as a cognitive principle, has argued that the exchange of meaning that it brings about is not just between two discrete terms but between two semantic fields, two domains of meanings, the structural properties of one being transposed upon the other.[50] This "field theory" of metaphor helpfully elucidates the punitive workings of the novel, for it is this confluence of semantic fields— the multiple inscription of prohibition and penalty—that gives rise not only to the jurisdictional scope of the novel but also, I would argue, to its peculiar harshness, its punitive zeal toward its signifying criminals.

It might seem odd to speak of the punitive as a signifying field, and yet Emile Durkheim, linking penal law to a residual religiosity, has alerted us to just this "metaphorical" dimension in crime and punishment (although, as he also says, "the metaphor is not without truth").[51] A crime is always "an offense against an authority in some way transcendent," Durkheim argues, and in avenging a wrong, in demanding that "the culpable ought to suffer because he has done evil and in the same degree," we are propelled by "an echo in us of a force which is foreign to us, and which is superior to that which we are."[52] As the enforcement of an "echo," punishment is symbolic and projective. Inscribed within its executed particular is always a broader, higher frame of reference, a broader, higher order of meaning.[53]

This appeal to a transcendent ideal is certainly true of the Kantian retributionists, who demand punishment in the name of justice. And with slight modification it is true even of Kant's adversaries, the utilitarians, who, in making "social utility" the ground for punishment, in effect turn *that* into a higher principle, not unlike "justice" in Kant. Punishment for the utilitarians (as we have seen in Beccaria) is thus strictly a means to an end, the particularity of each case being harnessed always to the supreme goal of crime prevention. As Bentham says, the "first object" of punishment is "to prevent, in as far as it is possible, and worth while, all sorts of offences whatsoever; in other words, so to manage, that no offence whatsoever may be committed."[54] For him as for Beccaria, punishment is not so much an act of reprimand as an act of preemption: it addresses not the accomplished deed but contemplated misdeeds, not the actual criminal but potential offenders. Bentham thus insists on the "exemplarity" of punishment, for "example is the most important end of all, in proportion as the *number* of the persons under temptation to offend is to *one*." And, as he further argues, "there is not any means by which a given quantity of punishment can be rendered more exemplary, than by choosing it of such a sort as shall bear an *analogy* to the offence."[55] The criminal is punished primarily as a sign, then, a salient example, condensing and displaying in his person an entire structure of prohibition. And, as a sign, he is posted mostly for the benefit of others, held up to serve them due warnings.

But as Bentham is the first to recognize, exemplary punishment can lead to excess, to a profligacy in signification, as it were. It is not surprising that immediately after his discussion of exemplarity, he should come up with a section on "frugality" (on the importance of not "produc[ing] any such superfluous and needless pain"), followed by another section in which he gingerly considers "exemplarity and frugality, in what they differ and agree."[56] Indeed, for all its talk about the salience of example, *The Principles of Morals and Legislation* (1789) is deeply committed to frugality as the law's operative principle. And so Bentham begins his discussion of penology with a chapter on "Cases Unmeet for Punishment" and concludes with a chapter on "The Limits of the Penal Branch of Jurisprudence"—thus anticipating, by more than a century, Oliver Wendell Holmes's recommendations in "The Path of the Law."[57] In the course of that intervening century, as criminal law became more and more frugal in its semantics, the luxury of signification became more and more a residual privilege of the novel. Here, then, is one instance of the uneven development between law and literature, although I should also add that such an unevenness is never quite absolute. Against the novel's semantic latitude, so continually in evidence, we should perhaps remind ourselves of a residual latitude in criminal law as well, an unacknowledged but perhaps unavoidable tendency to signify beyond its strict constructions, which suggests that even within its august precincts, a "crime" is never simply a given, external to or antecedent to its verdict, but is rather a semantic effect, given meaning by the very process of judgment.

This is not just a fanciful way of putting things. Some serious consequences follow, I think, from seeing crime as a semantic effect, shaped by the categories by which it is apprehended and represented. Indeed, if the debate among legal scholars is any indication, the very authority of criminal law—its claim to neutrality and rationality—would seem to rest on whether "crime" is to be understood as a substantive or interpretive phenomenon, whether it is seen as an autonomous given, with an objective existence in the world, or whether it is seen as a textualized effect, constituted by a meaning-giving procedure. Mark Kelman has argued, for example, that legal reasoning in criminal law is both propelled and constrained by its "interpretive constructs," which, by adopting a variably broad or narrow time frame with regard to causal antecedents and a variably broad or narrow compass with regard to intent, in fact prejudge the issue, since the verdict arrived at is a foregone conclusion given the choice of certain criminal law categories.[58] Kelman does not use the phrase "signifying field," but he might well have, because what he seems to be suggesting is that the criminal law can assign blame only by constructing its object as a *legally meaningful* object, the legal meaning here being strictly an effect of the temporal and spatial grid which composes the event, which defines not just its veracity but its very content and character. Given the priority of these general legal categories over each particular crime, the assignment of blame would appear to be procedurally weighted, procedurally overdetermined, and the entire system of criminal justice might begin to look like something that is itself criminally unjust.[59]

I mention Kelman at some length, partly to indicate the high stakes involved in speaking of crime as a signifying field, but partly also to distinguish my approach from his. Kelman is primarily concerned with the ground of judgment, or the lack thereof. Focusing on the "interpretive constructs" in criminal law, he calls into question its objective foundation, its descriptive transparency and adjudicative rationality. My chapter builds on his insight but reverses his direction of inquiry. Conceding at once that any verdict is interpretive, that it is enacted through a process of textualization and thus always semantically overdetermined, I want to focus all the same not so much on its arbitrary *ground* as on its abundant *figures*. What concerns me is the range of symbolic inscriptions brought into play by a particular act of judgment, the wealth of referents encoded in a seemingly discrete offense. Such a focus might seem unduly aesthetic, in a context where perhaps ethics alone ought to matter. And yet in the long run, the aesthetics of crime—its constitution as a signifying field and the semantic excess that accompanies that constitution—must end up leading us back to the question of ethics, must end up casting doubt not only on any particular instance of punishment but also on that higher idea which underwrites it and which it incessantly echoes: the idea of justice itself.

This much said, we can perhaps return to Judith, that signifying criminal, and to her crime, the crime of anonymity. If she is indeed a sign, what family of crimes does she stand for? What patterns of prohibition are adumbrated by her specific instance of punishment, what clusters of social meanings are encoded, elaborated, vicariously affirmed? We might begin to answer these questions by circling back to the "crime of anonymity" itself, which, as it turns out, is not at all unique to Judith. Indeed, E. P. Thompson has discussed an entire category of offense under that label, and it is helpful here to recall the sense of his initial usage. By the "crime of anonymity," Thompson refers to a phenomenon common in eighteenth-century England, the writing and sending of anonymous letters, usually from the lowly to the exalted, letters variously salacious, rambunctious, or plain extortive. According to Thompson, such crimes were especially prevalent in a stratified society, a society of ascriptive estates, which, "in myth if not in actuality, rested upon relations of paternalism and deference." In such a world, where social distinctions were both customary and compulsory, norms of conduct depended entirely on the denomination of identity. A proper name not only indicated who one was, it also indicated what was proper to one's social station. Crimes of anonymity were deeply unsettling (and were treated as a capital offense) for that very reason. As Thompson says, "anonymity was of the essence of any early form of industrial or social protest," because (or so it seemed to eighteenth-century Englishmen) to refuse denomination was to reject the norms of social estate.[60]

Judith, of course, is neither so political nor even so purposeful in *her* crime of anonymity. Still, it is worth noting that even in her case, names are intimately bound up with social station and social entitlement. She is glad to be temporarily without a name—to be "Judith, and Judith only"—because Hutter's name seems so clearly beneath her. He is a "coarse and illiterate" man; his marriage to her mother was a "horror," the two being "an ill-assorted pair," she being in "every way so much his superior" (399). The name "Hutter" ill becomes the mother, and, by the same token, it ill becomes the daughter as well. Judith's problem, a lifelong one apparently, is to find a last name that would consort equitably with the first, a last name that would give her a denotative parity.

Nor is Judith altogether without choice in this matter. Indeed, at various points the narrative teases us with the possibility of her finding a nomenclatural partner, even going so far as to couple her name with another name, holding up the compound as if to test for fit. The fit is not always ideal, however, as Judith is the first to notice. "No—no—Judith without a name would never consent to be called Judith March! Anything would be better than *that*!" she exclaims at one point. She can afford to be firm there, because a more suitable name seems to be awaiting her, and she is not too shy to tell its owner, "the name is a good one; either Hetty or myself would a thousand times rather be called Hetty Bumppo or Judith Bumppo than to be called Hetty or Judith Hutter" (409, 405).

Natty is not so sure. He points out, reasonably enough, that the proposed names are "a moral impossible, unless one of you should so far demean herself as to marry me." And, so as not to be uncivil, he adds, "There's been handsome women, too, they tell me, among the Bumppos, Judith, afore now, and should you take up with the name, oncommon as you be, in this particular, them that knows the family won't be altogether surprised." In spite of such encouragement, however, the name "Judith Bumppo" is actually unthinkable, and for obvious reasons. Natty, however, offers a kinder and gentler excuse: "Judith, you come of people altogether above mine in the world, and onequal matches, like onequal fri'ndships, can't often tarminate kindly" (405, 411). Judith and Natty would have been an "illassorted pair," not unlike Judith's mother and Hutter, since she too is "in every way so much his superior." Of course, Judith is not the one to raise any objections now, but the objections are raised for her and, we might add, against her. As a fallen woman she is manifestly not good enough for Natty; as the offspring of people "altogether above [him] in the world" she is manifestly too good for him. Sexual propriety and social station are inversely symmetrical here, in such a way as to bring about a curious alignment between being "too good" and being "not good enough." Judith is unacceptable on both counts, and it is now incumbent upon her to find a name she is neither above nor beneath, but perfectly equal to.

EQUALITY REPUBLICAN AND LIBERAL

Judith's search for a proper name is not just a search for legitimacy in marriage—a search conducted under the auspices of sexual propriety—but also a search for a proper place in the social hierarchy, a search conducted, surprisingly, under the auspices of marital equality. Equality is the ideal invoked here, invoked as the basis for conjugality. Nor is Cooper alone in this particular, for, as Jan Lewis points out, the ideal of a "symmetrical marriage"—a marriage of equal partners—was an integral feature of classical republicanism, widespread in the early republic.[61] More recently, Rosemarie Zagarri has traced this republican ideal to the influence of the Scottish Enlightenment (although, as she also points out, the espousal of such an ideal, with its emphasis on *marital* equality, also "effectively negated the possibility of political equality").[62] In any case, in the late eighteenth and early nineteenth centuries, marital equality was a subject weighty enough to be discussed by the likes of John Witherspoon, president of Princeton. A frequent contributor to *Ladies Magazine* and *Pennsylvania Magazine* (edited by Tom Paine), Witherspoon counseled that "a parity of understanding and temper [is] as necessary towards forming a good marriage, as an equality of years, rank, and fortune."[63] Numerous other magazine articles offered the same advice. It is not surprising, then, that in *The Deerslayer* inequality should be held up as the principal obstacle to a proposed marriage. In fact, on those grounds Natty is moved to reject not one but two such unacceptable proposals: not just an "onequal match" with Judith but another match, also unequal, with Sumac, widow of the recently killed Le Loup Cervier, who demands marriage even more vehemently. But, as Hetty observes, "Sumac is old and you are young," and, as Natty himself observes, "she's red and I'm white." Such a flagrant violation of equality makes death "more nat'ral like, and welcome, than wedlock with this woman" (473).

Equality, invoked as a marital ideal, foregrounds race as the ground of incommensurability.[64] It also foregrounds class. The social rankings of the marriage partners are very much at issue here, for paradoxically it is only by settling the question of rank—only by fixing upon one particular class to which both partners belong—that the marriage can be deemed equal. To give the paradox an even sharper edge, we might say that the ideal of marital equality proceeds from the fact of social hierarchy. It does not so much eliminate the concept of social station as accentuate it. Equality is a sorting principle here— it matches like with like—and, as such, it sets the protocol not only for gender relations but also for social distinctions. It is in this context, in the convergence of gender and class under the norm of equality, that proper names would come to figure so largely in the novel: they figure, above all, as signs, signs of something gone awry and of an ensuing sequence of retribution. Judith's lack of a name, her desire for one and her failure to get one, thus compresses into a single detail the punitive weight of two semantic fields, gender and class, joining both to a common purpose, mapping the lineaments of one onto the countenance of the other. That twofold verdict brings to the novel something like a twofold severity, a passion for justice redoubled in strength, and redoubled in its operative radius.

Nor is this punitive fervor at work only in the name Bumppo. Judith is deemed unequal to, and therefore unworthy of, another name as well. Captain Warley, the owner of that other name, makes it clear why that is so. She is "a lovely creature, this Judith Hutter," he concedes, but, he hastens to add, "I do suppose there *are* women in the colonies that a captain of light infantry need not disdain, but they are not to be found up here on a mountain lake" (511). The dalliance between Judith and Warley is glaringly, scandalously an "association between superior and inferior" (151), which is why the name "Judith Warley" is also glaringly, scandalously unimaginable in *The Deerslayer*. Unlike the other two names, "Judith March" and "Judith Bumppo," names tantalizingly held up for our appraisal, this one is not even allowed to materialize on the page.

Still, Judith is by no means an uncouth or ill-favored person vainly aspiring to a social station that is manifestly beyond her. If she is indeed an "inferior," as we are told, that inferiority is not at all self-evident. Quite the contrary. Judith is fastidious, overly fastidious, both in appearance and demeanor. "Her language [is] superior to that used by her male companions, her own father included." It displays no "mean intonation of voice, or a vulgar use of words." Indeed, "the officers of the nearest garrison [had] often flattered [her] with the belief that few ladies of the towns acquitted themselves better than herself in this important particular" (134–135). Judith's refined speech is an enviable asset, a sign, one would have thought, of her social elevation. After all, in *The American Democrat* (1838), Cooper had suggested that "a just, clear and simple expression of our ideas is a necessary accomplishment for all who aspire to be classed with gentlemen and ladies."[65] Judith's problem (an unforgivable one for Cooper, it appears) is that she talks like one of the "gentlemen and ladies" when she is in fact not one of them. She is an inferior who commands a superior manner of speech, a sign that deceives the beholder, signifying status and refinement where it ought to have signified ignorance and backwardness.

As a delinquent sign, one far in excess of its referent, Judith might

be said to have transgressed against the very idea of the commensurate. This crime makes her equal to no one, least of all herself. She is
both above and beneath any given identity, both superior and inferior, a predicament which, under a regime of marital equality, must
also make her sadly unmatchable. It is tempting here to describe her
in the idiom of Arnold van Gennep and Victor Turner: she is a "liminal" character, caught "betwixt and between all the recognized fixed
points . . . of structural classification," someone who is "neither one
thing nor another," "neither here nor there," "at once no longer classified and not yet classified."[66] The vocabulary of liminality *almost*
describes Judith, but in one crucial respect it does not, and it is instructive to see why. The liminal person for van Gennep and Turner
is not so much a deviant as a truant, a figure caught in transit, as it
were, between normative states, but whose progress is such as to
ensure an eventual restitution of the boundaries he or she momentarily ruptures. Judith's truancy has no such terminal limit, and no
such teleological guarantee. She will always remain "betwixt and between," always "no longer classified and not yet classified."

Judith is not a liminal person; she cannot be one, because there is
no final resting place for her, no stable identity into which she might
be inducted, no encompassing "structure that defines status and es-
tablishes social distance."[67] To say this is also to say that there is a
world of difference between the society Judith inhabits and the stable
tribal society described by van Gennep and Turner. Indeed, we might
even say that what van Gennep and Turner take to be a structural
aberration is in her world the norm. And so, the problem of equality—the problem of being commensurate, either with oneself or with
someone else—turns out to afflict not just Judith but virtually everyone in the book. Pervading *The Deerslayer*, indeed, is something like a
thematization of that problem, a thematization that gathers force as
each character subjects everyone else to yet another ranking, putting
this person above or beneath that person, trying to ascertain who is
equal to whom. And since the verdict changes from moment to moment and indeed from judge to judge, its sentencing power resides
not so much in its finality as in its endless reversals.

A brief conversation between Hutter and Hetty, for example, illus-
trates just how severe the problem of equality is and how intimately
it structures every person's sense of self as well as sense of others:

"You're by no means ugly, though not so comely as Jude."

"Is Judith any happier for being so handsome?"

"She may be, child, and she may not be. But talk of other matters, now, for you hardly understand these, poor Hetty. How do you like our new acquaintance, Deerslayer?"

"He isn't handsome, Father. Hurry is far handsomer than Deerslayer." (83)

In the space of a few lines, two different sets of people have been brought forward to be ranked, and two different sets of criteria have been invoked to facilitate that ranking. High marks in the department of beauty by no means translate into high marks in the department of happiness; this much even Hutter concedes. This drawback, however, does not prevent either term from generating an evaluative frenzy of its own. "Not as comely," "happier," "far handsomer"—these distinctions are all the more insistent for being incommensurable. Hutter, for example, offers beauty as the standard of judgment, which puts Judith considerably ahead of Hetty. Hetty, however, counters with a different standard—happiness—and on *that* count Judith does not fare quite so well. And yet, when Hetty herself proceeds to rank Hurry Harry and Natty, she abandons happiness as a criterion and returns to the earlier term, beauty, in order to pronounce Hurry the better of the two.

Social identities in *The Deerslayer* are judged by a profusion of terms, which, unfortunately, make ranking not easier but shakier. To return to the vexed question, for example, about the relative standing of Judith and Natty, how is one to decide? Natty, of course, has announced that Judith is "altogether above" him, but things are actually not so clear. Judith herself, for instance, far from agreeing with him, fancies herself quite his inferior. "But we are not altogether unequal, sister—Deerslayer and I?" she asks Hetty. "He is not altogether my superior?" Equality—between herself and Natty—is a burning question for Judith, and, working herself into a mania, she will go on to ask that question three more times in the course of the same conversation. "Why do you think me the equal of Deerslayer?" she asks Hetty again. And then again, "Tell me what raises me to an equality with Deerslayer." And finally, not satisfied with Hetty's answer, she asks yet again, "But I fear you flatter me, Hetty, when you think I can be justly called the equal of a man like Deerslayer. It is true, I have been better taught; in one sense am more comely; and perhaps might look higher; but then his truth—his truth—makes a fearful difference between us!" (302).

Judith is comically obsessed here, but in a way she is simply doing to herself (and to Natty) what everybody else has been doing throughout the book. She is ranking the two of them, and doing so through a profusion of terms—"better taught," "more comely," "look higher"—as intransigent as they are incommensurable. And the effect, once again, is to multiply the instances of inequality, making it more flagrant, more entrenched. As far as Judith is concerned, for example, literacy and good looks carry some weight, but "truth" carries infinitely more, so much more that it tips the balance altogether. Hetty, of course, disagrees. She is flabbergasted, in fact, that her sister would even entertain the thought of not being equal to Deerslayer. "To think of you asking me this, Judith!" she exclaims:

> "Superior, Judith!" she repeated with pride. "In what *can* Deer-slayer be *your* superior? Are you not Mother's child—and does he know how to read—and wasn't Mother before any woman in all this part of the world? I should think, so far from supposing himself *your* superior, he would hardly believe himself *mine*. You are handsome, and he is ugly—"
>
> "No, not ugly, Hetty," interrupted Judith. "Only plain. But his honest face has a look in it that is far better than beauty. In my eyes Deer-slayer is handsomer than Hurry Harry."
>
> "Judith Hutter, you frighten me! Hurry is the handsomest mortal in the world—even handsomer than you are yourself." (301)

Who is equal to whom? The question obsesses everyone, but Natty, Judith, and Hetty all seem to have different answers. With breakneck speed, the terms for comparison shift and the partners for comparison multiply. It is not just Judith and Deerslayer who are being ranked now, but also Hurry and Deerslayer, and then Judith and Hurry. One thing is clear, though, in this pandemonium: with each fresh ranking, it becomes less and less likely that those ranked will ever be found "equal" to one another. Here then, dramatized and perhaps ironized, is something of a cultural crisis—something like a crisis of equality— in which personal identities, evaluative norms, and social distinctions are all endlessly fluctuating, endlessly in transit. What is liminal, it would seem, is not so much one particular individual as the entire social structure.[68]

The "liminality" of nineteenth-century America is a commonplace

among historians, of course.[69] Here, I want to associate it more specifically with a moment of transition from the eighteenth to the
nineteenth century, from the highly rationalized political culture of
classical republicanism to the increasingly unrationalizable political
culture of modern liberalism. Such a transition, I argue, put a new
premium on the idea of equality, giving it a strongly individualistic accent, and, in thus wrenching it from the fabric of republican
thought, also transformed the concept, bending it out of recognition
and perhaps out of its original coherence.

Gordon Wood has described this transition, in a celebrated phrase,
as "the end of classical politics." "The eighteenth century had sought
to understand politics," Wood writes, by appealing to "a graduated
organic chain in the social hierarchy."[70] Classical republicanism celebrated hierarchy—not as the distinguishing mark among individuals, but as the operative condition for a civic order. For as J. G. A. Pocock points out, a healthy polity could come about only with organic
gradations, only with a "naturally differentiated people" "perform-
ing complementary roles and practicing complementary virtues."[71]
Complementarity was the operative tenet of a republican order, and,
to the extent that complementarity meant the joint workings of *unequal* subjects, inequality was not at all a problem here. It was not a
problem because it could be rationalized by politics, rationalized by
republican institutions, so that rather than sowing the seeds of dis-
cord, it instead furnished the structural grounds for civic participation. For as Pocock also points out, classical republicanism did not
presuppose a general equality among its citizens; it only legislated a
specific political equality, "an equal subjection to the *res publica*." The
political sphere, in other words, was the unifying ground, the ground
of commensurability for citizens unequal in every other respect, for
even "though by any standard but one, the shares accorded each
were commensurate but unequal, there was a criterion of equality (in
ruling and being ruled) whereby each remained the other's equal."[72]
To simplify Pocock's complicated argument (and bedeviling prose),
we might say that in classical republicanism, equality was defined
as an effect of the polity—an effect of its rational order—and in that
sense was both independent of and emendatory to the actual existential condition of its citizens. "Commensurate but unequal" was not at
all oxymoronic in this world, for commensurability, understood as an

institutional edict, could stand, in its very institutionality, as the rational ground subsuming and absorbing the brute fact of unequal distribution.

DECLINE OF POLITICAL RATIONALITY

What Woods calls the "end of classical politics" marked the breakdown of this political rationality. "The American Revolution introduced an egalitarian rhetoric to an unequal society," J. R. Pole sums up with admirable succinctness.[73] The complex accommodation between political equality and distributive inequality, once the working paradox of the republican order, now became the fault line along which the entire polity threatened to come apart. The egalitarian rhetoric which had once united the "oppressed" colonies against the "tyranny" of their British rulers was now directed inward, and, applied to the new nation, it quickly revealed the same drama of tyranny and oppression. And so civil society was now seen no longer as a rational entity, a "graduated organic chain" dedicated to the common good, but as a factious conglomerate, torn by competing interests. And to the extent that these competing interests were reproduced on the level of popular government, the political sphere itself was transformed into the home of furor and passion, rather than the home of reason and justice. For as Madison somberly noted in his famous entry (no. 10) to *The Federalist*, political equality was no longer an adequate answer to the "unequal distribution of property," no longer an adequate check on its cankerous passions:

> Hence it is that such democracies have ever been spectacles of turbulence and contention; have ever been found incompatible with personal security or the rights of property; and have in general been as short in their lives as they have been violent in their deaths. Theoretic politicians, who have patronized this species of government, have erroneously supposed that by reducing mankind to a perfect equality in their political rights, they would at the same time be perfectly equalized and assimilated in their possessions, their opinions, and their passions.[74]

In short, for Madison, the political sphere was no longer the ground of commensurability, no longer the seat of a rational order. It had been corrupted, instead, into a passional arena, overrun by "impulses of rage, resentment, jealousy, avarice, and other irregular and violent propensities," and given over to "ruinous contentions," as Alexander Hamilton also noted.[75]

Hamilton was writing in the aftermath of the 1786 Shays's Rebellion, which he identified by name.[76] That event seemed to epitomize the irrational nature of democracies, their tendency toward "ruinous contentions," for its participants, to the horror of all, were revealed to be not dyed-in-the-wool ruffians but ordinary farmers in distress, led by none other than a former militia captain. The rebels were put down, but, again to the horror of all, they were able to recoup in a matter of months under a new tactic, namely, by "promot[ing] their views under the auspices of constitutional forms," as Madison bitterly observed.[77] Those constitutional forms proved so hospitable that they were soon in a position "to establish iniquity by Law."[78] Such atrocities dramatized the extent to which the political sphere had been corrupted, transformed from the rational ground of a republican order into a theater of the absurd.[79] They also dramatized the extent to which the idea of equality itself had been redefined: from a republican to a liberal idea, from civic participation to personal entitlement, from a question of political rationality to a question of individual parity.[80]

The exact nature of the political changes in the late eighteenth and early nineteenth centuries is of course a much disputed issue. Inspired by the work of Bernard Bailyn, J. G. A. Pocock, and Gordon Wood, historians have engaged in a long and heated debate over the relative centrality of classical republicanism and modern liberalism in the early republic.[81] Without being unduly partisan, it is possible, I think, to argue for a new orientation beginning in the 1780s, moving away from the "republican" view of the polity as differentiation for the common good toward a modern "liberal" view, with its emphasis on differentiation as an individuating principle, a principle of centrifugal desires. Liberalism, John Rawls writes, affirms a "plurality of distinct persons with separate systems of ends."[82] This is what makes liberalism compelling and problematic in the twentieth century, as it was compelling and problematic in the nineteenth. And most problematic of all was, and is, the idea of commensurability, given the "plurality of distinct persons." Since commensurability would now have to be defined as equality, and since equality itself would have to be defined as a distributive category—distributing unequal resources through equal individuation—the liberal idea would seem to have embodied at its core a logical incoherence, thrown into ever sharper relief by an ever growing plurality of claims.[83] If "commensurate but unequal" was the paradox of classical republicanism, "equal but incommensurate" might turn out to be the curse of modern liberalism.

Modern liberalism was, to be sure, neither full-blown nor even fully articulated at the end of the eighteenth century. Still, by 1794 the problem of equality—and its vexed relation to individuation—had become so acute that Samuel Williams, historian of Vermont, was moved to offer the following attempt at synthesis:

> [Americans] all feel that nature has made them equal in respect to their rights; or rather that nature has given to them a common and an equal right to liberty, to property, and to safety; to justice, government, laws, religion, and freedom. They all see that nature has made them very unequal in respect to their original powers, capacities, and talents. They become united in claiming and in preserving the equality, which nature has assigned to them; and in availing themselves of the benefits, which are designed, and may be derived from the inequality, which nature has also established.[84]

Nature, that time-honored oracle, seemed more than a little confused here, wavering as it did between an egalitarian theory of rights and a hierarchizing theory of talents. No wonder the author, Samuel Williams, wrote with some confusion himself. Paying his respects, on the one hand, to the newly sanctified tenets of individual equality, Williams seemed to have one foot firmly planted in the liberal landscape. Convinced, on the other hand, that "benefits" were to be "derived from inequality," he seemed to be looking backward to a republican universe, "a graduated organic chain in the social hierarchy." Judging from this spectacle of divided allegiance, we can only agree with Lance Banning: "Logically, it may be inconsistent to be simultaneously liberal and classical. Historically, it was not."[85] However, even this formulation does not quite settle the problem, for to be "simultaneously liberal and classical" must entail a peculiar set of mental gymnastics, not to say a peculiar set of mental constraints. It must give rise, that is, to a peculiarly unstable notion of commensurability, at best supple and inflected, at worst punitive and repressive.

Cooper had no pronouncements as delicately balanced or as visibly perplexed as Williams's. Still, the problem of equality was important enough to merit two chapters in *The American Democrat* (1838), a work also haunted by the exigencies of being simultaneously liberal and classical. True to the latter, Cooper observed, quite bluntly, that "the celebrated proposition contained in the declaration of independence is not to be understood literally. All men are not 'created equal,' in a physical, or even in a moral sense." And he went on (in a litany worthy of *The Deerslayer*) to enumerate those items that made for hierarchical distinctions: "one has a good constitution, another a bad; one is handsome, another ugly; one white, another black[;] . . . one possessing genius, or a natural aptitude, while his brother is an idiot."[86]

Cooper's world remained—anachronistically—a republican universe, a graduated organic chain in the social hierarchy. Such organic gradations posed no threat to the idea of equality, for Cooper, true to his republican legacy, defined the idea strictly in political terms: not as an existential fact emanating from the individual, but as a legislative fact emanating from the polity. Equality, he argued, is simply the consequence of "a new governing principle for the social compact," so that "as regards all human institutions men are born equal." So far, Cooper would seem to be a quintessential (and belated) advocate of classical republicanism. And yet, writing as he did in 1838, he could no longer rest secure in his republican faith. Seeing political equality as an institutional artifact, he also saw it as a *groundless* artifact, for, as he said, "human institutions are a human invention, with which nature has had no connection."[87] Cooper's republicanism was thus republicanism infected with a liberal problematic: a republicanism that, in spite of its hopes in the structural rationality of the political order, nonetheless ended up doubting that political order, doubting its very ground of legitimacy. Here, then, was another way to be simultaneously liberal and classical. And just as Samuel Williams had previously ended up with a "nature" that spoke with a forked tongue, so Cooper's denaturalized polity also brought on something like a rationalizing crisis. After all, if equality is an artificial creation, not grounded in nature but legislated by man, what is there to give it a foundation, a sanctifying ground beyond its stipulated provisions? And if equality is "not to be understood literally" but to be taken rather as a figure of speech—a consensual metaphor instituted by a "social compact"—what is there to make that consensus absolute?[88] What is there to stop one particular individual from figuring equality in a different way? What is there to stop someone like Judith, for example, from claiming that though she is not "literally" equal to Natty, she might nonetheless be deemed equal, deemed, in fact, marriageable to him?

FEMINIZATION OF VIRTUE

On this point, however, *The Deerslayer* stands equipped with an answer. It is crucial then—crucial not just for the plot but for the general problem of commensurability—that Judith should be, as the preface says, "erring, and fallen." Where all else fails, the category of the fallen woman remains infallible. The strength of that category reconstitutes a signifying foundation, a consensual ground that seems not provisional but absolute, not legislative but natural, and makes it possible to say, with restored confidence, who is marriageable to whom and who is equal to whom. To say that is also to suggest that in *The Deerslayer* as in mid-nineteenth-century America, gender is a field of symbolic order: a field where meanings are affixed, identities rationalized, distinctions maintained. Female sexuality is not just a sign here, it is a sign whose referent has become so integral, and indeed so immanent, that it commands the stability almost of a natural fact. The distinction between a virtuous maid and a fallen woman is absolute and absolutely guaranteed, biology being adduced here as a kind of epistemological ballast.

The centrality of gender as a signifying field, then, would seem to stem from its capacity for naturalizing signs and hence its compensatory relation to other fields—for instance, the field of class, where signs are becoming newly unstable, newly denaturalized.[89] In the difficult transition from classical republicanism to modern liberalism, gender is invoked, above all, to restore a natural order to a newly denaturalized political order. Against the groundlessness of political institutions, gender works with the solidity of a natural fact. One knows exactly what it takes to be a fallen woman, what it means to be a fallen woman, and what will eventually happen to a fallen woman. And so in *The Deerslayer*, it is within the semantic field of gender that the idea of equality, elsewhere rendered so problematic, is reconstituted as a coherent notion. It does not matter that Judith and Natty are actually found to be unequal; this regrettable fact is acknowledged, even proclaimed, since its very regrettableness is a tribute to the idea of equality, all the more honored for being unattained. And just as equality is affirmed here in its absence, what is affirmed in absence as well is a rational universe, "commensurate but unequal," in which human institutions can furnish a unifying ground for human differences. Such a universe, of course, no longer existed in the mid-nineteenth century, and no doubt it had never truly existed in that degree of perfection. Through the semantics of gender, however, it could at least be intimated, memorialized, symbolically restored. In this context, Raymond Williams's idea of the "dominant, residual, and emergent" must be broadened to include gender as a primary site of residual signification.[90] In *The Deerslayer*, what is residually invoked is the idealized world of classical republicanism, as yet untouched by its infectious encounters with modern liberalism and as yet pristine in its rational harmony: a world once political in focus but now shadowed forth only through the relations between the sexes.

If sexual purity is ritually invoked, as Mary Douglas argues, to repair the perceived damage to the body politic, the figure of the fallen woman would seem to have a wide symbolic currency, indispensable to any society at odds with itself.[91] Still, at the particular historical juncture we are studying—a juncture marked by the lamented loss of rationality in the political sphere—the figure of the fallen woman would seem to occupy a special place in her culture's semantic landscape. Historians of the early republic have written primarily on the experiential status of women.[92] To their work, we might want to add a rhetorical supplement, focusing on the ways the figure of woman, her integrity or lack of integrity, is made to answer to (and perhaps to answer for) the integrity or lack of integrity of the body politic.

Nor is this political figuration altogether fortuitous. Classical republicanism has never been gender neutral—although we might also note that traditionally it was gendered in a way almost directly contrary to its later avatar. Virtue, that cornerstone of the republican polity, had for centuries been figured as masculine, manifesting itself in military heroism and civic activism. The word virtue "derives from the Latin *virtus*," Hanna Pitkin points out, "and thus from *vir*, which means 'man.' *Virtù* is thus manliness." Meanwhile, *fortuna*, which puts *virtù* at such hazards, is figured primarily (though not exclusively) as feminine. "Fortune is a woman," Machiavelli memorably observes, and, as Pitkin adds, "while he sometimes calls fortune a goddess, the means of coping with her that he suggests are not those usually applied to divinities."[93] The figure of woman has other meanings as well. In *The Spirit of the Laws* (1748), Montesquieu associates her with "luxury," a disease fatal to the republic. He cautions "good legislators" against the "public incontinence" that "causes women to corrupt even before being corrupted."[94]

Judith, whose love of luxury is copiously documented, is conceived very much in the spirit of Montesquieu. Still, this bad habit alone does not seem to be the cause for her downfall. Her capital offense lies elsewhere. Virtue—Judith's much decried loss of it—is what puts her completely beyond the pale of Natty Bumppo, and what disqualifies her forever as a claimant of names. But simply to state that is also to note the enormous distance the word has traveled, not only from its classical Renaissance roots but also from its more immediate use in Revolutionary America. To the Founding Fathers of the republic, virtue was still masculine, still political; and if there was some doubt about its availability, there was no doubt at all about its gender.[95] As the foundational attribute of the republic, the word had an authority almost tautological, as we can see in the circular incantation coming even from a skeptic like James Madison: "I go on this great republican principle: that the people will have virtue and intelligence to select men of virtue and wisdom."[96] Against that great republican principle, the prurient narrowing of focus in *The Deerslayer* must seem like a cruel joke. From being a civic ideal, conducive to the public good, virtue has come to denote a sexual standard, conducive to the acceptability of a marriage. And from being embodied by the manly citizen, virtue is now perilously lodged within the feminine subject.

The feminization of virtue might turn out to be the most important semantic transformation attendant upon the rise of a liberal political culture. Ian Watt long ago alerted us to this "tremendous narrowing of the ethical scale, a redefinition of virtue in primarily sexual terms."[97] More recently, Ruth Bloch and Carroll Smith-Rosenberg have related this semantic transformation to structural changes newly effected in the liberal polity, with its emerging party system, its conception of politics as a sphere of expediency, and, paralleling that development, its emphasis on private morality and relegation of the ethical domain to female tutelage.[98] In short, the feminization of virtue registered in the broadest sense a cognitive revolution, a revolution in the way institutional domains were conceptualized, organized, and differentiated. It had everything to do with the liberal philosophy of separate spheres, a philosophy which distinguished between the sexes even as it distinguished between the moral and the political, inscribing a realm of foundational certitude over and against a realm of partisan maneuverings.[99]

Proceeding further, we might say that nineteenth-century liberalism not only believed in separate spheres of life, it also attributed to each of those spheres a high degree of autonomy, which is to say, a high degree of reflexive resolution and internal equilibrium, imagining each as self-sufficient on its own terms, integrated by its own rationalizing principle. The Invisible Hand behind the self-regulating market was only the most dramatic example of such reflexive resolution. There were other examples as well. The moral domain, as it evolved under the aegis of modern liberalism, also came into its own through a declaration of independence—through a cognitive separation from the polity and from the path of the law—becoming, in the process, a fully autonomous domain, discretely conceptualized and reflexively integrated. And so here too, a self-adequating principle came to govern the structure of the moral agent, matching deed and consequence, character and desert, making the field internally commensurate and internally accountable.

Natty Bumppo, Cooper's prime exhibit in the way of the moral agent, offers a good illustration of its workings. As John P. McWilliams has persuasively argued, and as we see most vividly in *The Pioneers* (1823), Natty embodies the moral law as opposed to the civil law embodied by the lesser characters.[100] And the moral law, in *The Deerslayer*, is summed up by one word, "honesty," an epithet Natty virtually personifies. "I'll answer for his *honesty*, whatever I may do for his valor in battle" (63): this is Harry March's backhanded compliment, and, for the rest of the book, we are never allowed to lose sight of Natty's "honest face and honest heart" (74). "All proclaim your honesty," Judith tells him (128), "your honest countenance would be sufficient surety for the truth of a thousand hearts" (126). And she adds, "The girl that finally wins you, Deerslayer, will at least win an honest heart—one without treachery or guile" (130).

Honesty, understood as an antidote to "treachery or guile," harkens back to the eighteenth century, to what Gordon Wood has called its "paranoid style," a conspiratorial mode of thinking. Cooper's *The Pathfinder* (published in 1840, just one year before *The Deerslayer*) was an extravagant exercise in just that genre.[101] However, as

Wood also argues, the paranoid style must be seen not as a collective delusion or mania but as a "mode of causal attribution," which, in supposing that "every social effect, every political event, had to have a purposive human agent as a cause," implicitly "presumes a world of autonomous, freely acting individuals who are capable of directly and deliberately bringing about events through their decisions and actions, and who thereby can be held morally responsible for what happens." The paranoid style turns out to be a Kantian style. Assuming as it did a fully purposive, fully rationalized universe—a universe that admitted of no mismatch, no loss between will and consequence—this paranoid style sustained not only an eighteenth-century style of political discourse but, increasingly, a nineteenth-century style of moral reasoning. And as Wood also points out, this mode of causal attribution has not died with the eighteenth century: "its assumptions still permeate our culture, although, as our system of criminal punishment shows, in increasingly archaic and contradictory ways."[102]

Natty is not about to become a recipient of such criminal punishment. Still, his moral centrality in *The Deerslayer* would seem to suggest not only the extent to which the novel is even more archaic, even more contradictory than criminal law, but also the extent to which this archaic contradiction is simultaneously the rallying point for a new line of development. For what Natty embodies, in his formidable integrity—in the fully commensurate, fully matching relation between his "honest face" and "honest heart"—is nothing other than the newly sanctified image of the moral domain, understood now as a domain rationalizable on its own terms, a domain of reflexive resolution and internal equilibrium. And so it is fitting that the litmus test for him should be the act of promise keeping, an act which, if executed, would bear witness to just such a rationalizable universe. Promise keeping is thus central to Cooper as the criterion for a morality reflexively integrated within the individual.[103] And Natty's conduct here is exemplary. Captured by the Hurons, he is allowed to leave on a "furlough." Judith begs him not to return, but Natty would not think of it. For him, a furlough is "a thong that binds tighter than any chain. . . . Ropes and chains allow of knives, and desait, and contrivances, but a furlough can be neither cut, slipped, nor sarcumvented" (445).

Natty is bound by his promise, not only in the sense that he is compelled to honor it but also in the sense that he is reflexively integrated by it, becoming, in the process, a truly rational entity, recuperative in time as well as in space, its will always translating into its deed, the terminal effect always encompassed by the original intention. He is as good as his word. Here, then, is a version of the commensurate that would actually work. Problematic as a distributive category and endangered as a political category, commensurability remains coherent, it would seem, only as a moral category, reflexively unifying the trajectory of a single individual. On the strength of that commensurability, Natty is able to go through a succession of names—"Straighttongue," "Pigeon," "Lap-Ear," "Deerslayer," "Hawkeye"—without failing always to be equal to himself. Also on the strength of that commensurability, the novel ends, having rejected various unequal matches, with that curious, seemingly tautological, but by no means unequal union: between a man named Deerslayer and a gun named Killdeer.

The moral domain, as it is reflexively integrated by the moral agent, thus turns out to be the rational ground not only for the nineteenth-century novel but also, more generally still, for a liberalism increasingly faced with the erosion of that rational ground in other spheres of life. Especially for Cooper, sorely aware that the political order has no foundation in nature, the recovery of a moral foundation must seem all the more gratifying. Natty's "moral law," offered not only in contradistinction to civil law but also in transcendence of it, might be seen, then, as a kind of necessary fantasy, an attempt to redress the decline of reason in politics by looking beyond it, locating beyond its passional sphere a rational ground at once more innate and more permanent. In short, the moral law, to be moral, must now be *natural*; it must be anterior to and independent of politics. And it is the naturalness of this morality that the novel must demonstrate with particular insistence.

On that count, however, Natty himself would appear to be a rather inadequate specimen, for even though his promise keeping might look like an instance of natural morality, its naturalness nonetheless cannot be definitively proven. In fact, a hundred years before Cooper, in a well-known chapter in *A Treatise of Human Nature* (1739), Hume had argued just the opposite. "The rule of morality, which enjoins the performance of promises, is not *natural*," Hume said, because promises are merely "*symbols* or *signs* instituted, by which we might give each other security of our conduct." As such, they are strictly "human inventions, founded on the necessities and interests of society." Indeed, "a promise wou'd not be intelligible, before human conventions had establish'd it."[104] And since promise keeping is conventional, so too is morality itself. It is no more than an "artificial" institution, Hume argued, no more than a system of assumable signs: "It appears, therefore, that all virtuous actions derive their merit only from virtuous motives, and are consider'd merely as signs of those motives. . . . But 'tis usual . . . to fix our attention on the signs, and neglect, in some measure, the thing signify'd."[105]

A moral person, according to Hume, is simply a person who displays the signs of morality: signs anything but natural, anything but innate. Something of that unhappy thought, I think, haunts the moral landscape of *The Deerslayer*. And perhaps it is to overcome it that the novel would develop a twin focus, giving us not only a putatively moral character who keeps promises but also a certifiably immoral character who has grievously sinned. In other words, to be truly foundational, the judgmental weight of the novel would have to be borne not only by a man such as Natty, the naturalness of whose morality is a matter of surmise, but, even more crucially, by a woman such as Judith, the naturalness of whose "fallenness" is a matter of certainty, anatomically demonstrable and quite beyond dispute.

If the rise of modern liberalism marked the decline of political rationality, as I have tried to argue, the feminization of virtue would seem to be simultaneously a symptom and a remedy. A cognitive revolution such as this one testifies both to the emerging irrationality of the political sphere and to a spirited attempt to repair that damage, to locate a rational ground outside the vicissitudes of politics, in a natural morality commensurate with the natural order. The feminization of virtue, in this sense, might be seen as the naturalization of Reason itself, perhaps the ultimate dream of the Enlightenment. And as we have already seen in Kant's *Philosophy of Law*, Reason naturalized within the moral domain must make "justice" a natural dictate, a categorical imperative, its "Equalization of Like with Like" taking on the character of an axiom, its principle of commensurability doubling as a death sentence. To the extent that *The Deerslayer* is home to this naturalized justice, it too must be punitive at its core: punitive not out of wanton cruelty but out of rational necessity.

The fate of Judith amply attests to that punitive rationality. She, as we know, is someone inhospitable to the commensurate, being always above or beneath someone else. Such a problem, however, is not without its remedy. The remedy is suggested, in fact, by Hurry Harry in an oddly prescient remark to Thomas Hutter. Judith, he says, "hasn't her equal on the frontiers for good looks, whatever she may have for good behavior. . . . Give me Jude, if her conduct was only equal to her looks!" (73). Hurry begins by stating the problem— Judith, once again, has failed to be equal to anyone—but he quickly moves from the problematic to the optative, turning from the unequal distribution of beauty among persons to a more congenial topic, namely, the maintenance of equivalence between "looks" and "conduct" within a single person. As with Natty, it is the moral agent that is offered as the theater of the commensurate. And since that agent happens to be a fallen woman, the gender inflection neatly transposes as a disciplinary proposition what is problematically unstable as a distributive proposition. The persistence of retribution in the novel, the feminization of that phenomenon, thus represents something of a wish fulfillment on its part, its dream of a justice immanent within a natural order.

And yet if *The Deerslayer* is any indication (and the novel seems to me virtually generic in this regard), such a dream of justice must remain, first and last, a dream. Its frailty is underscored not least of all by the punitive excess of the novel—its tendency toward undue severity, redoubled execution—an excess which, in its refusal to limit its scope, must end up upsetting the very moral ground that underwrites it and gives it coherence. Something of that excess is seen in the fate of Hetty, who, caught "in the crowd of Huron women" (507) fleeing the British army, is fatally wounded by a stray bullet. "How this wound was received no one knew" (512). Judith, of course, assures her sister, " 'Twas an accident, poor Hetty; a sad accident it has been" (514). But Cooper also adds, "it was probably one of those casualties that ever accompany scenes like that related in the previous chapter" (512). What was related in the previous chapter was the triumph of the king's army, a triumph accompanied by the usual "shrieks" and "groans" of the vanquished, although, oddly, what Cooper chooses to dwell on is one particular aural detail, "a sound unusual to the woods." This was the "measured tread" of the army, an army of "trained men," a tread "regular and heavy, as if the earth were struck with beetles" (507). It is the sinister repetition of this sound, this "heavy, measured, menacing tread," which troubles the concluding pages of the novel, and gathers into a single detail the bugbear of republican thought, its fear of the "standing army." And it is against the complex inscriptions of that sound that we can see Hetty's death as complexly inscribed as well, a death afflicting her, to be sure, but also radiating outward to a web of referents.

Guiltless herself, Hetty must nonetheless pay the penalty of death. That exorbitant penalty is exacted from her, no doubt because, like Judith, she too is a signifying criminal, made to atone not only for a moral offense, the "sins of the family," but also in this case for a political offense, something like the sins of the nation, the sins of a republic gone liberal. For what is dramatized here, in the "accidental" death of Hetty, the senselessness of it and the randomness of it, is nothing other than the breakdown of Reason itself: once the hoped-for foundation of the polity and now the hoped-for foundation of nature, but, in the mindless killing of Hetty, proven unreliable on both counts. Perhaps that mindlessness matches the feeblemindedness of Hetty's own life; but, if so, this instance of commensurability must seem an obscene parody of the term. Unlike the death penalty in Kant, the guaranteed "Equalization of Punishment with Crime," the death penalty in Cooper brings with it no guarantee of a natural fit in the world. And unlike the path of the law, the broad mantle of novelistic justice is finally too broad for its own logic, too complexly inscribed and too richly particularized to pass for a model of full rationality. What is dispensed here, then, turns out to be a rather disconcerting kind of justice, intensely retributive, to be sure, but also hopelessly overwrought, hopelessly asymmetrical to its object, unnerving in its excess, and unedifying in its residue.

And so even Judith, the prime recipient of novelistic justice, is not completely dispatchable, not completely obliterated by the verdict which, barring her from Natty's affections, leaves her "with a heart nearly broken by the consciousness of undeserving" (531). Judith is undeserving of Natty, the voice of justice would like us to think. But given the lack of a syntactic predicate here—given the construction of "undeserving" as a detached substantive, rather than as an adjectival copula appended to a particular object—Judith might also be said to be the embodiment of "undesert" itself, embodying it as a morally vexing condition and embodying it, as always, in a glaring unfitness for the commensurate. If she is both too good and not good enough for Natty, she is also too good and not good enough for any fate that the novel might conceivably devise for her. Her banishment to England—to take up with Warley, "though she did not bear his name" (534)—dispenses justice only within the formal closure of the novel. It cannot eliminate her completely, for, fifteen years later, revisiting the scene, Natty "found a ribbon of Judith's fluttering from a log," a ribbon which "recalled all her beauty and, we may add, all her failings." Natty takes it and "knot[s] it to the stock of Killdeer, which had been the gift of the girl herself" (533). Together, in their knottedness and in their incommensurability, gun and ribbon testify both to the workings of novelistic justice and to the persistence of its residues.

2

Part and Whole

"Distributive justice is a large idea. It draws the entire world of goods within the reach of philosophical reflection. Nothing can be omitted; no feature of our common life can escape scrutiny." So writes Michael Walzer in the opening paragraph of *The Spheres of Justice* (1983), a book remarkably unorthodox in its refusal to look for a "singular conclusion" about justice, but somewhat less unorthodox, perhaps, in the operative scope it continues to claim for that term. Justice for Walzer is not only a large idea; it is the most comprehensive, indeed the most exhaustive, idea imaginable, the most fundamental guiding principle for any human community. Its sphere of action is coincidental with the "entire world," with the sum of lived experience, with "being and doing as [well as] having."[1]

Walzer's broad definition of justice thus carries with it a silent premise about the nature of human society: a society imagined to be a "whole" and justice imagined, in turn, as the ethical norm governing that whole. This conception of justice as a virtue pertaining to a totality—and a virtue presiding over that totality—is not at all unique to Walzer, being is a commonplace at least since Plato. In *The Republic*, for example, since it is the state that counts as a totality, Plato suggests that it is "in a State which is ordered with a view to the good of the whole [that] we should be most likely to find justice." Justice, in other words, is the integrating principle of any given society, here imagined as a corporate unit. For that reason, it must be regarded, like a statue, "not piecemeal," not by exaggerating some particular feature, "but as a whole . . . by giving this and the other features their due proportion."[2]

This chapter questions the notion of a "whole"—whether social or individual—both in the context of the century best known for its exposition and theorization, the nineteenth century, and in the context of a particular vision of justice it continues to underwrite. My discussion will feature Herman Melville and Rebecca Harding Davis at pivotal moments, though its initial engagement (in various senses of that word) is with the Marxist vision of justice. Marx is, of course, often taken to be an *anti*theorist of justice. His pronouncements on the subject are strictly ironic, some commentators have argued, because justice as he sees it is no more than the idealized self-image of a given economic regime, no more than the glorified abstraction from a reigning ideology.[3] Here, I take a somewhat different view, arguing that a nonironic theory of justice is traceable to Marx: traceable to his belief in a social whole and above all to his materialist conception of that whole.

Marxist materialism—a generalizing principle, moving always from a determinant to that which it determines—not only presupposes as its operative condition a social totality but presupposes, as well, a fully translatable (and therefore fully recoverable) totality of cause and effect. Like the concept of justice itself, materialism, at its most thoroughgoing, is above all a dream of objective adequation. Invoked as historical agency, as a material "base" translatable into corresponding social structures, it makes justice a matter of teleological guarantee (and, by the same token, perhaps also a matter of analytic indifference). Justice in Marx, I want to suggest, is both presumed and rendered moot by that presumption. Its imperfect enactment in history is guaranteed to be rectifiable in time, rectifiable by a social whole whose eventual materialization is the very promise of its materialism. The concept of the "whole," in other words, is both the operative premise and the inferential endpoint for Marx. And on this count (as on many others), he is perhaps more truly a nineteenth-century figure than we ordinarily think: committed to a discourse of part and whole that I call "metonymic" and committed, not least of all, to a vision of justice founded upon its generalizations.

METONYMY AND MATERIALISM

Not unique to Marx, the discourse of part and whole was very much a standard trope in the nineteenth century, a regular feature of its social critique. In a graphic moment in "The American Scholar," for example, Emerson would thrust before the reader a catalog of bodily parts, amputated and randomly assorted, "strut[ting] about" like "so many walking monsters—a good finger, a neck, a stomach, an elbow, but never a man." With this grotesque image he castigated a phenomenon he found equally grotesque, a phenomenon brought on by the modern division of labor and amounting, as he saw it, to a metonymic perversion, a substitution of part for whole. Every task is "so distributed to multitudes, . . . so minutely subdivided and peddled out," Emerson complained, that human beings too have become mere fractions of what they might have been.[4] Speaking of human fractions, Emerson's neighbor, Thoreau, was even more emphatic: "It is not the tailor alone who is the ninth part of a man; it is as much the preacher, and the merchant, and the farmer. Where is this division of labor to end? and what object does it finally serve?"[5]

Emerson and Thoreau were talking about the same phenomenon which, some sixty years earlier, Adam Smith had reported in thrilling terms.[6] The division of labor for Smith had meant a tremendous gain in productivity, his prime example being the worker who, once upon a time, had been capable of making "perhaps not one pin in a day," but who under modern management "might be considered as making four thousand eight hundred pins in a day."[7] For Emerson and Thoreau, such increased output could mean only a human loss, only a substitutive violence, by which the "ninth part of a man" was made to stand for the man who, they assumed, was once upon a time fully himself, organic and integral. "A man in the view of political economy is a pair of hands," Emerson had observed in an earlier lecture.[8] This sense of metonymic horror was vividly felt on both sides of the Atlantic. It was the burden of Ruskin's pointed rebuke to Adam Smith in *The Stones of Venice* (1853), when he complained about laborers being "divided into mere segments of Men—broken into small fragments and crumbs of life; so that all the little piece of intelligence that is left in a man is not enough to make a pin, or a nail, but exhausts itself in making the point of a pin or the head of a nail."[9] And it was the burden of Marx's even more pointed critique in *Capital* (1867). Capitalism, Marx wrote, institutes a regimen of "partial function" and "fractional work"; it "rivet[s] each labourer to a single fractional detail" and runs a "productive mechanism whose parts are human beings."[10] In so doing, it

> converts the labourer into a crippled monstrosity, . . . just as in the States of La Plata they butcher a whole beast for the sake of his hide or his tallow. . . . Not only is the detail work distributed to the different individuals, but the individual himself is made the automatic motor of a fractional operation, and the absurd fable of Menenius Agrippa, which makes man a mere fragment of his own body, becomes realised.[11]

The body of the worker, partitioned and fragmented, thus stands for Marx as a sign, a generalizable figure, for capitalist atrocity. I call this mode of figuration "metonymic," not so much in the sense of Roman Jakobson[12] as in the sense of Kenneth Burke and, more recently, in the sense now current among cognitive linguists, especially George Lakoff. For Kenneth Burke, metonymy is the trope that "conveys some incorporeal or intangible state in terms of the corporeal or tangible"; it is thus a form of reduction, capturing an immaterial order within a material index and an attribute of consciousness within a "bodily equivalent."[13] George Lakoff, meanwhile, links metonymy to what he calls the "prototype effect" in human cognition: the tacit derivation of an overarching, integral, and silently normative category from a term construed to be its part.[14] Metonymy operates most broadly then as a principle of commensurability, the immaterial here being encapsulated by (and equated with) the material in a generalizable relation, a relation of representational adequacy or logical inferability. Deriving a presumptive whole from an actualized part, metonymy not only instantiates but also contains, focusing on a salient detail only to project from it a bounded totality. In this particular example, the bodily parts adduced by Emerson and Thoreau, Marx and Ruskin, would seem to be projections, however monstrous, of a normative wholeness, shadowed in its very loss.

This chapter is an argument against the presumed integrity of such a "whole." It is also an argument against the presumed commensurability of the material and the immaterial. Still, my hope here is not to develop a general critique of metonymy but to challenge one particular instance of its deployment. What concerns me is a quite specific juncture, the juncture at which Marx (like Emerson, Thoreau, and Ruskin) should choose to expose the injustice of capitalism by invoking the ideal of an integral unit—equated with its physical body, here called "the individual himself"—a unit whose current dismemberment he lamented but whose original (and eventual) wholeness he apparently never questioned.

The nineteenth-century concept of a "whole," including Marx's and perhaps most especially Marx's, was thus "materialist" in a quite literal sense, in that it was derived from (and imaged after) the boundedness and integrity of the physical body. What this corporeal derivation made possible was a new assurance about the boundedness and integrity of the world, based on the commensurability between the

see M. D. Bell's
Resumption of
romanticism.

material and the immaterial, an assurance I here call "metonymic."
Here I also depart from Hayden White, who, in identifying metonymy as a central trope in Marx, has emphasized its opposition to the
metaphoric (and thus fragmenting) exchange imposed by capitalism.[15] Yet in its very denial of the fragmented, in its reduction of all
differences to a form of the commensurate, metonymy in my view
would seem to be instituting an exchange of its own. It was through
metonymy, after all, that the idea of the person was here equated with
the physical fact of the person, making the bodily subject synonymous with the subject as an epistemological category.

Charles Taylor has referred to this principle of commensurability—this equation of the epistemological with the corporeal—as the
"strong localization" of the self. He links it not only to modern individualism but also to modern materialism, the paradoxical union of
which, he argues, would usher in the equally paradoxical spectacle of
a "radical subjectivity" consorting with a "radical objectivity." Under
this new dispensation, this collapse of the immaterial into the material, "we come to think that we 'have' selves as we have heads."[16] It
was this equation of "selves" with "heads" that prompted these nineteenth-century thinkers to make the bodily subject a founding unit,
an empirical whole, integral not only in physical space but also in the
nonphysical space of a polity, an economy, and a morality.

Following Taylor, then, I want to link the preeminence of the bodily
subject not only to nineteenth-century individualism but also, more
surprisingly, to nineteenth-century materialism, especially its Marxist variant. "Materialism," from this perspective, is something rather
broader than the position usually attributed to Marx and summed
up in his much-quoted preface to the *Critique of Political Economy*
("The totality of these relations of production constitutes the economic structure of society, the real foundation, on which arises a legal
and political superstructure and to which correspond definite forms
of social consciousness").[17] Understood as a form of economism, materialism has had more than its share of critics. Rather than rehearsing
their familiar arguments, I want to give the term a different definitional scope and situate it within a different order of vulnerability.
Taking materialism to be above all an epistemology, I want to take
issue not with its thematic dependence on the economic but with its
cognitive dependence on the commensurate: its dependence on the
translatable relation from part to whole, from the tangible to the in-

tangible. It is in this sense that I want to charge Marxist materialism with being "metonymic," metonymy here being not just a style of representation but also a style of cognition. And it is this cognitive style that underwrites Marx's dream of an integral body as an adequate figure for "the individual himself," as well as his dream of a total revolution as an adequate figure for justice, an adequation based on the translatability of the economic into the legal, the political, and the social.

BODIES PHYSICAL AND NONPHYSICAL

Marx is not alone, I should add, in being intelligible within a metonymic tradition. We too are intelligible within it, for the legacy of metonymy is still with us today, still current in the debates in contemporary political theory, between, say, Michael Sandel and John Rawls, about the degree of coincidence between the bodily subject and the epistemological subject.[18] It is current as well, I would further argue, in the institution of literary criticism, in our shared habit of referring routinely to the "body" of the text, as if its epistemological horizons were objectively bounded: bounded by its contents, and bounded (most currently) by its material circumstances, circumstances generalizable into something called History, a whole at once social and textual. Metonymy dies hard, it would seem. Still, its longevity notwithstanding, such a cognitive form has not always been in ascendancy, and historically the material and the immaterial have been otherwise correlated, the image of part and whole otherwise configured.

In the *Nicomachean Ethics,* for example, the imagined whole turned out to have something other than a material body, and it answered to something other than a personal name. It was the *community* that counted as an integral unit for Aristotle, the community that represented the ideal of some fundamental and plenary wholeness. Not surprisingly, then, it was the nonphysical ideal of the community—rather than the physical body of the individual—that struck Aristotle as being in danger and in need of fortification against the fragmenting effects of the division of labor. Since there was no natural bond between the builder and the shoemaker, and between the shoemaker and the farmer, Aristotle worried that "a community or association between them would be impossible." Indeed, if it were not for that fortunate necessity, the necessity of "reciprocal exchange," which reunited those separated by the division of labor, binding them to-gether "as if they were one single unit," the always precarious whole called the community might otherwise "not hold together."[19]

I have highlighted the degree to which the bodily subject was not deemed an endangered unit (or a unit of concern) for Aristotle, not only to supply a foil to Marx but also to bring into focus a different epistemological tradition, one that, to my mind, stands less as an al-ternative to materialism than as a reminder of its limits. The example of Aristotle is especially instructive here. His well-known defense of concrete particulars notwithstanding, Aristotle was not willing to equate an epistemological entity with its physical embodiment, not willing to imagine the immaterial as being commensurate with, ex-hausted by, or generalizable from a material unit. In this regard at least, he was firmly within the tradition of ontic logos, a tradition prevalent in Greek antiquity and dramatized most memorably in Plato's Theory of Forms.[20] This subtle but crucial space of epistemo-logical difference—a space left open (and left opaque) by the explana-tory inadequacy of the material world—would persist for the next two thousand years, with obvious changes but also with significant continuities. It was kept alive, not least of all, by Christian theology, under whose auspices the explanatory inadequacy of the material world would become not only a point of contention but also a cause for celebration.

It was the "body" of Christ, after all—the body and its enigmatic materiality—that fueled the major doctrinal battles of the eleventh and twelfth centuries. The problem with the term "body," as exas-perated church fathers noticed from the outset, was that it had "mul-tiple" meanings: at least three, in fact, referring simultaneously to "the body of Christ in human form, the body of Christ in the Sac-rament, and the body of Christ in the church."[21] The apostle Paul hardly clarified matters when he offered the following exegesis: "The bread which we break, is it not the communion of the body of Christ? For we being many are one bread and one body, for we are all par-takers of that one bread."[22] Augustine, puzzling in turn over this sup-posed gloss, thought that "the communion of the body of Christ" meant "the unity of the body and blood of Christ," which he inter-preted as "the society of his body and members, which is the holy church in those who have been predestined and called."[23] The holy church as the "body of Christ" was indeed a central tenet of medieval theology, but it was also a central enigma, as imperfectly grasped by human reason as it was imperfectly registered by the physical senses, a "body" in no way coextensive with the corporeality of its members. The efficacy of the church, its power to secure salvation for all, was based on this very incommensurability, this ineffable (but not unimaginable) margin of discrepancy between the two kinds of "bodies." For it was only in the midst of—and only in its nonreduction to—the mortality of physical bodies that the corporate church would shine forth in its immortal majesty: a body in nonphysical space, at once immediate and intangible, available to sensory apprehension and indeed sensory adulation, but hardly encompassed by its limits.

The enigma of the corporate church—the sense that it was somehow not just a body, somehow more than a body, though it was nonetheless a body—attested not only to the commingling of the material and the immaterial in medieval thought but also to the complex lack of adequation between these two orders of reality. As much as anything else, the corporate church was marked by its cognitive slipperiness, its refusal to conform to the bounds of the senses. Even so, it was less of an enigma, and less of a knotty theological issue, than the problematic materiality suggested by the other meaning of the "body of Christ," revolving around the character of the sacramental host in the Eucharist. Almost to a man, Christian exegetes rejected the cheap excuse that the "body" might be no more than a figure of speech. Almost to a man, they agreed that the body was material, a "real presence," and that, in the act of consecration, the bread actually stopped being bread and was "converted into the nature and substance of the flesh" of Christ.[24] What was unclear, however, was how this "conversion" came about. In what sense could the bread and wine be said to be the body and blood of Christ, and what relation did this eucharistic "body" bear to the historical body of Christ, the body received from the womb of the Virgin Mary and sacrificed on the cross? In the eleventh and twelfth centuries, these theological fine points would flare up into debates of the most gargantuan proportions.

Berengar of Tours, author of *De sacra coena* (*On the Holy Supper*) and one of the chief antagonists in this controversy, argued that the eucharistic body could not possibly be that historical body, because otherwise it would "have been in existence already for a thousand years and more." Even if one could stomach the idea of eating some thousand-year-old meat, Berengar thought it unlikely that the body of Christ in heaven would be daily cut up and "a particle" daily "sent down to the altar."[25] And, in any case, what did it mean to "eat" this Christic flesh? Guitmond of Aversa, an opponent of Berengar's, but like him driven by an overliteral imagination, began to worry about a mouse nibbling on the consecrated host. Would that animal be eating the "body of Christ"?[26] Clearly, these were questions not everyone would like to entertain. Berengar was condemned by a succession of councils and synods (fourteen in all). In 1059, he was forced under duress, in Rome, to recant his position and to affirm that "the bread and wine are the true body and blood of our Lord Jesus Christ," even to the point where that body might be "ground by the teeth of the faithful."[27] This did not quite settle the controversy, however, which waged on for another hundred and fifty years, until finally, in 1215, the Fourth Lateran Council established the doctrine of transubstantiation (the actual presence of the body and blood of Christ "under the outward appearances of bread and wine"),[28] a doctrine that survived even the challenge of the Reformation, being reaffirmed by the Council of Trent in 1551.

The debate about the eucharistic body reflected not only the complex discrepancy between the material and the immaterial in medieval theology but also the complex discrepancy between "reason" and "sense."[29] As Galileo would say (in a different context), the Christian theologians were "able to make reason so conquer sense that, in defiance of the latter, the former became the mistress."[30] And so, even though the "holy mystery of the Lord's body" was not exactly comprehensible as a *sensory* phenomenon, the theologians were nonetheless able to argue for its *rational* defensibility.[31] The "rationality" at work here, then, would seem to be of a distinct, and distinctly premodern, stripe, not predicated on the evidentiary adequacy of the senses, and certainly not on the generalizability from the material to the immaterial. Within the terms of our discussion, we might say such a rationality was profoundly antimetonymic. The material and the immaterial commingled, that is, only in enigmatic apposition and not at all in explanatory adequation: it would be folly to start out from the physical bread and wine and generalize about the "body of Christ." Acceding, then, to the explanatory limits of the material world, the Christian theologians acceded as well to an order of reality only imperfectly fathomed by the senses.

This premodern rationality, with its tolerance for conceptual enigmas, was discernible not only in Christian theology but also in that most sober and unmystical of domains, jurisprudence. The complex discrepancy between the material and the immaterial would prevail even here, for it was here, as Ernest H. Kantorowicz has shown, that one would encounter the legal fiction of the "King's Two Bodies," a fiction kept alive for hundreds of years, providing one of the most important threads of continuity from the Middle Ages through Tudor and Stuart England and reappearing, as late as 1765, in Blackstone's *Commentaries on the Laws of England.*[32] And so the king too, like Christ, had a "body" that amounted to a kind of sensory mystery, a mystery that nevertheless did nothing to prevent the most determined as well as most virtuoso sort of legal reasoning, displayed, on this occasion, by the learned judges in the celebrated case of the Duchy of Lancaster (1562). The king, they reasoned, had a body politic at once insepar-able from but also irreducible to the body natural:

> So that he has a Body natural, adorned and invested with the Estate and Dignity royal; and he has not a Body natural distinct and divided by itself from the Office and Dignity royal, but a Body natural and a Body politic together indivisible; and these two Bodies are incorpo-rated in one Person, and one Body and not divers, that is the Body corporate in the Body natural, *et e contra* the Body natural in the Body corporate. So that the Body natural, by this conjunction of the Body politic to it (which Body politic contains the Office, Government, and Majesty royal), is magnified, and by the said Consolidation hath in it the Body politic.[33]

The syllogism, self-announced as it was, was not strictly speaking sensible—if one defines "sense," that is, by the reckoning of the phys-ical senses. Like the Christian theologians, the learned judges here seemed to be doing some fancy footwork with arithmetic and with physical concepts such as spatial location and extension. Bacon, con-fident New Physicist that he was, and supremely intolerant of such mysteries, complained that this was "a confusion of tongues [having] their foundations in subtlety and imagination of man's wit, and not in the ground of nature."[34] That confusion of tongues was tolerated even less, in the twentieth century, by Frederic Maitland, the great legal historian, for whom the King's Two Bodies had now become nothing but a joke. He would "not know where to look," Maitland said, "in the whole series of our law books for so marvelous a display of metaphysical—or we might say metaphysiological—nonsense."[35]

Maitland is right, of course. Or at least he is right within a particular cognitive universe, in which the "metaphysical" and the "metaphysiological" have come to mean the nonsensical, and in which "sense" itself has come increasingly to be equated with human reason itself. This conflation of sense with reason—a phenomenon traceable to the seventeenth century, to the new fascination with the physical and mechanical properties of the mind—would, in the succeeding centuries, profoundly transform the relation not only between body and mind but also between the mind and the world. Henceforth the mind would engage the world only in its material intelligibility, only through the evidence furnished by the physical senses, on the assumption that such empirical data would unlock mysteries elsewhere operative. Enlightenment rationality—linked most directly to secularization and more obliquely to Protestantism—might be seen critically, then, as an alternate form of mystification: the mystification of empirical reason itself into what Bacon called "the ground of nature." That "ground" was thus very much a materialist ground, giving pride of place always to the materiality of the body—or rather, to the materiality of the world as registered by the materiality of the body—a materiality which was then adduced as an account of the mind as well as an account of the world.[36] In sharp contrast then to the enigmatic apposition of the material and the immaterial in medieval theology, a relation of explanatory adequacy would now prevail, subordinating the immaterial to the material as a logical derivative, or perhaps even, as Michael McKeon suggests, as an "analogy."[37] Within the terms of our discussion, we might also call Enlightenment rationality an instance (and an especially long-lasting instance) of metonymic practice, operating always on the presumed commensurability between two ontological orders: between body and mind, between thought and world, between evidence tangible and empirical and inferences intangible and presumed.

To press home the distinction between the modern and the premodern rationality that I have tried to outline, we might point to one particular area of contrast, having to do with the postulate of "generalizability" and with the cognitive practices it underwrites. Unacceptable (and indeed inconceivable) to premodern reason as a hermeneutic relation between material and immaterial realms, this postulate has become, since the Enlightenment, none other than the founding tenet of modern rationality.[38] Unlike medieval cognitive practice, then, which assigned to the senses no evidentiary primacy and to the material realm no explanatory adequation, Enlightenment rationality came into being not only through the elevation of the senses into evidentiary ground but also through the elevation of physical evidence into generalizable evidence. Now sense and reason, materiality and reality would all be strung together into a series of equivalences: symmetrical, airtight, mutually entailed, mutually reflexive. Materialism—understood as a dream of objective adequation—thus imposed on the world a new texture, thinning it out into a translatable order, a grid of inferable correspondences. No longer opaque, no longer a paradox of the sensible and the enigmatic, it would henceforth acquire a uniform comprehensibility, submitting without fail to empirical proofs and causal explanations. The collapse of reason into sense, in short, went hand in hand with the attribution to the world of a kind of anticipated (and therefore compulsory) transparency. We usually associate these imperial claims of reason with modern science, but such claims would seem to have been shared by a much broader spectrum of Enlightenment epistemologies. Modern materialism, in particular, would seem to stand or fall on those claims, for, embracing a physicalized world as its evidentiary ground, it would effectively invert the Cartesian mind/body dualism into an *explanatory* dualism, so that the material would be separated from the immaterial only to serve as its epistemological foundation, the foundation upon which the immaterial might be explained as a secondary effect.[39]

This Enlightenment tradition of physical evidence and explanatory adequacy was thus very much the philosophical tradition inhabited by Marx.[40] To be sure, he was witnessing its darkening moment, the moment when, as Foucault suggests, the field of knowledge was increasingly troubled by a new sense of "obscure verticality," of "great hidden forces" invisibly controlling the "visible order."[41] Still, this darkening world would seem only to have inspired and not deterred Marx, propelling him toward material explanations of antithetical clarity, if equal verticality. His critique of the commodity form (punctuated by the word "mystery" as a kind of incantatory accusation) was driven very much by an explanatory passion, by a desire to make sense of the world, to deliver it from its intolerable opacities through an attribution of cause. For him, the idea of an immaterial order—incommensurate with, inexplicable by, and nongeneralizable from material facts—was nothing if not an intellectual affront. And as his grudging tribute to Bacon, Hobbes, and Locke made amply clear, not the least of the attractions of materialism was its epistemological certitude. Praising Bacon, for example, for the "rational method [he applied] to the data provided by the senses" and for his "teaching [that] the senses are infallible and are the source of all knowledge," Marx acknowledged that "materialism is the son of Great Britain by birth."[42] And as if further to underscore that kinship, he here had recourse to the same argument (and indeed the same vocabulary) that Frederic Maitland would use fifty years later, noting with some vehemence that "an *incorporeal substance* is just as much a nonsense as an *incorporeal body. Body, being, substance* are one and the same real idea."[43] It was this equation of "body" with "being"—and the casual relegation of the incorporeal to the realm of "nonsense"—that made for the explanatory texture of Marxist materialism, an evidentiary model predicated not only, as we all know, on the primacy of the economic but, just as crucially, on a conception of man as a *"corporeal, living, real, sensuous, objective being."*[44] As an entity whose physical wholeness was an undisputed given, the bodily subject thus stood at the very heart of the Marxist dream of objective adequation. The bodily subject was the locus of metonymy in Marx, we might say: the point of inferential projections, the point where he could derive his generalizations from matter to spirit, from part to whole, from a physical fact to a presumptive totality.

But to say that is also to suggest a certain tropism, a certain gravitational pull, between Marxist materialism and nineteenth-century individualism. For within an evidentiary universe of the physical senses, it is only the corporeal subject—only the individual as actualized by his or her body—that can ever be demonstrable as "real." As Marx says, "Since only what is material is perceptible, knowable, *nothing* is known of the existence of God. I am sure only of my own existence."[45] Only the bodily subject can ever stand, empirically and incontestably, as a founding unit of Marxist epistemology. And since the relation between the material and the immaterial is now one of explanatory adequation (rather than, as previously, one of enigmatic apposition), it is the bodily subject that must now stand as the ground of generalizations, the ground out of which bodily shapes can be derived for otherwise nonphysical bodies: "bodies" such as society, or such as class.

MARXIST INDIVIDUALISM

To give the paradox an even sharper edge, we might say that the Marxist image of society is, almost by necessity, an inferential derivation from Marxist individualism, the "social" here being derived always from a prior notion of the bodily subject. The suggestion is not as outrageous as it might seem. It is not entirely fortuitous, after all, that Marx should be found, on at least one occasion, in the company of Emerson and Thoreau. And Alasdair MacIntyre pointed out some time ago that Marxism is a nineteenth-century philosophy "as much because of what it has inherited from liberal individualism as because of its departures from liberalism."[46] That inheritance, I would argue, is less substantive than cognitive. The bodily subject is central to Marxist thought, in other words, not as a matter of thematic description but as a matter of inferential projection. It enables Marxism to make sense of the world by reflexively incorporating the world, fashioning it into an integral unit, and generalizing from body to person, from person to class, and from class to a totally "just" society.

Still, the notion of a "Marxist individualism" might seem like an oxymoron, since Marx (unlike Emerson and Thoreau) was on record as having rejected the individual as a legitimate category of thought. He had begun the *Grundrisse*, for example, with the acid remark that "the individual and isolated hunter and fisherman, with whom Smith and Ricardo begin, belongs among the unimaginative conceits of the eighteenth-century Robinsonades." "The more deeply we go back into history," he said, "the more does the individual, and hence also the producing individual, appear as dependent, as belonging to a greater whole."[47]

When Marx went on, however, to imagine this "greater whole," when he tried to offer a historical survey of this "whole" as a counterpoint to the individual, the terms with which he did so turned out to be surprisingly individualistic, derived to a surprising degree from the physical attributes of the body. Thus, the "first form" of community as he envisioned it (an "initial, naturally arisen, spontaneous" development) also happened to be a "comprehensive unity." And since this "unity is the real proprietor and the real presupposition of communal property, it follows that this unity can appear as a particular entity above the many real particular communities," so much so that it "exists ultimately as a *person*."[48] Similarly in classical antiquity, the "second form" of human association: even though the community was no longer "the substance" integrating its members into "purely natural component parts," Marx noted with satisfaction that the city-state was still a *"political body,"* still a "presence," a "whole," indeed "a kind of independent organism."[49]

As Marx's organic language suggests, the social for him—whether as historical reconstruction or (as I will argue) as dialectical forecast—turned out to resemble nothing so much as a physical body, a body integral and objective, imaged forth as a natural unit. And since this nonphysical "body" now stood to its physical counterpart not in a relation of discrepancy (as the medieval church once did) but in a relation of analogy, we might speak of the social in Marx as the effect of a metonymic entailment. The nonphysical body, in other words, took on all those attributes—the empirical objectivity as well as the corporeal integrity—which characterized the physical body. The latter, then, was not only constitutive of the former but fully descriptive of it, fully representative of its nature and disposition as a "whole." The logic of metonymy in this sense dispensed with the need to theorize about the social, for it was already accounted for, its defining features already immanent and inferable from those of a material given. And so it turned out that for Marx an immaterial phenomenon was imaged after the materiality of the corporeal subject, an entity objectified even as it was generalized.

Raymond Williams, in one of the most illuminating discussions of materialism I have seen, has singled out this generalizing logic as the central problem within Marxism. Materialism, Williams writes,

> grounded on the rejection of categorical hypotheses of an unverifiable kind, and basing its own confidence in a set of provisional working procedures and demonstrations, finds itself pulled nevertheless towards closed generalizing systems: finds itself material*ism* or *a* materialism. There is thus a tendency for any materialism, at any point in its history, to find itself stuck with its own recent generalizations, and in defence of these to mistake its own character: to suppose that it is a system like others, of a presumptive explanatory kind.[50]

The tendencies of materialism, so succinctly outlined by Williams here, are especially problematic (but also, in a sense, problematically utopian) when its generalizations are derived from the bodily subject, when its image of the world is founded upon the image of a containable physicality. It was this odd compound of materialism and individualism—this projection of the bodily attributes of integrity and totality onto a historical canvas, as the ultimate attributes of human existence—that enabled Marx to imagine a just society as the organic issue, the natural given and the natural end, of the coming of age of the proletariat.

Marx's image of the proletariat was thus not so much that of a *collectivity* as that of an *individual.* Or, more accurately, we might say that Marx's image of a collectivity *was* in fact the image of an individual. If capitalism was that monstrous machine whose "parts are human beings," class was that integral body within which those human parts could once again be made into a political whole. "The proletariat" in Marx was the effect of a generalization, then, extrapolated from and imaged after what (following Marx and Engels) we might call the figure of the "abstract individual." Of course, the "abstract individual" was the very thing Marx and Engels set out to critique, in their attack on Bruno Bauer and, most famously, in the eleven *Theses on Feuerbach*.[51] And yet it is possible to argue that this figure was never clearly foreign or antecedent to Marxism, that it was in fact the derivational ground for its historical projections:

> Since the abstraction of all humanity, even of the semblance of humanity, is practically complete in the full-grown proletariat; since the conditions of life of the proletariat sum up all the conditions of life of society itself in all their human acuity . . . it follows that the proletariat can and must free itself. . . . The question is not what this or that proletarian, or even the whole of the proletariat at the moment considers as its aim. The question is *what the proletariat is,* and what, consequent on that *being,* it will be compelled to do.[52]

What empowered the proletariat, then, was its particular mode of "being," its status as the "abstraction of all humanity," its agency being not only underwritten by but actually objectified within that integral character. It was this derivation of a historical necessity from an objective identity,[53] and the projection of that objective identity upon a human collectivity, that made the proletariat a historical *subject* for Marx. And since that subject was a metonymic container for "all the conditions of life," the unfolding of which was "practically complete in the full-grown proletariat," there was also a sense in which this "full-grown" body would bring with it a unified "whole," a complete subsumption of differences. For this reason Marx wrote that even though "proletariat and wealth are opposites . . . it is not sufficient to declare them two sides of a single whole." Rather, he argued, "when the proletariat is victorious . . . it is victorious only by abolishing itself and its opposite. Then the proletariat disappears as well as the opposite which determines it, private property."[54]

In this account of the birth of communist society, the proletariat not only eliminated its antagonist but, in the same gesture, eliminated itself as an antagonist and so ushered in a unified humanity, marked by its undifferentiated pristineness no less than by its dialectical completion.[55] This image of an integral whole allowed Marx, in *Critique of the Gotha Programme*, to speak of revolutionary justice as if it were a natural issue, growing out of the development of a single body, the unfolding of a single life. Having gone through its difficult childhood (when it is "still stamped with the birthmarks of the old society from whose womb it emerges"), this revolutionary "body" will grow into a state of maturity, Marx said, a state where justice will prevail as a natural condition of life and where "society [can] inscribe on its banners: from each according to his ability, to each according to his needs!"[56]

"From each according to his ability, to each according to his needs": this dream of commensurability—this exchange of effort and satisfaction—remains, even in the late twentieth century, one of the most compelling visions of justice. Still, its utopian faith—its faith that its two stipulatory clauses could somehow balance out, that its two prepositions, "to" and "from," would somehow flow in organic harmony—could proceed only from an assumption of wholeness, only by imagining the social body as if it were actually a physical body.

The Marxist dream of justice, as a dream of objective adequation, thus rested on what Louis Althusser would call a postulate of "philosophical fullness" as well as a postulate of "simple original unity."[57] For Althusser, such postulates are sheer anathema, which he lays at the door of Hegel and, to some extent, the early Marx himself.[58] What they amount to, he argues, is a blithely homogenizing principle, a kind of cosmic equation mark, liquidating all differences, making them all subsumable, all immaterial:

For the unity of a simple essence manifesting itself in its alienation produces this result: that every concrete difference . . . [becomes] no more than "moments" of the simple internal principle of totality, which fulfils itself by negating the alienated difference that it posed; further, as alienations—phenomena—of the simple internal principle, these differences are all equally *indifferent*.[59]

Against this "indifferent" epistemology, which turns all differences into epiphenomena, into secondary evidence, Althusser offers an elaborate defense, by painstakingly (and some would say casuistically) distinguishing the Marxist dialectic from its Hegelian precursor. Of course, the Hegelian legacy might be said to have influenced not only Marx but virtually every modern thinker, including Althusser himself.[60] Still, the point remains that in making the immaterial a simple translation from the material—in making the former an epiphenomenon of the latter—Marxist epistemology would seem to have conferred upon the "indifferent" an analytic primacy, embracing it not only as its cognitive ground but also as its cognitive horizon. This reign of the indifferent might be seen, I would argue, not only as a consequence of Marxist materialism but, above all, as a consequence of Marxist individualism, dictated by its generalizations from the integrity and totality of the corporeal subject. Like an entire spectrum of nineteenth-century individualisms, Marxist individualism adduces signs of difference only to affirm the primacy of identity.[61] Against this identitarian logic, then, against its ceaseless subordination of the differentiated, its ceaseless subordination of the nonintegral, I want to bring into focus one particular critique of Marx—initiated by Engels and elaborated by Max Weber, Emile Durkheim, and most recently Anthony Giddens—a critique directed at his subordination of the nonintegral in one especially crucial category, the category of the "social."

MARX AND DURKHEIM

The social is, arguably, the category that has the most to suffer from a Marxist epistemology. It suffers, that is, from a presumption of generalizability, a presumption about its "indifferent" givenness as an epiphenomenon. In reclaiming it, I want to challenge not only the broadly materialist and individualist premises of Marxism but also their implicit claim to adequation, to "philosophical fullness." Toward that end, I want to highlight what I see as the necessary blurriness of the social in Marx and contrast it with its sharp clarity in, say, Max Weber, or (perhaps most pertinent here) Emile Durkheim. I have in mind, in particular, the contrasting evidentiary domains—and the contrasting degrees of analytic precision—set forth by Marx and Durkheim to discuss what might look like the same phenomenon, namely, the division of labor.

For Marx, the division of labor was very much an *economic* phenomenon; it was an industrial arrangement, peculiar to the factory and the assembly line. He was at pains, indeed, to show how the "division of labor in the interior of a society, and that in the interior of a workshop, differ not only in degree, but also in kind." The former, the social division of labor, being pervasive and seemingly universal, was for that reason also unanalyzable, since it "springs up naturally," a "spontaneous growth," "caused by the differences of sex and age, a division that is consequently based on a purely physiological foundation."[62] True to his logic of corporeal generalizations, society was figured here as a natural body, and social division of labor, being also "physiological," was thus a matter of analytic indifference to Marx.[63] All his critical energies were directed elsewhere, against the division of labor in the workshop, clearly no work of nature but a man-made horror, involving as it did the carving up of natural individuals into industrial parts. In short, for Marx, the domain of the "social" (to the extent that it was distinguishable from the economic) turned out to be only a secondary order of evidence, subsumable under the category of the "natural." Only the economic, only the primary evidentiary domain, merited the scope as well as the care of his analysis.

There was a hierarchy of evidence in Marx, we might say, a hierarchy seen all the more clearly when it is seen in reverse—when we turn, for example, to Durkheim. What was immaterial to Marx was consequential for that very reason to Durkheim. And so, tersely noting that "the division of labor [is] a fact of a very general nature, which the economists, who first proposed it, never suspected,"[64] Durkheim went on to discuss the phenomenon not as a feature unique to the workshop but as a feature common to all organized society. As the principal investigatory site, the social also sustained the finest analytic distinctions in Durkheim. Far from being a derived postulate or a collapsible epiphenomenon, it was here a field of primary relations with an evidentiary domain in its own right, out of whose complex differentiations Durkheim would elaborate an equally complex theory of social integration.

Durkheim's insistence on the social as primary evidence—his sense of its irreducibility to some other explanatory ground—serves as a challenge not only to the evidentiary logic of Marx's economism[65] but also to the logic of his bodily generalizations, his inferential reasoning from the physical to the nonphysical, from part to whole. The social might be seen, indeed, as a challenge to the very concept of a "whole." This is not, of course, Durkheim's own sense of its possible usage; for him, society is very much a whole, and the "social" very much synonymous with the functionally integral. Still, in rejecting a hierarchy of evidentiary planes, Durkheim himself would seem to be pointing the way toward a *non*integral conception of society, predicated not on the linear translatability of structural determinism but on the supple permutability of structural interaction.[66] Especially in the context of justice, the "social" for Durkheim turns out to be the chief antidote to the reign of the commensurate, replacing the *lex talionis* of primitive society with various forms of mediation, forms increasingly complex in their "volume" and "density."[67] Seen in this light, the social would seem to open up the possibility of a field incompletely unified, incompletely integrated, a field characterized neither by the fit among its constitutive terms nor by the fit among its evidentiary planes. Justice, in such a world, can no longer be seen as a simple given, an immanent relation among things. In short, theorized as a domain of *difference*, difference at once irreducible and irreconcilable, the social would seem to turn justice into a vexed concept not only as a matter of implementation but, above all, as a matter of commensurability, a matter of internal adequation.

Using Durkheim against himself, then, I want to invoke the social both to question the notion of a commensurate totality, and—going even further out on a limb—to argue that the very concept of "social justice" might turn out to be itself an oxymoron. My thinking here is guided by Ernesto Laclau and Chantal Mouffe's powerful argument against our usual conception of "society" as a "founding totality of its partial processes."[68] Taking seriously their suggestion that the social is "unsutured," that there is no seamless rationality, no perfect adequation between part and whole, I want to bring into critical focus various permutations of the incommensurate—relations of unevenness, nonalignment, untranslatability—that challenge the idea of the "whole." And with the disturbance of that concept, I want to disturb as well the concept of justice which invokes it and rests on it, deriving from its supposed totality its own claim to descriptive adequacy and philosophical fullness.

NEW HISTORICISM
AND THE PREPOSITION "IN"

For my purposes, then, the social is less important as an autonomous domain than as an analytic pressure, a challenge not only to any notion of "total" justice but also to any notion of an immanent (and therefore containable) equivalence among things. Differently put, we might also say that the social, as a field imperfectly integrated, imperfectly contained, is a vital challenge to that most familiar and most peremptory of spatial concepts, inscribed by the preposition "in," a concept which, as Charles Taylor reminds us, has "come to seem as fixed and ineradicable from reality as the preposition is from our lexicon."[69] And since this spatial concept is crucial not only to the materialism and individualism of Marx but also to a broad spectrum of modern epistemologies (beginning, perhaps, with Descartes's location of ideas "in" the mind, as mental "contents"),[70] I want to take this occasion to digress somewhat and to reflect more specifically and more critically on this prepositional regime, as it informs, inspires, and inhibits many of our linguistic practices. I am thinking especially of the practice of literary criticism and its time-honored ambition to interpret what is *in* a literary text.

What is in a literary text is, of course, a matter of attribution, varying with our critical interests. With our current historicist turn, it is the "social" itself that is most often offered up as a complement to that preposition, offered up as its substantive notation as well as its syntactical end. The social is invoked, that is, both as an operating theater and as a functional logic, both of which are understood to govern the text, to be objectively immanent "in" it, giving it a resident identity, an indwelling purpose, and turning it into a kind of verbal container for a thing called History.[71] In our hasty retreat from deconstruction, we seem to have forgotten one of its crucial insights: that a text has no interiority, no objective circumference it can be said to encompass, and no unified space, no unified field of intention it can be said to contain, certainly not an intention unified under the name of History. One conceivable outcome of deconstruction might actually have been a radical challenge to the entire discipline of literary studies: a challenge to its image of the text as a bounded object and to its image of reading as an attempt to match that boundedness, to be commensurate with what is "in" it. This was not what in fact happened. New Historicism, to the extent that it reinstates reading as the search for a containable identity, a context-bound identity, would seem to mark a return to an earlier epistemology, one that, in this case, reads History not only as the indwelling agency in Literature but also as its hermeneutic limits, its bounds of meaning. The text is thus imagined once again to be a spatial unit, embedded in History and filled with its contents, contents inferable if not ultimately provable, answering always to a History which accounts for it, translates into it, and integrates it into a hermeneutic whole, dictating and containing its possibilities for meaning. The task of critic is thus once again to "unpack" those contents, to effect a reverse translation, as it were, by locating the historicity "in" the text and locating the text "in" history.

As must be obvious by now, I want to take issue with this prepositional regime. I want to propose a mode of literary studies not premised on a spatialized image of the text, and not premised on meaning as a *containable* category. The hermeneutic relation between history and literature is thus necessary but insufficient. Just as the meanings of history might not be fully generalizable from one particular work of literature, so the meanings of literature might not be fully derivable from one particular historical moment. Rather than limiting ourselves to a search for "historicity" (and rather than equating historicity strictly with determinacy and locatability), we might want to turn instead to a hermeneutics that is less spatially ascriptive, less discretely periodizing, and more alive, perhaps, to the continuing meaningfulness of a text, more willing to study that meaningfulness beyond any function it might conceivably have performed at one particular moment. Engaging the text not as a part of a *concluded* whole—not as a piece of cultural work that has already served its purpose, that has meaning only in reference to the past—we might instead want to think of it as an evolving cluster of resonances, its semantic universe unfolding in time rather than in space, unfolding in response to the new perceptual horizons that we continue to bring to bear upon it and that never cease to extend to it new possibilities of meaning. The accumulating resonances of a text, its subtle but non-trivial shifts in nuance and accent, are a tribute, then, to the socialness of language, to the unending conversations of humanity over time. Inflected by those conversations, inflected by the historical life of language—a life at once more ancient and more recent than any locatable circumstance—the very linguistic character of a text must make it permeable in time, polyphonic over time, its resonances activated and reactivated with each new relation, each mutating meaning.

To equate the text with any single explanatory context would seem, from this perspective, to be unduly metonymic: unduly collapsing an immaterial order into a set of material circumstances, and unduly collapsing a semantic universe into a narrow grid of instances. Against the violence of that reduction, much might be said, I think, for a criticism that makes no attempt to produce a containable identity for a text, no attempt to devise a fit for its semantic contours. And even as "fitness" is rejected here as a hermeneutic ideal, "doing justice" is also rejected as a hermeneutic practice, on the ground that justice (with reading as with much else) is dangerously close to a form of impoverishment. Not doing justice to the text, not sentencing it to a designated slot in history, such a criticism will perhaps not be "historicist" in the current understanding of that term. All the same, it will remain historically minded, although it will imagine history not as a domain of full inscription, in which the meaning of literature is given once and for all, given because of its determinate place in a hermeneutic totality. Indeed, skeptical of that totality, and skeptical of the preposition "in," it will perhaps turn to some other relational categories—"between," "beside," "residual to," "in spite of," "above and beyond"—categories that engage the text not as the predictable part of a historical whole but as a perpetual witness to a history perpetually incomplete.

READING THE INCOMPLETE: HERMAN MELVILLE

What might a reading look like that has no desire to imagine a whole, no desire to devise for the text a hermeneutic totality? I want to pursue that question by way of a practical demonstration, by turning now to Herman Melville's "The Paradise of Bachelors and the Tartarus of Maids," a story that, almost providentially, brings together questions of the material and the immaterial, part and whole, and all against the background of a literary form that makes justice an un-avoidable (if implicit) issue. As the title suggests, this is a diptych, made up of two contrasting, complementary parts, evenly divided and inversely matching. On one side, there is convivial ambience, culinary delight, and carefree association, a world occupied exclu-sively by men. On the other side, there is a brutal environment, regi-mented labor, and physical misery, a world occupied monotonously by women.

Given this complementary structure—this antithesis of privilege and oppression—it is hardly surprising that the men should happen to be bachelors. For bachelorhood, here and elsewhere in Melville, is a species of manhood singled out for its privilege and distinguished, in that privilege, from manhood of the more run-of-the-mill sort, ex-emplified by the "Benedick tradesmen," who, being married, must spend their lives attending to the "rise of bread and fall of babies."[72] The bachelors, by contrast, are free from all obligations, marital and paternal, free, it might seem, even from the necessity of work. Of course, we know that the bachelors actually do work. They are prac-ticing lawyers, hailing from such places as Grey's Inn and Lincoln's Inn. However, as they are here presented they are eminently at lei-sure. The bachelors are portrayed, that is, as if they were gentlemen of means, banded together, first and last, by their pleasure in idle-ness. Reveling as they do in a unique gender privilege, they make up a class by themselves.

The mapping of an aristocratic identity upon a bachelor iden-tity—the mapping of class upon gender—is, of course, something of a convention itself. As Eve Kosofsky Sedgwick points out, the "aristocratic," as perceived (no doubt wishfully) by the bourgeoisie in the nineteenth century, was marked by a cluster of attributes including effeminacy, unspecified homosexuality, connoisseurship, and dissipation, all of which were conveniently personified by the pleasure-loving, leisure-flaunting bachelor.[73] Sedgwick is speaking of nineteenth-century England, but her insight applies equally to nineteenth-century America, where an even keener suspicion of the "aristocratic" prompted the same indictment of class through gen-der, making the effete bachelor a metonym for the entire upper order, real or imagined. This is certainly the case with Ik Marvell's *Reveries of a Bachelor* (1850), which makes that most unmanly of luxuries, daydreaming, the essence of well-heeled bachelorhood. And it is the case as well with "The Paradise of Bachelors and the Tartarus of Maids," which, in making effete aristocrats out of effete bachelors, would seem to be operating within a well-defined tradition of populist critique.

"The Paradise of Bachelors" is thus pervaded (ostentatious references to "paradise" notwithstanding) by an aura of the degenerate, an aura of declension from a heroic past to a feminized present: "the iron heel is changed to a boot of patent-leather; the long two-handed sword to a one-handed quill"; "the helmet is a wig." Instead of "carving out immortal fame in glorious battling for the Holy Land," as the Crusaders once did, the modern-day bachelor is now reduced "to the carving of roast-mutton at a dinner-board" (317–318). There is a time-honored quality to this portrait of degenerate leisure: time-honored, but, it would seem, also endlessly repeated. Melville was hardly alone, then, in his dire intimations, for as Francis Grund observed in 1837, Americans as a rule "know but the *horrors* of idleness."[74] And so it was that in 1843, when Henry Ward Beecher gave a series of Sunday evening lectures to his congregation (subsequently collected in his *Lectures to Young Men*), the first lecture should be devoted to the subject of idleness. Like Melville's story, this also featured a certain *seedsman*:

> When Satan would put ordinary men to a crop of mischief, like a wise husbandman, he clears the ground and prepares it for seed; but he finds the idle man already prepared, and he has scarcely the trouble of sowing, for vices, like weeds, ask little strewing, except what the wind gives their ripe and winged seeds, shaking and scattering them all abroad. Indeed, lazy men may fitly be likened to a tropical prairie, over which the wind of temptation perpetually blows, drifting every vagrant seed from hedge and hill, and which—without a moment's rest through all the year—waves its rank harvest of luxuriant weeds.[75]

Such harsh judgment (not to say such figurative extravagance) might seem surprising. It is especially surprising coming from Beecher, who happened also to be the author of a popular novel, *Norwood* (1868), whose idealized hero, Reuben Wentworth, was not only idle in his youth but actually contemplated a career in idleness. He discussed the matter with his Uncle Eb, who, when asked whether one could "be a gentleman in any respectable calling," had answered, "Oh, dear, no. *My* gentleman must take all his time to it, spend his time at it, be jealous of everything else." Wentworth ends up not being a gentleman—he becomes a doctor—but what Uncle Eb said about the gentleman might equally be said of him: "He [is] so fine that he accomplishes more while doing nothing than others do with all their bustle."[76]

Elsewhere in Beecher, there are further examples of people who accomplish more while doing nothing than others do with all their bustle. In an essay entitled "Dream-Culture" (1854), for instance, he went so far as to argue that "the chief use of a farm, if it be well selected, and of a proper soil, is, to lie down upon." He called this unusual kind of husbandry "industrious lying down," and contrasted it with the other, more usual variety, practiced by farmers, which involved "standing up and lazing about after the plow or behind his scythe." *That* kind of farming was ordinary enough. "Industrious lying down," on the other hand, produced crops that were far more extraordinary: "harvests of associations, fancies, and dreamy broodings." And to those who objected that such "farming" was "a mere waste of precious time," Beecher replied that it was completely justified "if it gives great delight[,] . . . if it brings one a little out of conceit with hard economies, . . . and the sweat and dust of life among selfish, sordid men."[77]

Beecher certainly seemed to be speaking out of both sides of his mouth.[78] He was not alone, however, for there was in fact very little agreement in the mid-nineteenth century about the merit of leisure and recreation.[79] The controversy attracted a good many commentators, especially clergymen, a significant fact in itself. In a book called *The Christian Law of Amusement* (1859), for example, James Leonard Corning, pastor of the Westminster Presbyterian Church in Buffalo, described the battle as being waged between those who denounced amusement "with most dogmatic intolerance as if nothing could be said in its favor" and those who praised it to the skies, "as if the progress of civilization depended on it."[80] However, this did not prevent Corning himself from joining the fray, determined as he was to prove that the necessity for amusement was a "Christian law."

As for Henry Ward Beecher, the battle seemed to be going on inside his head and among his various pieces of writing. But there was a pattern as well behind these seemingly contrary pronouncements.[81] In *Norwood*, for example, it was the gentlemanly Dr. Wentworth who, alone of all the townspeople, could afford to be seen standing under a cherry tree, "watching with a kind of sober smile the workmen" laboring away at their tasks.[82] Leisure clearly meant different things when it was enjoyed by different people. Cheap amusements—such as the popular theater and the circus—were sinks of iniquity: a "universal pestilence," an "infernal chemistry of ruin," indeed "hell's first welcome."[83] More genteel pastimes, however—such as visiting the Louvre and the National Art Gallery, or summering in the country—actually turned out to be morally uplifting and indeed were recounted by Beecher as fond episodes in his own life. *Star Papers*, his collection of occasional essays, offered a record of his tour of Europe as well as his "vacations of three summers."[84]

Beecher is something of a pivotal figure from this perspective, testifying not only to the fluidity of class attributes in the nineteenth century but also (perhaps more crucial for my argument here) to the contending valences within the social field, its failure to exhibit anything like a rationalized totality. Leisure, once flung in accusation at the feet of the upper class, was now claimed by the middle class, gingerly but also quite openly, not just as a birthright but as something of a requisite, at once identity imparting and identity certifying.[85] The social meaning of leisure would thus seem to be more variously marked, more variously nuanced and accented, than might appear generalizable from any simple economic given. It is against this complex semantic history of leisure that we can begin to gauge the dissonances in Beecher's own writings, or the dissonances between him and Melville. And it is against this complex semantic history, as well, that we can begin to gesture toward a historical criticism that is nonetheless not bound by the preposition "in." For the great interest of the Melville story is surely not what is *in* it: not the fact that leisure is here linked with degeneracy but the fact that it is so linked in accordance with an earlier, more populist, faintly anachronistic conception of class. Unlike the blandly decorous leisure in *Norwood* or *Star Papers*, leisure in "The Paradise of Bachelors" remains overrich, too savory, too alluring.[86] And unlike Henry Ward Beecher, who apparently has come to accept leisure by accepting a selective version of it—the version newly sanitized by its association with the middle class—Melville has kept alive an older dynamics of attraction and revulsion, or attraction *as* revulsion, so that the spectacle of gentlemen at leisure becomes not so much a presumption in favor of leisure as a presumption against the gentlemen themselves, who as leisured men are also shown to be lesser men.

From that perspective, it is difficult to speak of the story as a "social critique"—as if that critique were its resident identity—for the critique is hardly located "in" the story, but is intelligible only in relation to Beecher and only in relation to an earlier conception of class that, in the mid-nineteenth century, was just about to be superseded. Furthermore, even with this expanded semantic horizon, the text does not seem to possess a meaning integral enough or binding enough to give it anything like a *concluded* identity. For the Melville story, in its very polemical energy, in its metonymic attack on the leisured gentleman as effete bachelor, also carries with it something like a polemical overload, with consequences unintended, unexpected, and quite possibly unwelcome. One such consequence is that even though the story is probably not "meant" to be homophobic, homophobia is nonetheless more than a dim shape on the horizon.[87] The resonances of the story (and for us, in the 1990s, they are troubling resonances) must far exceed anything Melville himself might have imagined. Given this signifying surcharge, and given the continual evolution of that surcharge, any attempt to devise a hermeneutic totality for the text is bound to fail—woefully, but perhaps also happily. For that failure is surely a tribute to the story's continuing vitality, its continuing ability to sustain new meanings, even troubling meanings, over time. The semantic horizon of the text is thus commensurate neither with the sum of its parts nor with the sum of any number of readings. Taking these incommensurabilities as reminders of a nonintegral universe, we should perhaps also take to heart their intimations of shortfall, as well as intimations of possibility, in order to rethink the very idea of adequation, both as it informs a reading of a text and as it informs a theory of justice.

The question of justice is, of course, the implicit burden of the Melville story itself, a question that, to my mind, is also better pondered as an instance of the incomplete rather than an instance of descriptive fullness. As we have seen, what Melville offers is a contrasting tableau of privilege and oppression, rendered in the idiom of class as well as the idiom of gender. The female operative, a casualty on both counts, thus stands as a metonym for injustice, an injustice done to all workers. This gendering of injustice is very much a deliberate invention on Melville's part, for, as Judith A. McGaw points out, even though there were actually *both* male and female workers in the Dalton paper mill that Melville visited, the story takes as its exhibit only the latter.[88] This metonymic focus on the woman worker is in turn doubled upon itself, for the focus is hardly on her general well-being, but on one particular feature of her person. It is her sexualized body that is being dramatized here, the oppressions and deprivations of that body serving as a metonym for the full range of her oppressions and deprivations. Female sexuality, in short, becomes the generalized sign for the injury of class. Beginning with the journey to the paper mill (a protracted affair, vividly rendered as a grotesque encounter with the female anatomy), economic injustice is equated throughout with sexual violation, industrial capitalism being figured here as a mechanized rape of the female body.

It is this metonymic logic that confers on female sexuality its signifying primacy. To the extent that this signifying relation is understood to be a *complete* relation, however—to the extent that this "rape" is understood fully to summarize the female operatives as well as the entire working class—the women are also turned into naturalized signs, welded into and subsumed by what they signify. There they stand, "like so many mares haltered to the rack," tending machines which "vertically thrust up a long, glittering scythe . . . look[ing] exactly like a sword" (329). Not surprisingly, they give birth not to babies but to industrial products. The narrator reports a "scissory sound . . . as of some cord being snapped, and down dropped an unfolded sheet of perfect foolscap . . . still moist and warm" (332). In short, the sights and sounds of industrial production cruelly mimic the sights and sounds of biological reproduction, underscoring at every turn the simple equation between perverted womanhood and industrial victimhood.

Melville was not the only one to have lighted on the denaturalized woman as a metonym for the sufferings of the working class. Joan Wallach Scott, studying the representation of women workers in France during the same period, has come upon strikingly similar images of female sexual disorder metonymically equated with the problems of the entire industrial order. As Scott points out, this mode of cultural figuration—this deployment of a class critique upon the symbolic body of woman—is not altogether disinterested. Indeed, as she documents it, political economists such as Jules Simon (who wrote a book called *L'Ouvrière*) not only routinely lamented the sexual plight of the women workers but also proposed, as a remedy, "the return of the mother to the family," for, as he said, "It is necessary that women be able to marry and that married women be able to remain at home all day, there to be the providence and the personi-fication of the family." Given this view of things, it is not surpris-ing that, according to Michelet, *ouvrière* was an "impious, sordid word that no language has ever known." Jules Simon, meanwhile, went so far as to say that "the woman who becomes a worker is no longer a woman."[89]

There is, of course, nothing quite so outspoken in "The Paradise of Bachelors and the Tartarus of Maids," nor anything that hints of the Cult of True Womanhood, the American counterpart to those pro-nouncements offered by Michelet and Simon.[90] Still, given Melville's anxieties about his literary career in an environment dominated by "scribbling women," it is certainly possible to see, in this story about "blank-looking girls" working on "blank paper" (328), a half-resent-ful, half-wishful, and not especially well-disguised fantasy about women who wrote too mechanically and too much.[91] Such specula-tions aside, we might note as well that in his metonymic logic—in the implied equation between industrial victimhood and perverted womanhood—Melville, like Marx, would seem to have begged the very question of justice his writing so powerfully brings into focus. In his case, injustice is both self-evident and beside the point, both natu-ralized and rendered moot by that naturalization. Its spectacle excites only an obligatory apostrophe—"Oh! Paradise of Bachelors! and oh! Tartarus of Maids!"—an apostrophe almost "equal" to its object, we might even say, not only in repeating the diptych form of the story but also in completing it, turning its metonymic conceit into a natural circumference, a natural totality.

Against this formal closure—this inscription of a figural reality as full reality—I want to suggest an avowedly "incomplete" read-ing, one designed, that is, to go against the grain of the story, and most certainly against the grain of metonymic thinking. I want to sug-gest a reading predicated on the improbable presence of a historical "whole" in the text, an improbability whose consequences I take to be pragmatic rather than self-deprecatingly rhetorical. In other words, if we concede that the meaning of literature is not a containable cate-gory, we would have to concede, infinitely more, that the meaning of history is also not containable: not as a hermeneutic totality, and espe-cially not as a hermeneutic totality in a text. Taking this hermeneutic incompleteness as an energizing relation between history and litera-

ture and as a tribute to the evolving vitality of both, we might want to
focus on those moments in the text where its historicity seems most
tenuous, most problematic, using these moments to question the very
idea of a unified "whole," both as it bears on the determining ground
of literature and as it bears on the determinate shape of history.

Reading "The Paradise of Bachelors and the Tartarus of Maids,"
then, *not* as a totality, I want to engage it obliquely, engage it by dwell-
ing on what it does *not* represent, which in this case happens to be
an alternative account of the woman worker. That alternative figure
casts a new light, I think, not only on the presumptive totality of
Melville's story, but also on the presumptive totality of the historical
process itself. For that figure was nothing if not emblematic in the
1830s and 1840s. Gleefully adduced—by company officials and ecstatic foreign visitors—that woman worker was considered the pride
of America and was routinely contrasted with the debased operatives
in Manchester, England.[92] Charles Dickens, who admitted to having
"visited many mills in Manchester and elsewhere," reported with
much-dramatized surprise that the American women workers "were
all well dressed. . . . They were healthy in appearance, many of them
remarkably so, and had the manners and deportment of young
women: not of degraded brutes of burden." Indeed, "from all the
crowd I saw in the different factories that day, I cannot recall or separate one young face that gave me a painful impression; not one young
girl whom, assuming it to be a matter of necessity that she should
gain her daily bread by the labour of her hands, I would have removed from those works if I had had the power."[93]

For Dickens, the American woman worker cut a different figure for
obvious reasons: in being so happily unrecognizable to the English
reader, she showed up everything that was wrong with industrial
England. This juxtaposing function was, in fact, the standard function
assigned her by English visitors. The Reverend William Scoresby,
who visited the "factory girls" expressly to report to his congregation in Bradford, England, devoted chapters of his book, *American
Factories and Their Female Operatives* (1845), to "Their Literary Pur-
suits," "Their Leisure Employments," "Their Moral Condition," and
"Causes of Their Superiority." Scoresby found that these women
were "clothed in silks, and otherwise gaily adorned," that it was "a
common thing for one of these girls to have five hundred dollars (a
hundred guineas, nearly) in deposit" at the Lowell Institution for

Savings, that their literary publication, the *Lowell Offering*, was "fair and comely," quite "a phenomenon in literature": in short, though "having no possible motive for flattering our transatlantic sisters," he must nonetheless conclude that in "general moral character, or superior intelligence, or great respectability—these factory girls do greatly surprise and interest us" and that they must commend themselves to "those who feel an interest in the improvement of the condition of our working population."[94]

These glowing nineteenth-century accounts are echoed by some twentieth-century historians, who, reacting against mainstream labor history, have called attention instead to the *benefits* of factory work for women.[95] Thomas Dublin, in particular, emphasizes the importance of industrialization not only to women's individual well-being but also to their potential for collective action. Dublin finds that—contrary to our usual view—the New England factory girls had not been driven to work by dire necessity. Indeed, according to him, the property holdings of the fathers put them in the broad middle ranges of wealth in their home towns; fully 86 percent of the fathers had property valued at $100 or more. These women came because they wanted to, he argues, because they wanted the freedom of urban living, away from their rural families; what they gained along the way was a sense of solidarity born out of the social relations of production. Work sharing at the mills and communal living at the company boardinghouses socialized the women in a way that the household economy would not, and that experience led directly to the collective action exemplified by strikes of the 1830s and the Ten Hour Movement of the 1840s, which saw the growth of a permanent labor organization among women, the Lowell Female Labor Reform Association (founded in December 1844). Dublin concludes that the factory experience "placed the Lowell women squarely within the evolving labor movement and indicated that crafts traditions were not the only legitimating forces in labor protests of the period."[96]

Such arguments, striking in their own right, do not pose as severe a challenge to the Melville story as they do to our current habit of reading. Any attempt to read the story as a metonym—as a container of history, an index to history—is bound to flounder here, for what is most striking about the story is surely its oblique relation to the lives of nineteenth-century women workers, its nonencapsulation of anything that might be called a "historical whole," and its unavoidable

slipperiness as the ground of historical generalizations. To acknowledge this is not, of course, to argue for a lack of connections between
history and literature. It is, however, a call to rethink the *nature* of
those connections, to set aside our current metonymic premise in
favor of concepts such as unevenness, off-centeredness, nonalignment. Such concepts, in their challenge to the idea of a fully integrated totality, qualify not only the hermeneutic relation between
history and literature but also the epistemological foundation of yet
another idea which requires a "whole": the idea of justice itself.

THE LIMITS OF TOTALITY:
REBECCA HARDING DAVIS

For the nineteenth-century women workers themselves, it was the
very nonexistence of a whole that made their lives livable, bearable,
and, in the end, not simply a metonym for "injustice." Their stories
and poems, letters and memoirs thus stubbornly refused to bear witness to a principle of full integration, full adequation,[97] a refusal that,
at the very least, should compel us to rethink the category of "commensurability," with its attendant constructs of body and mind, part
and whole, material and immaterial, and its attendant suppositions
about the ground for justice. Almost without exception, these women,
even those writing for house organs such as the *Lowell Offering*, commented on the physical ordeal of work, the fatigue and often the dis-
figurations suffered by the body. In a series entitled "Letters from
Susan," one author, Harriet Farley, complained that

> the hours seemed very long . . . and when I went out at night the
> sound of the mill was in my ears, as of crickets, frogs, and jewsharps,
> all mingled together in strange discord. . . . It makes my feet ache and
> swell to stand so much, . . . they almost all say that when they have
> worked here a year or two they have to procure shoes a size or two
> larger than before they came. The right hand, which is the one used in
> stopping and starting the loom, becomes larger than the left.[98]

What is remarkable, however, is that, such bodily afflictions notwithstanding, Farley also went on in the same letter to report that the
factory girls "scorn to say they were contented, if asked the question,
for it would compromise their Yankee spirit. . . . Yet, withal, they are
cheerful. I never saw a happier set of beings. They appear blithe in the

mill, and out of it."[99] From aching ears and swollen feet, it might seem a long way to cheerfulness, happiness, and blitheness. But it was just this strange transport—this improbable outcome given the point of departure—that structured the daily lives of the women workers. Harriet Hanson Robinson, who started working in the Lowell mills in 1834 at the age of ten, offered yet another account of this phenomenon in her memoir, *Loom and Spindle*, published in 1898 when she was seventy-three years old. From the distance of some sixty years, she could still remember the excitement of gainful employment, of having money in the pocket for the first time, and of the magical transformation the women underwent:

> [A]fter the first pay-day came, and they felt the jingle of silver in their pockets, and had begun to feel its mercurial influence, their bowed heads were lifted, their necks seemed braced with steel, they looked you in the face, sang blithely among their looms or frames, and walked with elastic step to and from their work. And when Sunday came, homespun was no longer their only wear; and how sedately gay in their new attire they walked to church, and how proudly they dropped their silver four-pences into the contribution-box! It seemed as if a great hope impelled them,—the harbinger of the new era that was to dawn for them and for all women-kind.[100]

For women not accustomed to having earnings of their own, not accustomed to the luxury of city clothes or the luxury of church patronage, leaving home and working in a factory brought with it a psychological well-being that shone forth in spite of the physical ordeal of repetitive labor and long working hours. One was not reducible to the other or generalizable from the other, and that was precisely the point. For what was most remarkable about these accounts of factory life was surely the persistent lack of fit—the lack of absolute determination or absolute entailment—between standards of discomfort and states of mind, between the generalized conditions of work and the specific affect reported by the women workers. The women workers were workers, to be sure; they were bodies bound to machines, bodies that became aching ears and swollen feet. But they were women as well, and, as women, they had a prehistory significantly different from that of the men and a capacity for transformation (not to say a capacity for benefit) also significantly different. The experience of industrialization, it would seem, was not at all an integral experience, not at all evenly registered or universally shared, but locally composed for each particular group, its composition being directly related to the antecedents out of which that group emerged.[101] In the case of the women workers, coming as they did from under the shadow of the patriarchal household, the emotional satisfaction as newly independent wage earners might turn out to be as nontrivial a benefit as the physical drudgery of labor was an oppression. It is here, in the perpetual lack of adequation between these two registers, that we can speak of the "nontrivial" as a crucial evidentiary category, a crucial supplement to any model of presumptive totality and generalizability. And here as well we can speak of gender as an exemplary instance of the nontrivial, both in the relays it multiplies between body and mind and in the challenge it poses to their supposed integration.

What emerged, then, from these writings by women workers was a set of determinations that, while acknowledged, were also carefully kept from being too seamless, too absolute. Between the body and the person, and between the person and the class, there was always the possibility for inconclusiveness, always the possibility for imperfect alignment and contrary articulation. The bodies of the women told one story, their letters told another, and their organized strikes, it would seem, told yet a third. Lucy Larcom was speaking only in one of the many possible voices of the woman worker when she wrote:

> One great advantage which came to these many stranger girls
> through being brought together, away from their own homes, was
> that it taught them to go out of themselves, and enter into the lives of
> others. Home-life, when one always stays at home, is necessarily narrowing.
> That is one reason why so many women are petty and unthoughtful
> of any except their own family's interests. . . . For me, it
> was an incalculable help to find myself among so many working-girls,
> all of us thrown upon our own resources, but thrown much more
> upon each others' sympathies.[102]

Speaking in a voice related but not exactly identical, Larcom also mentioned that she was "dazzled" by the thought of "Mount Holyoke Seminary . . . as a vision of hope" and that "Mary Lyon's name was honored nowhere more than among the Lowell mill-girls."[103] And it was in yet another related but not exactly identical voice that Sally Rice wrote the following letter, explaining why she did not want to leave the factory and go home to the "wilderness":

I can never be happy in among so many mountains. . . . I feel as though I have worn out shoes and strength enough walking over the mountains. . . . [A]nd as for marrying and settling in that wilderness, I wont. If a person ever expects to take comfort it is while they are young. . . . I am most 19 years old. I must of course have something of my own before many more years have passed over my head. And where is that something coming from if I go home and earn nothing. . . . You may think me unkind but how can you blame me for wanting to stay here. I have but one life to live and I want to enjoy myself as well as I can while I live.[104]

We would be hard put to find a unified identity in these letters and memoirs by women workers.[105] What confronts us instead are many *circumstances* for identities, identities imagined as well as lived, all rhetorically mediated and only partially harmonized. The women were not speaking out of a singular body called the "working class." They were not even speaking out of a singular body called the "person." For the person, in every respect, turned out to be less than a singularity but also more than a body. Like the human voice itself, at once rooted in the body which nourishes it but also miraculously unencompassed by that body, the person too is at once material and immaterial, at once a determinate presence and a field of incipience, no part of which—neither the swollen feet, nor the letter-writing self—could "do justice" to the whole, the very integrity of which was now shown to be something of a fiction.

In this sense, the writings of the women workers suggest one way to think about Rebecca Harding Davis's *Life in the Iron Mills* (1861), to my mind one of the most interesting nineteenth-century attempts to write in defiance of a whole, in defiance of the canon of objective adequacy, and therefore also one of the most interesting experiments in what we might call "incomplete justice"—if that is not too much of a contradiction in terms. That experiment begins, significantly, with a series of carefully specified nodal points where the story's transparency of determination is allowed to become opaque, to modulate into a paradox, an enigma, a relation of untranslatability. One such moment revolves around the central female character, Deborah, whose "thwarted woman's form," "colorless life," and "waking stupor that smothered pain and hunger" would seem to make her "fit to be a type of her class."[106] The "fit" is by no means absolute, however, for generalizable as Deborah might seem, one can nonetheless never be sure she is just that and no more than that. Certitude extends, in other words, only to what is verifiably there, not to what is unverifiably not. There is no final proof, for instance, that there is

> no story . . . hidden beneath the pale, bleared eyes, and dull, washed-out-looking face, [where] no one had ever taken the trouble to read its faint signs: not the half-clothed furnace-tender, Wolfe, certainly. Yet he was kind to her: it was his nature to be kind, even to the very rats that swarmed in the cellar: kind to her in just the same way. She knew that. And it might be that very knowledge had given to her face its apathy and vacancy more than her low, torpid life. (22)

If the opaqueness of Deborah begins with a postulate of the unverifiable, something that might or might not be in her, it ends with something like a tribute to the inexhaustible, a condition that makes any determinate cause inadequate to the felt effects. Of course, what is inexhaustible here turns out to be Deborah's capacity for suffering, a capacity well in excess even of what her "low, torpid life" so amply supplies her. This fact, lamentable from one point of view, nonetheless gives Deborah something almost akin to the cheerfulness, happiness, and blitheness reported by Harriet Farley, Harriet Robinson, and Lucy Larcom—akin, in the sense that it also saves her from being a transcript of her material conditions, affirming in her the density and dignity of the unknown, untypified, unspoken for. Her greatest suffering comes not from her bodily deprivations but from the particular sort of *kindness* with which she is treated. In this unexpected fastidiousness (where one would have imagined simple gratitude), Deborah emerges less as a whole than as a qualification to that concept. She cannot be read metonymically for just that reason, for her identity is both overflowing and undersaturated, both unexhausted by her materiality and only partially accounted for by its determinations.

In the enigma of affect which Davis puts at the heart of a story that is otherwise relentlessly transparent, relentlessly determinate, *Life in the Iron Mills* stands as a testimony to the limits of totality, and perhaps to the limits of justice itself. Justice is clearly very much an issue in the story, though, I would argue, a vexed issue, at once invoked and circumscribed in the very terms of its invocation. "I want you to come down and look at this Wolfe," the narrative voice tells us, "that you may judge him justly." And it goes on:

> Be just: when I tell you about this night, see him as he is. Be just,—not
> like man's law, which seizes on one isolated fact, but like God's judg-
> ing angel, whose clear, sad eye saw all the countless cankering days of
> this man's life, all the countless nights, when, sick with starving, his
> soul fainted in him, before it judged him for this night, the saddest of
> all. (25–26)

In spite of Davis's repeated injunction to the reader to "be just," to
arrive at a verdict that would presumably encompass the entire life of
Hugh Wolfe, such a panoramic vision actually seems only to be the
privilege of "God's judging angel," whose omniscient eye is in a position to see "all." Human laws, by contrast, would always be imperfect, limited by their partial vision, a limit imposed not only by the
unavailability of justice as a fully viewable category but also by the
unavailability of any human life to be judged as a "whole." That unavailability is further compounded by the phenomenon of loss in the
routine of living, an involuntary attrition which, in making human
agency porous in its effect, must render porous as well any notion of a
recuperative universe.

"Something is lost in the passage of every soul from one eternity
to the other,—something . . . which might have been and was not"
(64), Davis writes at the end of *Life in the Iron Mills*. The "loss" here
is perhaps loss in a general Wordsworthian sense, the loss incurred
by the very unfolding of a human life. But, more specifically, it also
seems to be the loss incurred by any attempt to engage the world,
any attempt to translate from one experiential register into another. It
is this loss that renders excruciating Deborah's love for Hugh—her
nightly, mile-long walk to bring him dinner and, most fatally, her
decision to steal for his sake—a love so untranslatable as to be virtually meaningless to its object. And it is this loss that renders excruciating Hugh's last attempt to engage the world in conversation.
As he says good-bye to the last passerby outside his jail window, on
what he knows to be the last day of his life, "a longing seized him to
be spoken to once more":

> "Joe!" he called, out of the grating. "Good-bye, Joe!"
> The old man stopped a moment, listening uncertainly; then hurried
> on. The prisoner thrust his hand out of the window, and called again,
> louder; but Joe was too far down the street. (59)

The fragility of the human voice—its utter lack of guarantee, utter
dependence on the recipient, its helplessness and involuntary silence

in the face of physical distance—thus dramatizes, for Davis, not only the incommensurability between the material and the immaterial, but also the incommensurability between self and world: a world that refuses to envelop us in reciprocity, to render back to us, in sonorous fullness, our need for attention, expression, conversation. The single most haunting image in *Life in the Iron Mills* is the fate of what is not translated, not received, not noticed. In ways at once accidental and agonizing, the sum of the parts is always greater than the whole here, for the whole, the supposed whole, is not so much an effect of our plenitude as an effect of our loss.

And yet it is through this loss—through the incommensurability of the material and the immaterial which occasions it—that Davis is able to offer the consolation (dubious to some, perhaps, but a consolation nonetheless) of human lives that are only partially determined, partially accounted for. That consolation marks the breakdown in a panoramic view of justice, a breakdown in its ability to tell a complete story, either about the collective life of the working class or even about the circumscribed life of a woman named Deborah. And indeed, to our surprise, Deborah, unlike Hugh, is allowed to survive, living a life "pure and meek" among the Quakers, in a "homely pine house" overlooking "wooded slopes and clover-crimsoned meadows" (63). That ending, improbable as it is, nonetheless seems nonabsurd to me: nonabsurd, not because it fully summarizes, fully integrates what has gone on before, but because it does not. There is no total justice here, only incomplete justice, incomplete both in the narrowness of its action and in the dissonance of its effects. With that incompleteness, and the nontrivial difference it nonetheless makes, *Life in the Iron Mills* enjoins us to rethink the very object of political philosophy—to rethink it outside its dominant claims of adequation and totality—an injunction that, thus far, would seem not only more humanly bearable but also more humanly precise.

3

Luck and Love

The narrator in Borges's story "The Lottery in Babylon" is a man with a wildly checkered career, an odd fact true also of everyone else in that society. "Like all men in Babylon," he says, "I have been proconsul; like all, a slave. I have also known omnipotence, opprobrium, imprisonment." What gives his life this "almost atrocious variety" is "an institution which other republics do not know or which operates in them in an imperfect and secret manner." That peculiar institution is the lottery. In Babylon, it is not only sanctified and perfected but also adopted as a total institution, distributing every burden and benefit, every misery and felicity, and including everyone in its jurisdiction. With each drawing, the fate of each citizen is shuffled one more time, sometimes drastically improved, sometimes drastically worsened, leaving everyone in a state of equal risk, equal uncertainty. But the narrator is not complaining. His society is governed, he says, by "the sinuous numbers of Chance," given form by "the Celestial Archetype of the Lottery, which the Platonists adore."[1]

JUSTICE BY LOTTERY

Borges does not say whether or not Babylon counts as a *just* society, but the lottery, as a mechanism that delivers to each recipient a particular fate and that moreover advertises its reason—or lack of reason—for doing so, must occupy the same terrain reserved for the question of justice. To be outrageous, one might even propose it as a means to the latter. This, as it happens, is the very argument put forward by Barbara Goodwin, in a seemingly wacky but actually remarkably astute and tough-minded recent work, unblushingly titled *Justice by Lottery* (1992).[2]

Goodwin calls for a "Total Social Lottery," one that distributes all goods and offices and that, according to her, is simpler, fairer, and less brutalizing than any distributive principle to date. The lottery abolishes all human distinctions; it treats everyone alike, giving everyone an equal chance. Since it has no foreknowledge of its outcome, it also has no biases, no vested interests, no preconceived notions about particular ends. And so, bizarre as it might seem, the lottery actually fulfills those very conditions of procedural neutrality ordinarily taken as requisite for justice. Furthermore, since there is no attempt at justification here, no attempt to explain reward by reference to merit, what the lottery distributes is also distributed without judgment, carrying neither moral approval nor moral opprobrium. The burden would be in the tasks themselves and not in any invidious nuances we attach to them. According to Barbara Goodwin, then, allocation-by-lot might turn out to be our best bet for social justice, more egalitarian than any allocation we have thus far been able to implement and more humane than any we have thus far been able to imagine.

And indeed, dubious and outlandish as it might now seem, the lottery actually has a genealogy which might prove surprising to some of us. As James Wycliffe Headlam-Morley has shown in his pioneering (and still astonishing) study of the Athenian democracy, the lottery was its central political instrumentality. Elections in Athens were strictly "the verdict of chance," Headlam-Morley writes. "It is scarcely too much to say that the whole administration of the state was in the hands of men appointed by lot: the serious work of the law courts, of the execution of the laws, of police, of public finance, in short of every department (with the exception of actual commands in the army) was done by officials so chosen."[3] More recently, E. S. Staveley, in corroboration of this view, has described in great detail the *klērōtērion*, the Athenian allotment machine, in steady use after the fifth century B.C.[4]

Even in our own time, the lottery is by no means an unheard of proposition, and some influential thinkers have been its advocates. Most of them have championed it, however, not as a first principle but as a last resort, to be used in exceptional cases when the idea of "rational choice" is rendered especially disconcerting, distasteful, or impossible. Guido Calabresi and Philip Bobbitt, describing situations which they call "a nightmare of justice,"[5] have suggested that, in these instances, the lottery—the "choice not to choose"—would be an acceptable recourse. Such nightmares of justice include, for example, choosing one hostage from among a group of children; here, the blindness of the lottery works with a "simple, sweeping conception of egalitarianism" which "allows us to choose when we can no longer tolerate choice."[6] Bernard Williams, thinking of similar situations where choice is a burden and an unchosen choice a blessing and a respite, has also argued for the instrumental benefits of randomization, though with the important proviso that "the 'random' element in such events, as in certain events of tragedy, should be seen not so much as affording a justification . . . as being a reminder that some situations lie beyond justification."[7]

In making choices that are patently random—patently without adducible reason—the lottery openly proclaims its arbitrariness. It offers no justification for what it does and, in so doing, it also raises the question whether justification is *ever* possible, whether *any* choice can carry a rationale with the requisite moral weight. What the lottery challenges is perhaps nothing less than the idea of "rational deliberation" itself: not only its situational efficacy but also its epistemological ground, its premise that competing claims are commensurate, weighable and resolvable by the scales of reasoning. In jettisoning those scales and in resorting to the dice, the lottery thus throws into jeopardy considerably more than the outcome of some particular decision. It also throws into jeopardy something like the adjudicative power of reason, something like its claim to justice.

This deep skepticism about the adjudicative power of reason is very much a live issue for contemporary philosophers, who, confronting choices that are necessarily arbitrary and unjustified, have begun to see them not as peripheral aberrations but as central embarrassments, embarrassments that challenge our long-standing faith in the scope and efficacy of reason.[8] The work of Bernard Williams is especially illuminating here.[9] In a series of influential essays collected into *Moral Luck* (1981) and *Ethics and the Limits of Philosophy* (1985), Williams seizes upon the inadequacy (or sheer absurdity)[10] of justification to critique what is arguably the central tradition in Western philosophy, a Kantian tradition, based on the morality of reason. Kant, aspiring always to a moral foundation sufficiently general and sufficiently unconditional, has tried to locate that foundation in the deliberative rationality of the moral subject: a being supposedly capable of (and held accountable for) reasoned choices, choices not only universally possible but possible in ways that make "justification," or the lack of it, ethically meaningful. Rational choice for Kant is the primary activity of the moral subject, and the entire edifice of philosophy might be said to stand or fall on the intelligibility of this concept.

It is the noncontingency of rational choice—the fact that everyone is capable of it and accountable for it—which allows morality itself to be seen as a categorical imperative: absolute, foundational, and underived.[11]

Against this Kantian ideal of noncontingent reason, Bernard Williams introduces luck as a nuisance, a complication, and an intellectual puzzle. As a web of unwilled occurrences that nonetheless interferes with any willed decision, luck makes the concept of "rational choice" shaky, unduly optimistic, perhaps even blindly fatuous. In "choosing" to attend one school rather than another, does the college-bound teenager also "choose" the particular friendships and opportunities, the particular shapings of life and work, that follow as a consequence? Luck undermines not only the extensional integrity of choice, its ability to retain its intended shape in time, but also its autonomous justifiability, its ability to be judged in its own right as intrinsically right or wrong, just or unjust. Williams, in fact, believes that justification is never self-executing, never a feature resident in any particular choice, but always retrospective, always conferred after the fact, rendered possible only by subsequent occurrences. There are no decisions that are inherently wrong, only decisions that go wrong, decisions that are proven wrong by unfolding events and conspiring circumstances—which is to say, by luck. The agency of luck, the vexing uncertainty that it introduces between choice and consequence, thus appears for Williams as an exemplary instance of a pattern of disjunction in the world: a disjunction that undermines not only the instrumental claims of deliberative reason but also the moral judgment issuing from it and reflecting upon its exercise.

For choice, according to Kant, is of course eminently *judgeable.* One chooses deliberately and lends oneself to the verdict of moral rightness or moral wrongness. If we were to agree with Williams, however, about the intervening agency of luck—about its ability retrospectively to prove a choice right or wrong—then the judgeability of any decision may no longer be taken for granted. Choice, in other words, is no longer so clearly located within the domain of morality: no longer strictly exercisable on its own terms, analyzable within its limits, or justifiable under its auspices. Indeed, to push Williams's argument to its logical (if extreme) conclusion, we might say that *all* choices, whether rational or not, whether deliberated or not, are necessarily arbitrary, necessarily without intrinsic justification, and so are no different from the action of the lottery, or else they differ only in that the latter professes its arbitrariness rather than disguising it. In this sense, the lottery might even be said to be at the cutting edge of a new philosophical doctrine. It reminds us, as Jon Elster writes, that "some decisions are going to be arbitrary and epistemically random no matter what we do, no matter how hard we try to base them on reasons."[12]

Still, even given this philosophical appeal, probably not everyone would agree with Barbara Goodwin's sweeping (and only slightly tongue-in-cheek) proposal for a "Total Social Lottery." Fewer, no doubt, would agree with her conjectural portrait of those human beings who would make such a lottery work. For as she herself is the first to admit, her theory of justice (like every other theory of justice) is ultimately a theory about the political subject, about those human beings whose humanness, however defined and however hypothesized, must underwrite and validate her proposal for their ideal terms of association. Goodwin, of course, would like to believe that this humanness consists above all in an overriding *identity*, an overriding sameness among these beings, for the lottery can work only if people are more alike than they are different, so that the task randomly assigned to one can just as fitly be assigned to another, and benefits just as fitly reapportioned. Indeed, for her, "personhood" means not so much the particularity of persons as its opposite, something like the substitutability or interchangeability between persons. Only on that premise can the blind justice of the lottery not count as a handicap, for the blindness, cast among persons of overriding sameness, is hardly a liability but rather is a boon to justice.

It is this assumption of sameness—of substitutability and interchangeability—that strikes me as the fatal flaw in a "Total Social Lottery." My aim in this chapter, then, is to acknowledge the force of Goodwin's proposal but also to think through the implications of her unpersuasiveness. Like Goodwin, I want to bring "arbitrariness" into the analytic foreground as an ethical (not to say political) consideration. Unlike her, however, I want not so much to instrumentalize it, turning it into a vehicle of justice, as to emphasize its irreducible presence, its status as a conundrum (perhaps even a counterpoint) to our thinking about justice, about reason, and about the supposed coincidence or entailment between the two. What I have in mind, then, is something like a constitutive theory of luck, one that studies its arbitrary agency not only in our actions but in our very selves, in that accidental conjunction of circumstances and attributes which make us what we are. Understood as something that constitutes us (rather than something that merely confronts us), luck fits awkwardly, or perhaps not at all, into the idea of justice—an awkwardness which helps to explain, I think, not only its limited presence within the language of Kantian philosophy but also the limited ability of that language to describe the world as we know it.

The language of justice, I want to suggest, precisely because it is a language of rational adequation, a language that refines out of existence the category of luck—the category of what is not amenable to reason—is also a language that refines out of existence much of what most compels us or frightens us, a language too porous, finally, to render intelligible the particular delights and vulnerabilities of our lives. It is with this sense of linguistic porousness—this sense that the language of justice is both thinner and coarser than our experiential sense of ourselves and of one another—that I turn to luck as an undertheorized and for a long time barely noticed concept, one that has slipped through the sievelike fabric of our political discourse. And rather than rehabilitating it in one specific domain of experience (in the domain of rational choice, as Bernard Williams has done), I want to claim for it a kind of troubling ubiquity, a ubiquity which alters the very landscape—the very scope and authority—of justice itself.

My argument, for the most part analytic, is to some extent historical as well, winding up (after an estimable detour) in a tradition more ancient and more venerable than Kant's. Christian theology, with its doctrine of grace—espoused by Augustine, revitalized by Luther, and further elaborated in the American context by Jonathan Edwards—for centuries taught what, from the human perspective, had amounted to a doctrine of luck.[13] Grace was freely, gratuitously, and incomprehensibly given by God; it had nothing to do with the desert of the recipient. Edwards would not have used the word "nonfoundational," but that was what justice was in his cognitive universe, a universe governed by what he called "mere and arbitrary grace."[14] Christian theology, wary of the discrepancy between human reason and divine action, had historically treated justice with a kind of nonabsolutist circumspection, which makes it, to my mind, one of the most important challenges to the discourse of philosophy. In the nineteenth century, it was the "sentimental" women writers—the true heirs to Edwards, I would argue—who would keep alive this nonabsolutist circumspection, as they continued to wrestle with the problem of justice in a world of inescapable arbitrariness. The novels of these women—novels of mere and arbitrary grace, mere and arbitrary affections—not only darkened the democratic hopes of a poet like Whitman but also revised, reinvigorated, and (their authors' professions notwithstanding) recast into a secular idiom the complex thinking about justice that had animated their theological predecessors.

LUCK AND DESERT: JOHN RAWLS

Mindful of these beckoning figures, I want nonetheless to begin my argument about luck with a contemporary text, one all the more instructive for being so unlikely. John Rawls's *A Theory of Justice* (1971), perhaps the most celebrated text in twentieth-century political philosophy, and the work of a self-acknowledged Kantian, is very much dedicated to the idea of noncontingent reason, understood as a principle of "absolute necessity," absolute enough to be the "ground of obligation" and "cleansed of everything that can only be empirical and appropriate to anthropology," as Kant had counseled in the *Groundwork of the Metaphysics of Morals* (1785).[15] Justice, for Rawls as for Kant, is incompatible with circumstantial vagaries; but for both it is also imaginable outside of those vagaries. It is imaginable, that is, as a hypothetical construct, as the endpoint to an idealized exercise of reason, the endpoint to a deliberative process freed from all compromising particulars.

To his great credit, however, enamored as he is of noncontingent reason, Rawls never tries to naturalize it, never imagines it as effortlessly at home in the world, in the state of nature. Indeed, his "state of nature," the starting point for his political theory, is notable for being harshly arbitrary. For it is here, at the outset, that we are faced with the most glaring instance of distributive injustice: the random inequality of natural endowments. At the heart of Rawls's theory of justice, then, is something like a constitutive theory of luck. It is the sense that luck has always been there, from the very beginning—the sense that we are its creature, its handiwork—that pushes him to some of his most radical conclusions, especially his argument about desert and its relation to distributive entitlement.

Desert is, of course, seen by most sensible laymen (and mainstream political philosophers) as the basis of our entitlement and therefore as the moral foundation for distributive justice.[16] Rawls disagrees. He rejects the idea that "distributive shares should be in accordance with moral worth," that reward should match a corresponding merit.[17] For him, such an idea is not only undemocratic in practice but unpersuasive in theory. He argues, instead, that what counts as our "merit" is actually something that accrues to us through the accident of birth, through "luck in the natural lottery."[18] We cannot be said to deserve it, any more than we can be said to deserve those material advantages that accrue to us through the same accident. In short, to allow "the distribution of wealth and income to be determined by the natural distribution of abilities and talents" is to do no more than to submit to "the outcome of the natural lottery, and this outcome is arbitrary from a moral perspective."[19]

Rawls's vigorous rejection of desert is therefore the starting point for an alternative theory of justice. It is also the starting point for an alternative theory of the person. Since we do not actually deserve those attributes that happen to be lodged in us, we also cannot be said to own them. For Rawls, this thought gives rise to an exhilarating (and some would say phantasmagoric) vision of the world: here, natural talents are imagined to be showered upon the earth, like manna from heaven (the phrase is Robert Nozick's),[20] unowned, unmarked, undeserved by any particular person, and free to be used for the good of all. This notion of common usability—applied to attributes long considered private and personal—makes for a distributive domain larger than anything previously imagined. Out of this radically enlarged pool of resources, Rawls is able to argue for an equally radical mode of distribution, based not on the moral reflexivity within particular persons, not on the supposed correlation between merit and reward, but on the political will of the community, on its concerted policy decision. In other words, the benefit each person receives would not be self-evident or self-executing, would not reflect the sort of person he or she happens to be or the sort of work he or she happens to have done. It would express instead the principles of fairness of the entire society, the distributive choices that it makes regarding the individual and collective well-being of its members.

Such principles would speak not only to those lucky enough to be naturally talented but also to those so unlucky as to be without rewardable talents.

Critics of Rawls have, of course, objected to his theory of justice as an elegant but thinly disguised scheme for the redistribution of wealth, a scheme that, in refusing to reward excellence in particular persons, must end up destroying the ethical (not to say the economic) primacy of the person. This objection, forceful as it is, also seems to me somewhat beside the point. Rawls himself, indeed, is reassuringly emphatic here. "Each person," he announces on the first page of *A Theory of Justice*, "possesses an inviolability founded on justice that even the welfare of society as a whole cannot override."[21] What is especially fascinating here, then, both in the context of thinking about luck and in the more general context of thinking about the political consequences of personhood, is the way Rawls has managed to jettison the notion of personal desert without jettisoning, at the same time, either the category of the "person" or its political centrality within a theory of democratic justice. The challenge for him is thus to defend a distributive justice based on policy decision rather than on private endeavor and to demonstrate (appearances to the contrary) that this rejection of individual desert is nonetheless not a violation of individual rights, not incompatible with a respect for persons.

Differently put, we might say that Rawls's challenge is to adjudicate between—to devise a rational court of appeal for—two conflicting sets of claims: between the communitarian claims of the welfare state on the one hand and the individualistic claims of the liberal subject on the other. His strategy is to effect a formal solution to the problem, which is to say, a solution by virtue of an idealized noncontingent procedure. His celebrated construct, the "veil of ignorance"—a hypothetical situation in which the deliberating parties, knowing nothing about their yet-to-be-assigned fortunes, are asked to work out a principle of justice fair to all concerned, fair especially to those least advantaged—is one such solution. The virtue of such a construct is that it would allow reason to work with optimal freedom, which for Rawls also means that it would allow justice to emerge as a matter of procedure, because under these idealized conditions, justice would simply be the endpoint of our deliberative rationality. It would be "the choice which rational men would make."[22] Central to Rawls's theory of justice, then, is a mechanism to purify contingent man into rational man, a mechanism to extract the deliberating subject from all those circumstantial prejudices, all those accidental attributes, which hamper his exercise of reason.

As befits a Kantian, Rawls's is a strictly categorical conception of the person.[23] This is true not only of those hypothetical figures behind the veil of ignorance but also of his political subject, which to be a *democratic* subject must also be theorized into a suitable state of noncontingency. Indeed, any tangible or rewardable attributes, any marks of excellence or lack of excellence—all these particularizing features of the self—must be relegated to a domain defined both as prior to democracy and, in the end, as amendable by it. For Rawls, such redefinitions are crucial if the "person" is to remain democratically defensible, for a democratic subject must be first and foremost a universal subject, one whose political dignity is absolute, about whom one can make a categorical claim. To arrive at such a subject, actual selves would have to be stripped bare, would have to be removed from all those accidental features, all those inequities of chance, which make them unfit for such a categorical description.[24]

The upshot of this exercise is ultimately to bring about a refinement in the Rawlsian syntax of the self, a small but crucial distinction that he implicitly depends upon: namely, between what a person *is* and what a person *has*, between what is *me* and what is *mine*. It is a matter of luck that I am some particular person, that I have attributes I can call my own. But because those attributes that are "mine" are assigned to me by luck, because they just happen to have attached themselves to me, they cannot properly be said to be "me." Indeed, to give the paradox an even sharper edge, what is "mine" is, for that very reason, not "me." Rawls's theory of justice therefore operates on something like a postulate of detachability. It both assumes and requires a categorical subject apprehensible apart from all its substantive descriptions. Only such a "me," conceived in contradistinction to what is "mine," can make justice more than an apology for the accident of birth. Only such a "me" can make democratic equality not just a policy but also an epistemology.

This rigorous distinction between "me" and "mine" thus commits Rawls to what he himself acknowledges to be a "thin" theory of the person, one that bears, if not exactly an inverse relation, then at least a suspended relation to people as they ordinarily appear and as they are ordinarily perceived, people thick with particular traits, which they innocently call "his" or "hers," "yours" or "mine." Such usages are unacceptable to Rawls, because the person, to be democratically defensible, must be defensible as a categorical idea rather than as people with actual features and attributes. This is, in a sense, the logical consequence of yet another (and perhaps analytically prior) paradox in Rawls: his simultaneous acknowledgement of and revulsion against luck, his sense not only of its abiding centrality in human life but also of its unconscionable tyranny. For if his rejection of desert is based on the insight that desert is merely luck in disguise, the ubiquity of luck is at the same time a grievous wrong for him, one that carries with it a silent directive, a demand for rectification. And so, as Rawls himself admits, his theory of justice is very much a theory to combat luck, a theory to "nullif[y] the accidents of natural endowment and the contingencies of social circumstance."[25] His cleansing of the political subject is an effort in that direction, an effort to free the self of the incrustations of luck, to save the essential "me" from the accidental "mine," so that the category of the person can finally be categoric, and justice can finally be noncontingent.

SYNTAX AND DEMOCRACY: NOAM CHOMSKY

Central, then, to Rawls's political theory is a syntactic proposition about the self—a distinction between "me" and "mine"—a syntactic distinction which is then transposed into an ontological distinction. I use the word "syntax" advisedly, knowing that the word is not neutral but heavily accented by its association with Noam Chomsky, an association which, as it happens, Rawls himself has likewise remarked upon. He calls attention, indeed, to a parallel between his theory of justice and Chomsky's theory of linguistics. Both, he says, operate at some remove from "familiar common sense precepts," and both involve "principles and theoretical constructs which go much beyond the norms and standards cited in everyday life."[26] And both aspire, we might add, to a level of noncontingency which can only be found in what Chomsky calls a "formalized general theory."[27] I want to explore further this point of contact between Chomsky and Rawls, as a way to focus more precisely on the linguistic properties of Rawls's language of justice. Chomsky is uniquely helpful here, for not only is he a formidable practitioner in both linguistics and democratic politics, but his syntactic theory, in its ambitions and limits, also casts an admonitory light on the ambitions and limits of a syntax of political personhood.

Chomsky begins his challenge to traditional linguistics by taking issue with its self-conception as a taxonomic discipline; he urges, instead, that a proper study of language should focus not on its classifications but on its "generative" character. And for him, syntax above all is what makes a natural language "generative"—because it not only assigns structural properties to the semantic and phonological components of a sentence but also enables us to substitute words within the same structural category, and so to create an infinite number of new sentences, all equally rule observing and all syntactically equivalent. Substitutability and interchangeability, in short, are the central generative features of syntax. They make syntax the wellspring of language, its source of perpetual renewal as well as perpetual regularity. Indeed, for Chomsky, syntax represents not only the deep structure of sentences in one particular language but also (in its "transformational" capacity) the deep structure of *all* natural languages. It is the foundation of a "universal grammar," common to all human beings, at work in all mental processes, and indistinguishable from human cognition itself.

Chomsky's virtual equation of syntax and cognition, of course, comes at the expense of semantics, a time-honored area of linguistic (and philosophical) inquiry.[28] Chomsky, however, is openly impatient of semantic analysis, an impatience having to do, I suspect, with the way he defines the objectives of linguistics and the way he delimits its domain. While it is, "of course, impossible to prove that semantic notions are of no use in grammar," Chomsky cannot help pointing out that the "correspondences . . . between formal and semantic features in language" are so "imperfect" and "inexact" that "meaning will be relatively useless as a basis for grammatical description." For that reason, "grammar is best formulated as a self-contained study independent of semantics."[29] In short, semantics is not a fruitful object of study for Chomsky because, being always at the mercy of context, it is highly erratic, cannot sustain a grammar, does not lend itself to formalizable rules, and does not exhibit the properties of substitutability and interchangeability, whereas syntax does.[30]

Chomsky's elevation of syntax over semantics, in turn, opens outward into a set of definitional demarcations that map out the domain of linguistics as he understands it, demarcations that assign primacy, in every instance, to terms that are universal and noncontingent. Chomsky thus distinguishes between *competence* and *performance*, arguing that linguistics can adequately study only the former, only the grammatical knowledge common to all speakers of a natural language, rather than the specific verbal behavior of some particular user.[31] He also argues that language is primarily a vehicle of thought, an activity self-sufficient unto itself, rather than a vehicle of communication, an activity dependent on an audience.[32] And since he equates syntactic knowledge with cognitive capability, he also argues, most controversially of all, that linguistic competence is innate, that it resides in a congenital faculty of language, unindebted to educational input and environmental influence. Putting himself squarely in the camp of the rationalist tradition associated with Descartes,[33] Chomsky thus turns language acquisition itself into a noncontingent phenomenon, "free from the control of detectable stimuli, either external or internal,"[34] not varying with particular environments or even with particular individuals. It is instead a guaranteed feature of human cognition, uniformly and universally present to all, "independen[t] of intelligence, motivation, and emotional state."[35]

Chomsky's peculiar insistences might be better gauged, I think, if we contrast him briefly with the later Wittgenstein, whose position on natural language, on grammar, and on grammatical rules is close enough to Chomsky's for their divergences to be instructive. Like Chomsky, Wittgenstein believes that grammatical description is constitutive of thought, that "grammar tells us what kind of object anything is."[36] Also like Chomsky, he believes that the "various transformations and consequences of the sentence" are possible only "in so far as they are embodied in a grammar," a grammar which "has the same relation to the language as the description of a game, the rules of a game, have to the game."[37] Unlike Chomsky, however, Wittgenstein has no desire to produce a *foundational* theory of grammar, no desire to locate a necessary basis for syntactic knowledge in human cognition. He argues, to the contrary, that "grammar is not accountable to any reality" and that the "only correlate in language to an intrinsic necessity is an arbitrary rule."[38] Language cannot be foundational for Wittgenstein because it is an artifact rather than a guarantee, a form of mediation rather than a form of emanation, and can only render back to us our customs, our communities, our shared agreements about how things are. It has its being not in the innateness of cognition but in the socialness of convention; or, as Wittgenstein puts it in his famous dictum, "to imagine a language means to imagine a form of life."[39]

Against Wittgenstein's emphatic rejection of the innateness of language, Chomsky's equally emphatic assertion of that innateness becomes all the more striking. He has been savagely attacked, in fact, on just this point.[40] Questioned about this in an interview with the *New Left Review*, Chomsky replies:

> I would like to assume on the basis of fact and hope on the basis of confidence in the human species that there are innate structures of mind. If there are not, if humans are just plastic and random organisms, then they are fit subjects for the shaping of behaviour. If humans only become as they are by random changes, then why not control that randomness by the state authority or the behaviourist technologist or anything else?[41]

For Chomsky, then, "innate structures of mind" are above all a defense against the threats of "randomness," which for him mean especially political threats, threats from the state against its citizens. It is in this context, against the historical gravity of that threat, that we can best understand his foundationalist impulse, his desire to locate and to affirm linguistic "principles that are universal by biological necessity and not mere historical accident."[42] An unlearned competence, an innate grammar, a knowledge of syntax embedded in human cognition—these issues, brilliantly technical as they are, are nonetheless not strictly technical for Chomsky. They are so many bulwarks against the political vulnerabilities of human life, against the intolerable odds in favor of tyranny and oppression. And so, even though Chomsky's acknowledged intellectual debt is Cartesian rather than Kantian,[43] we might nonetheless speak of a categorical imperative in his linguistic theory, a desire to imagine an ethical domain free from contingency, free from the less than benign presence of the arbitrary, and free, for that reason, to pass judgment on the arbitrary. For him as for Rawls, the postulate of an ontological given—a guaranteed linguistic knowledge, a guaranteed deliberative rationality—is also the founding moment of political faith. And it is from this point of faith, this point of ethical inviolability, that the contingencies of politics might be adjudged, amended if necessary, resisted if necessary.[44] Chomsky's linguistic theory, then, like Rawls's political theory, is a tribute to, a protest against, and a self-conscious battle with that all-too-elusive, all-too-ubiquitous demon of luck, whether it inheres in the "lottery" of life or whether it inheres in the "randomness" of unjust regimes. And ultimately the triumph of democracy is measured by the elimination of luck: by replacing its inequities and irregularities with something like a syntax of justice, so that the political subject can finally resemble the grammatical subject, its basic rights as uniform and as categoric as the structural properties of the latter.

The language of justice, then, for Chomsky as for Rawls, is very much a language of syntax. In Wittgensteinian terms, we might also think of this language as a descriptive "net,"[45] held out to the world to capture it and to render it intelligible, a net, in this case, made of necessarily coarse mesh, since it is meant to retrieve from the world only those features that are invariant, features that can yield a foundational principle. This is what I mean by its linguistic "porousness." The language of justice, precisely because it is a language of syntax, a language of structural *guarantee*, demands from the world a grammatical uniformity. It prohibits irregularities, and it also ignores miracles, occurrences so extraordinary as to exceed its grammatical description. It is thus a language of the lowest common denominator, one that, if adopted, would explain why we might have no quarrel with the world. But it would not explain why we might love the world.

For the world is indeed not lovable within the language of justice, being less like a world than like a grid. And most gridlike of all is the self conceived in its image, a self so thinly constituted and minimally featured that it too is not exactly lovable. The language of justice equips us only to act in those domains where we can think of one another as categoric persons: as possessors of equal rights, claimants of analogous liberties, recipients of similar attention. It cannot explain why we make friends with some and not others, fall in love with some and not others, talk to some and not others. Or rather, it can explain those things only by setting them aside, as matters of preference, unworthy of ethical or political consideration. In this sense, the language of justice not only aspires to transform the world into a grammar, a collection of syntactic subjects, it also enjoins us to treat actual persons as if they were syntactic ones, attending only to those features structurally assigned and formally generalizable.[46]

Within such a grammar, human attachment thus becomes something of an enigma, a conceptual puzzle. For given the thinness of the subject, it is not at all clear how that attachment is to be anchored, let alone what it is anchored to, or what inferences one might draw from its being anchored to one particular object and not to another. Rawls, oddly, remains untroubled by this problem; in a passage memorable for its equanimity, he writes:

> The active sentiments of love and friendship, and even the sense of justice, arise from the manifest intention of other persons to act for our good. Because we recognize that they wish us well, we care for their well-being in return. Thus we acquire attachments to persons and institutions according to how we perceive our good to be affected by them. The basic idea is one of reciprocity, a tendency to answer in kind. . . . For surely a rational person is not indifferent to things that significantly affect his good; and supposing that he develops some attitude toward them, he acquires either a new attachment or a new aversion.[47]

The key word here is clearly "a rational person," liberally defined, for it is only under the most liberal definition that love and friendship can proceed with such commendable regularity, as an exchange of goodwill beneficial to both partners: routine, unvarying, matter-of-fact. There is nothing arbitrary about the loves of the rational person; they are strictly proportionate, strictly accountable, always "answering in kind" to the love he receives. His outgoing affection will always match the incoming goodwill. And, since it is a category of sentiment—rather than some particular individual—that he is responding to, we can assume that substitutability and interchangeability will be guaranteed features of his affective life. Without much exaggeration, then, we might call Rawls's "rational person" a grammatical subject, for his affections are happily rule observing, governed by a generative syntax that not only maintains a structural form but also endlessly renews that form by substituting any given term with an infinite number of syntactic equivalents.

If this sounds jarring, no doubt it is because we are not always so grammatical in love and friendship. A theory of formal universals, in this case, is virtually a parody of itself. Rawls, of course, is not the only philosopher to have trouble making ethical sense of affective preferences. As Gregory Vlastos has pointed out, personal affection also fares badly in Plato, for whom the highest form of love turns out to be "one furthest removed from affection for concrete human beings."[48]

Even so, there is something particularly comical, particularly thread-bare, about Rawls's account of love and friendship. Michael Sandel, one of Rawls's ablest commentators, has seized upon just this point not only to highlight the unpersuasive thinness of the Rawlsian self but also to put forward a sustained critique of the language of justice, focusing especially on its inability to account for the phenomenon of friendship except as a secondary (and indeed derivative) virtue. The thinness of the Rawlsian self means that it will have no responsive chord, that its capacity for friendship will always be limited by its "restricted access to the good of others," so that "every act of friendship thus becomes parasitic on a good identifiable in advance."[49]

My own critique of the language of justice, while indebted to Sandel's, will focus less on its trivialization of love and friendship than on its tendency to locate these phenomena in a relation of externality to itself, as that which philosophy is not and cannot be concerned with. I have in mind not only Rawls's respectful dismissal of love and friendship as "higher-order sentiments,"[50] higher than the supposedly lowly domain of political philosophy, but also the obsessively repetitive pages in the *Groundwork of the Metaphysics of Morals*, where Kant insists, over and over again, that "the highest and unconditioned good can alone be found" in those instances when one acts "not from inclination, but from duty." Kant concedes that there might be those who actually "take delight in the contentment of others as their own work," but "an action of this kind, however right and however amiable it may be, has still no genuinely moral worth."[51] Indeed, for him, the only genuinely moral person is someone who does good not because he likes to but because he has no fondness for it, someone who is

> cold in temperament and indifferent to the sufferings of others—
> perhaps because, being endowed with the special gift of patience and
> robust endurance in his own sufferings, he assumed the like in others
> or even demanded it. . . . It is precisely in this that the worth of charac-
> ter begins to show—a moral worth and beyond all comparison the
> highest—namely, that he does good, not from inclination, but from
> duty.[52]

Kant's moral agent, then, confronts a world he does not love, but which, for just that reason, he is bent on fulfilling his duty toward. To the extent that Kant remains the central figure in Western philosophy, the language of justice is thus centrally premised on the opposition between "duty" and "inclination": the former acquiring the status of ethical sufficiency, the latter suffering the fate of ethical dismissibility. And to the extent that these principles of sufficiency and dismissibility do not coincide with what attaches most of us to the world, the language of justice must render a good part of our lives ethically meaningless. The return of the repressed, then, can appear only as a fatal contradiction, a fatal clashing of opposing claims: between democratic equality on the one hand and affective preferences on the other, between our political need for formal universals and our emotional attachment to substantive particulars. Since philosophy is unhelpful on this point, I turn now to two other genres of texts, literary and theological, to investigate within their confines the terms of this contradiction and, through their alternative traditions, to explore further some other, possibly more complex, possibly more nuanced ways of thinking about justice, in which "inclination" might have a place.

GRAMMATICAL SUBJECTS: "SONG OF MYSELF"

I begin with Walt Whitman, a poet whose commitment to democratic justice is, not least of all, a formal commitment, whose poetry, with its endless catalogs, its endless collections of attachable, detachable parts, one as good as the other, one substitutable for the other, is perhaps as close as any poetry can come to being a generative grammar. Within the terms of our discussion, we would expect this to be a poetry governed by syntax, and that is indeed the case in "Song of Myself." Perhaps also not surprisingly, then, at the heart of the poem is a grammatical entity, the "myself" who is both the author and subject of his song. And, since this "myself" is democratically defensible only as a formal universal, it too has to be purified, extracted, turned into a categorical idea, so that it can remain structurally inviolate even as it goes through any number of substantive variations, even as it entertains any number of contingent terms. By means, then, of a series of grammatical distinctions—a series of complexly articulated and carefully differentiated uses of "me," "mine," and "myself"— Whitman too (even more than Rawls) works his way through the various syntactic modes of the subject in order to recover a truly foundational self, one whose democratic dignity is absolute, transcendent, and unconditional.

Given this categorical conception, the problematics of the subject that we have seen in Rawls—its much-discussed "thinness," its tendency to propagate a corresponding thinness in human affections, its rational practice of substitutability and interchangeability—would perhaps plague Whitman as well. In any case, as much as it is a poetry of accumulation, "Song of Myself" is also a poetry of divestment, a poetry that spins out an endless catalog of the self's many attachments only to distinguish the self from all those attachments. We see this in familiar lines such as the following, in which, beginning with things that are obviously external, Whitman moves on to things that are less obviously so, things that might even have been thought of as intrinsic to him. These he nonetheless disavows and imagines as being somehow distinct from him, distinct from the "Me myself" which is anterior to, and curiously untouched by, what he happens to be possessing or even experiencing at any given moment:

> My dinner, dress, associates, looks, business, compliments, dues,
> The real or fancied indifference of some man or woman I love,
> The sickness of one of my folks—or of myself . . . or ill-doing . . . or loss
>   or lack of money . . . or depressions or exaltations,
> They come to me days and nights and go from me again,
> But they are not the Me Myself.[53]

By the time Whitman is through, quite a few things that might have been considered a part of him—things like physical well-being and emotional affliction or satisfaction—are all consigned to the realm of the fortuitous, which is also to say, the realm of the unessential. To consecrate a democratic subject, Whitman, like Rawls, is quite willing to do some ontological cleansing, rearranging the very contents of the person. In practice, this means removing the self from all its contingencies and defining these contingencies as the "not Me Myself," so that, finally detached from them, the self can also be defined against them, as a principle of absolute necessity. As Whitman spins out his catalogs, then, the domain of the "*not* Me Myself" thus becomes broader and broader, more and more crowded, even as the "Me Myself" is increasingly stripped bare, put through an increasingly rigorous set of refinements, until it is purified into no more than an idea, an empty form, but, for that very reason, a form of transcendent dignity. Like Rawls, Whitman is quite willing to give up what is "mine," to write it over to the world as part of its bounty as well as part of its caprice, in order to rescue "me" as an absolute concept, free from all circumstantial encumbrances, free from the vagaries of the accidental.

In the 1855 preface to *Leaves of Grass*, Whitman writes that the poet "judges not as the judge judges but as the sun falling around a helpless thing" (9). This statement stands not only as a democratic manifesto but also, I think, as a noncontingent poetics, which, in its unfastidious, unconditional generosity, in effect eliminates luck by eliminating the invidious distinctions it fosters, so that the whole world is now taken in, wrapped in a kind of cosmic tenderness, without exception and without fail, leaving nothing to chance. The objects of Whitman's attention are admitted as strict equals, guaranteed equals, both by virtue of the minimal, universal "Me" they all have in common and by virtue of a poetic syntax which greets each of them in exactly the same way, as a grammatical unit, equivalently functioning and structurally interchangeable. To say this is perhaps to say the obvious: there is an intimate connection between Whitman's poetic language and political philosophy, a shared commitment to syntax. This grammatical disposition not only underwrites the universality of the self in "Song of Myself" but also inscribes in it a democratic hospitality to the world, a refusal to tolerate exclusions, a refusal, indeed, to register distinctions, an openness as impartial as it is impersonal.[54]

The problem in Whitman (to the extent that it is one) can be restated, then, as one version of the conflict we have been discussing: a conflict between the opposing claims of universality and particularity in the definition of personhood, and between the opposing domains of experience to which each corresponds. How can we reconcile the categoric conception of the self in democratic theory with our experiential sense of the self in human attachments, attachments that are, after all, not universal but highly particular, anchored to the self not in its commonality but in its distinctive features and substantive attributes—anchored, in short, not to what is "me" but to what is "mine"? How can we reconcile the grammatical dictates of substitutability and interchangeability with the phenomenon of memory, with our selective attachment to our past and to figures from our past, and with the sense that people never matter to us uniformly, not at any given moment, and certainly not over time? How can we, in short, imagine a "me" adequate both to the requisite impartiality of political life and to the requisite partiality of personal affections?

These questions have been raised by Whitman himself—or at least raised by him in the form of a statement—in section 3 of "Song of Myself": "Out of the dimness opposite equals advance. . . . Always substance and increase / Always a knit of identity, always distinction, always a breed of life" (27). Identity and distinction, the contrary claims of personhood and the contrary claims, I have tried to suggest, of democratic politics and affective preferences, are here conjoined by Whitman, made to appear as syntactic equivalents: in a parallel construction, with neither one subordinated to the other. But if this raises one's hopes, there is also a sense in which the hope is rigged, since the form itself of the syntax, the logical primacy it assigns to equivalence, would seem to have foreclosed the very question it is meant to address. This sense of foreclosure—of a conclusion syntactically settled ahead of time—is especially noticeable in the lines we examined earlier, Whitman's catalog of all those things that compose the "not Me Myself."

In that fateful passage, a succession of objects and events are adduced, paratactically, as analogous terms: equally contingent, equally peripheral to the self, and equally detachable from the self. Since the syntax here focuses only on the phenomenon of equivalence—only on the fact that all the items enumerated are equally "not Me Myself"—what cannot be registered is not only the appositional difference between those items but also the sequential difference generated by each, the legacy or constraint each might bring to what comes after it. In "Song of Myself" that difference hardly exists, since the fact of prior occurrence is in no way a determining condition for what follows. To mention just one example, "the real or fancied indifference of some man or woman I love" is offered here as a sequel, a syntactic equivalent, to "My dinner, dress, associates, looks, business, compliments, dues," and is in turn followed by yet another syntactic equivalent, "The sickness of one of my folks—or of myself . . . or ill-doing . . . or loss or lack of money . . . or depressions or exaltations"—as if all three were comparable, separated by no emotional distance, and as if the significance of each were exhausted by its appearance, so that each departs as it arrives, leaving behind no residue, no constraints on the syntax, nothing to make it less open or less ready for more parallel additions.[55]

"Song of Myself" is thus a poetry of sequence without sedimentation, a poetry that sallies forth, its syntactic vitality unmarred by what it has been through. It is a poetry that dwells ever in the present, not because it refuses to look back but because past events are so strangely foreshortened, so devoid of any weight of time, that they have the effect of being contemporaneous with all events subsequent to them. The operative process here is something like the transposition of seriality into simultaneity—the constitution of memory as a field of spatial latitude rather than temporal extension—a process that, I argue, makes for the perpetual openness of the poem, its boundless horizons of experience. Since I see this as a crucial feature of Whitman's democratic poetics, I want to discuss in some detail one particular stanza in "Song of Myself"—the famous encounter with the runaway slave in section 10—in which the word "remember" actually figures, and figures curiously:

> The runaway slave came to my house and stopped outside,
> I heard his motions crackling the twigs of the woodpile,
> Through the swung half-door of the kitchen I saw him limpsey and
>   weak,
> And went where he sat on a log, and led him in and assured him,
> And brought water and filled a tub for his sweated body and bruised
>   feet,
> And gave him a room that entered from my own, and gave him some
>   coarse clean clothes,
> And remember perfectly well his revolving eyes and his
>   awkwardness,
> And remember putting plasters on the galls of his neck and ankles;
> He staid with me a week before he was recuperated and passed north,
> I had him sit next me at table . . . my firelock leaned in the corner.
>   (33–34)

In its scrupulousness and restraint, restraint especially from undue effusiveness or familiarity, this passage must stand as one of the most compelling moments of democratic affections in "Song of Myself." The runaway slave is not a *particular* slave, he is *any* slave, for the poet would have done as much for anyone bearing that generic identity. His goodwill is also offered generically, occasioned not by any qualities peculiar to this slave but by his membership in a collective category, and it is transferable, one would imagine, to any other member of that category. The poet is behaving "grammatically," then, as I have disparagingly used that word. But if so, what becomes clear in this passage is the tremendous need for grammar in this world, the tremendous need for structural provisions unattached to particular persons and responsive to all analogous persons. Substitutability and interchangeability, from this perspective, hardly detract from human dignity. They guarantee it.

Still, it must be said as well that this dignity, while guaranteed, is also carefully shielded from that very substitutability and interchangeability which make it possible. And so, the object of the poet's attention is introduced not as *a* runaway slave but as *the* runaway slave, as if he were some previously mentioned figure, specially known to the poet, rather than the categoric person which he is. What Whitman encourages us to forget, then, is the very condition under which the slave is admitted into "Song of Myself," as one of its representative figures, one of its formal equivalents, succeeding the trapper and his Indian bride in the previous stanza and to be succeeded, in turn, by the twenty-eight young men bathing by the shore in section 11. Indeed, these other figures—the trapper and his bride, and the bathing young men—must be forgotten as well, their lack of connection to the slave being not at all a lapse but a necessity, a desired effect. This tender forgetfulness—this ceaseless transformation of "a" into "the"—thus generates a peculiar shape of time in "Song of Myself," turning it into an arena of simultaneity, an arena in which antecedence carries no particular weight because it is simply not registered as antecedence.

The transposition of seriality into simultaneity thus makes memory in "Song of Myself" democratic in a rather troubling sense, in that no particular event can claim to have a special place in it, no particular event can claim to be more cherished or more enduring.[56] The extension of time, or rather the emotional weight inhering in that extension, is something of an incomprehensible (or inadmissible) phenomenon, and it is this, I think, that accounts for that strange confusion of tenses here surrounding the word "remember." That fateful word is used not once but twice, in two consecutive sentences: "And remember perfectly well his revolving eyes and his awkwardness, / And remember putting plasters on the galls of his neck and ankles." Indeed the entire stanza, from the "swung half-door of the kitchen" to the famous "firelock leaned in the corner,"[57] might be read as a tribute to the minuteness and tenacity of memory. And yet, this tribute notwithstanding, the exact status of memory, its location and extension in time, remains more than a little puzzling. After all, the most striking feature of the stanza is surely the odd, incongruous placement of the act of remembering—something supposedly being done in the present—among the recorded deeds of the past. Presided over by the conjunctive "and," "remember" becomes syntactically equivalent to all the verbs that precede it: "went," "led," "brought water," "filled a tub," "gave him a room." It is made analogous to, and put into the company of, verbs depicting concrete acts of definite duration and tangible result, acts begun in the past and ended in the past.

Yet what makes memory special is surely that it resembles none of the above: it is not concrete, has no definite duration or tangible result, and knows neither beginnings nor endings. It can be put in the midst of the others, can be pronounced the equivalent of the others, only through a syntactic dictate that amounts to a kind of epistemological violence. Being harnessed in this manner by the syntax, memory becomes coterminous and coextensive with the event that occasions it. It is woven into the incident that it recalls, sealed and sewn within it. This is what gives memory in Whitman its tapestry-like quality, its strange sense of being without compulsion, without mobility in time. Relieved from the weight of antecedence, past events can now become cheerful additions to the present, swelling its ranks and multiplying its opportunities. The transposition of temporal extension into spatial amplitude thus makes for a self so resilient, so able to accommodate all contingencies as to be beyond contingency. This is, of course, the fantasized ideal in "Song of Myself": a self endlessly renewed by its procedures, a self whose perennial innocence translates into a democratic largesse, a self always open to new experience but always unencumbered by that experience.

An "unencumbered self," Michael Sandel has argued, is the ideal citizen for a "procedural republic,"[58] a Kantian political utopia, observing always the imperatives of the categorical and generalizing those imperatives into the idea of a universal subject, one who might "be made the ground for all maxims of action."[59] If so, "Song of Myself" must count as one of the most compelling portraits of that utopia, an experiment to devise for the unencumbered self a credible embodiment and a credible home. From the poem, though, we might glimpse not only the political necessities for such an ideal but also some of its experiential difficulties. For more dramatically here than elsewhere, we see the extent to which the language of democratic justice is a language of syntax, a language signally porous both in relation to the varieties of human experience and in relation to the particularities of affective life. It captures for us the openness of space but not the endurance of time, the rhythms of fresh beginnings but not the music of familiar affections, the renewability of syntax but not the sedimentation of meanings.

SEMANTICS AND MEMORY

In this context, it is worth returning briefly to Noam Chomsky and recalling some of *his* problems in elevating syntax into the primary (or perhaps even sole) object of study. From the first, Chomsky's critics have argued that the phenomenon of language is richer, more contingent, and less formalizable than a syntactic theory would allow and have called for a supplement, in the form of a *semantic* theory.[60] John Searle, one such critic, has objected (not surprisingly) to the inability of syntax to account for actual speech behavior, actual linguistic performances. Language, Searle argues, is not primarily an instrument of thought and only secondarily an instrument of communication (as Chomsky would have it) but is irreducibly, constitutively shaped by its communicative needs, and thus centrally organized by semantics, the production and reception of meaning.[61] Of course, Searle himself is speaking from a partisan position—that of speech-act theory, of which he and J. L. Austin are the leading exponents. That tradition, in giving pride of place to the contexts of utterance, has built its case, understandably, not on the formal universals of syntax but on the substantive contingencies of semantics. The meanings of words—their situational variations occasioned by different rules and intentions, and their etymological variations occasioned by historical change—make up the life of language as Austin and Searle understand it. Words come to us "trailing clouds of etymology," Austin writes, for "a word never—well, hardly ever—shakes off its etymology and its formation. In spite of all changes in and extensions of and additions to its meanings, and indeed rather pervading and governing these, there will still persist the old idea."[62]

Semantics, then, is that domain in which the historical life of language is honored and preserved, and in which human history itself is also silently but diligently recorded. Words have memories here, and the passing away of a usage, a manner of speaking, or a mode of association is never without residue, never without a shower of deposits, clouding up the orthographic clarity of words, giving them their particular texture and opacity. Unlike syntax, then, which begins as a clean slate each time it is used anew, empty of any traces of the words that previously composed it, semantics is a slate that can never be wiped clean, being written upon over and over again, accumulating meanings that settle and thicken in time. This is what Mikhail Bakhtin has in mind when he refers to semantics as a domain in which language becomes "saturated," each word pervaded by the "tastes of the context and contexts in which it has lived its socially charged life."[63] Bakhtin is speaking of the saturation of words within the historical life of an entire society, but, on a more modest scale, we might also imagine the same process of saturation within the biographical life of a single individual, or within the textual life of a long poem such as "Song of Myself." Here, too, prior usages might have left behind memories of their passing, accumulated nuances and inflections that make it impossible for words to be quite innocent, quite neutral, quite pristine, impossible for them to begin unencumbered.

This historical memory of words is what the poetic form of "Song of Myself" is out to combat. The "subject of language interests me—interests me: I never quite get it out of my mind," Whitman writes. "I sometimes think the *Leaves* is only a language experiment." It is a language experiment designed, most especially, to imagine "new words, new potentialities of speech" to match the "new world, the new times, the new peoples."[64] Such newness can come only with the primacy of syntax, and it is this that gives "Song of Myself" its peculiar resilience and regularity, its promise of substitution and guarantee of permanence. This is its great source of strength, a strength that, in Whitman as in Chomsky, comes from a necessary abstraction, an insistence on formal universals, that transforms the randomness of the world, its accidents and its vulnerabilities, into the pristine form of its syntax. "All goes onward and outward . . . and nothing collapses, / And to die is different from what any one supposed, and luckier," Whitman writes at the end of section 6, his famous paean to the grass which, like language, and most particularly like syntax ("so many uttering tongues!"), is ever substitutable, ever renewable, and therefore ever emblematic of our luck (30). And he immediately goes on, in section 7, to repeat that crucial last word all over again: "Has any one supposed it lucky to be born? / I hasten to inform him or her it is just as lucky to die, and I know it" (30).

Luck, that bane of democracy, is here mentioned by name, three times in the space of three lines and even in the face of death, its most terrible ally. It can be mentioned because, like the self which it overshadows, it too has been formalized, neutralized, made amenable to reason through the agency of syntax. In a complex play of crescendo that might be called the rationalization of luck, the syntax here focuses on the different degrees and gradations of it—"lucky," "luckier," "just as lucky"—using them to ask some rather abstruse questions (is it luckier to live or to die, or are both just as lucky?). What is happily missing here, among the available options, is one item which ordinarily would perhaps be of greatest concern to most people: namely, the category of the "unlucky." Indeed, even in "Song of Myself," that category is not altogether unknown (in section 4, Whitman has alluded, after all, to "The sickness of one of my folks—or of myself . . . or ill-doing . . . or loss or lack of money"), and yet it is just that memory that the syntax here works to erase, as it holds out for our contemplation a logical progression beginning with luck. The Whitmanian self is thus always lucky, he can only be lucky, all memories to the contrary being forgotten in the inflectionless use of the word. That inflectionlessness also makes him as lucky as everyone else. In being so assured of that fact, in having so little room for surprise, let alone for complaint, he might also be said, paradoxically, to be beyond luck, beyond its caprice and, above all, beyond its inequities.

What does it mean for a self to be beyond luck? Martha Nussbaum has argued that an ethical life that aspires to be noncontingent is also one that is necessarily impoverished. There can be no goodness without vulnerability, she suggests.[65] "Song of Myself" affirms her insight, qualifies it, and offers perhaps an alternative political context for its interpretation. Taking the noncontingent self, then, both as a necessary foundation of democratic justice, as Whitman urges, and as a potential case of experiential impoverishment, as Nussbaum warns, I want to think further about the epistemology underwritten by such a figure, and about the shape of the world radiating outward from its particular form. Whitman, as always, has indirectly supplied an answer here. In section 7 of "Song of Myself," immediately following his declaration that "it is just as lucky to die," he goes on to invoke a world of "manifold objects, no two alike, and every one good, / The earth good, and the stars good, and their adjuncts all good" (31).

These particular lines, celebratory in a way that borders on the syrupy, might perhaps lend themselves to the charge of facile optimism, but it would be unfair to read them in that light. They rather have to do, I think, with a democratic impulse (driven perhaps as much by anxiety as by hope) to so construe the world as to render the faculty of discrimination unnecessary. After all, judgment can cease, can truly cease, only in a world where there is no occasion for it. Luck of the Whitmanian sort, commissioned by a syntax so pristine as to be memory-proof, makes such a world thinkable, credible, habitable. Under its oversight, one can indeed live one's life "judg[ing] not as the judge judges but as the sun falling around a helpless thing," unburdened by the thought that the "helpless thing" might turn out to be a snake, a porcupine, a snapping turtle. It is this image of luck, disarmed and discharged, that enables Whitman to imagine a world that is epistemologically democratic, a world in which he can dispense with preference altogether, so that even among objects "no two alike," he can still surrender himself to a syntax that is nothing if not a chant of equivalence: "and every one good, / The earth good, and the stars good, and their adjuncts all good" (31).

Good, good, good, good. That chant of equivalence brings to a head the hope as well as the frailty of a democratic poetics, as of a democratic polity. The equivalence is secured, of course, by the regularity of the syntax, which neutralizes luck by making all eventualities equally *indifferent*, both in the sense that none is distinguishable from the others and in the sense that none is preferred to the others. For preference is indeed hard to justify, hard even to imagine, given the blanket attribution of goodness. In a world filled with objects all generated by the same syntax and all described by the word good, how can we make sense of the fact that some particular objects, some particular persons, will appeal to us in a manner altogether disproportionate to their grammatical description? And how can we make sense of the fact that some other objects, some other persons, will not appeal to us, certifiably (because categorically) good though they are?

A self that is beyond luck is not simply *beyond* the contingent, it is also *barred* from the contingent. It is barred, that is, from that circumstantial domain, inhabited by densely featured people, some of whom are miracles and some of whom are just unhappy freaks of accident, but all of whom, whether as objects of affection or as objects of aversion, can materialize for us only through a particularizing language. Whitman's democratic poetics, in short, can have no access to that chaotic world of special loves and hates. It is silent about those objects that, for us, are not categoric, not interchangeable or substitutable, not adequately described by grammar or fully accounted for by syntax. In that silence, "Song of Myself" is at one with the entire philosophical tradition from Immanuel Kant to Noam Chomsky and John Rawls. It is not at one with that tradition, however, in making that silence so eerie, so restless and untranquil in its willed uniformity. If nothing else, Whitman makes us long for what he does not and cannot offer: an ethics of preference, one that, in foregrounding what is not exhausted by a language of formal universals, what remains as its conceptual or emotional residue, might suggest some way of acknowledging both the democratic and the affective, some way of rethinking the very terms and limits of justice itself.

PREFERENCE HUMAN AND DIVINE:
THE WIDE, WIDE WORLD

As it turns out, it is not Whitman but his contemporaries, the so-called sentimental women writers of the mid-nineteenth century,[66] who are tough enough, hard-headed enough, to give us a literary tradition organized around such an ethics. It is they who take it upon themselves to confront, to fret over, and to draw a kind of reluctant sustenance from that most arbitrary and most invidious of phenomena: the phenomenon of human preference. And, in doing so, they also gesture toward a nonreductive (and often not even moral) account of human misery and felicity, thus proving themselves heirs to the complex thinking about grace and justice in Christian theology, a tradition as old as Christianity itself. It is this extended tradition that I want to claim as a long background for the women writers, not only to construct a different genealogy for their supposed sentimentality, but also to suggest something about the historical memory of American Protestantism itself and about *its* claim as an important historical supplement to the discourse of philosophy.

To take one of the most notorious examples, Susan Warner's *The Wide, Wide World* (1850), a novel so sentimental as to be continually awash in tears, is also a novel so stark as to be continually under the shadow of chance, a novel as relentlessly driven by unforeseeable randomness as *Moby-Dick* (1851), its contemporary and in many ways its antithesis, is relentlessly driven by foreseeable destiny. Luck is the principal actor in *The Wide, Wide World*, for its heroine, Ellen Montgomery, is quite a lucky girl, helped always by the hand of providence. Unlike the lucky self in Whitman, however, for whom the category of the "unlucky" simply does not exist, Ellen's good luck is a fearful reminder of the reign of its evil sibling, because it never appears as a positive good but always as a corrective, coming in the nick of time to terminate a bad situation. The intervention of the old gentleman in the store, for example, saves Ellen, but it does not negate the petty malice of Saunders the clerk; the timely arrival of Mr. Van Brunt again saves Ellen, but it also does not negate her utter sense of helplessness as Nancy, with the sadism "that a cat shows when she has a captured mouse at the end of her paws,"[67] ransacks her trunk, looks over the contents of her workbox and her writing desk, and forces hot gruel down her clenched throat. And in the most frightening scene in the book—a scene not of rape, but comparable to it—the arrival of John certainly saves Ellen, but, just as certainly, it does not negate her terror as her horse is whipped by Saunders, whose spite, at this accidental second encounter, has gone from petty to maniacal. Ellen is the recipient not only of gratuitous kindness but also of gratuitous malice. Her random good luck alternates with her random tribulations. There is no question of desert here, no question of moral causality. Events simply befall Ellen: unwilled, unchosen, undeserved. They turn the idea of justice into an enigma, not so much the logical endpoint of reason as the beginning of a conceptual riddle.

It is in the midst of this "wide, wide world"—a world wider than the language of justice can make of it—that Ellen is revealed to be something of an unjust person herself. She is capricious in her affections, capricious most of all in her self-acknowledged inability to love those for whom her love ought to have been easy, natural, and axiomatic. Asked, for example, by the kind gentleman on the boat whether she is one of God's children, Ellen replies with the usual tears, but her answer is more unusual than one might expect:

> "No, sir," said Ellen, with swimming eyes, but cast down on the ground.
> "How do you know that you are not?"
> "Because I do not love the Saviour."
> "Do you not love him, Ellen?"
> "I am afraid not, sir."

"Why are you afraid not? What makes you think so?"

"Mamma said I could not love him at all if I did not love him best; and oh, sir," said Ellen, weeping, "I do love mamma a great deal better."

"You love your mother better than you do the Saviour?"

"Oh yes, sir," said Ellen; "how can I help it?" (70)

Ellen cannot help loving her mother a great deal better than she loves her heavenly father. Earlier, she also cannot help loving her mother a great deal better than she loves her earthly father. (The scene in chapter 3, the "perfect fidget of impatience," with which Ellen awaits her father's departure so that she might be alone with her mother, must be one of the most memorable portraits of filial invidiousness in all of American literature.) Love here is a matter of arbitrary attachment, discriminatory likes and dislikes, sharp and sharply hierarchical senses of delight and solicitude. It is also a matter of involuntary compulsions, fueled by the phrase "cannot help." Ellen does not choose to love her mother, does not arrive at that decision with the help of her deliberative rationality. Her love is, on the contrary, strictly a *preference*, without any moral content whatsoever, innocent of volition, and therefore also innocent of justification.

The lack of moral justification is especially striking when Ellen's involuntary preference happens to take a negative turn, when it shows up as an unreasonable aversion toward someone. This is the case with Miss Fortune, Ellen's aunt, whom she describes in a letter to her mother:

> I wish there was somebody here that I could love, but there is not. You will want to know what sort of a person my aunt Fortune is. I think she is very good looking, or she would be if her nose were not quite so sharp: but, mamma, I can't tell you what sort of a feeling I have about her; it seems to me as if she was sharp all over. I am sure her eyes are as sharp as two needles. And she don't walk like other people; at least sometimes. She makes queer little jerks and starts and jumps, and flies about like I don't know what. (111)

Ellen's objections to Miss Fortune are not only uncharitable, they are downright irrational. She objects to things the latter cannot help: her sharp nose, her needlelike eyes, her jerky movements. But then Ellen, in turn, cannot help herself either: she feels what she feels. This maddening realm of tautology—you are what you are, I love what I love, a realm that, as Wittgenstein might say, can only be described, not explained—makes *The Wide, Wide World* a fine supporting document for Rawls's argument against the "lottery of birth." For Warner, though, the lottery would go on forever, endlessly churning out undeserved attachments as well as undeserved aversions, for in making human preference a matter of caprice on the one hand and a principle of invidiousness on the other, she has in effect created a world of cosmic arbitrariness, so that what appears small and puny here is not just Ellen Montgomery, and not just some particular human being, but the very idea of justice itself.

This sense of cosmic arbitrariness no doubt has something to do with the sharp reversal of fortune in Warner's own life.[68] But the book's religious fervor suggests as well that cosmic arbitrariness is not just a sudden insight, born of personal disaster, but also a long-standing tenet within the Christian tradition, in existence for almost two thousand years. It was Augustine, of course, who gave this cosmic arbitrariness its classic expression, in the form of the doctrine of grace.[69] Grace was God's sovereign and gratuitous love, love unoccasioned by human endeavor, undeserved by human merit. As Augustine insisted, "a gift, unless it be gratuitous, is not grace."[70] But grace gratuitously given also meant justice arbitrarily rendered, rendered, that is, to recipients unaccountably divided up, unaccountably labeled the saved and the damned. Augustine was thus a theologian of love much as Warner was; like her, he too saw love as the ground for gradations, exclusions, invidious distinctions, the ground for concepts such as "less" and "more." In the human realm, for example, a man who "lives in justice" is someone who "neither loves what should not be loved nor fails to love what should be loved; he neither loves more what should be loved less, loves equally what should be loved less or more, nor loves less or more what should be loved equally."[71] These invidious distinctions carried over into the divine realm as well, for here "grace alone separates the redeemed from the lost, all having been mingled together in one mass of perdition." Augustine insisted that human beings were basically alike, that, left to our own devices, we would all belong together. However, out of our common humanity, out of that "same mass of perdition, God maketh one vessel for honorable, another for ignoble use; the ones for honorable use through his mercy, the ones for ignoble use through his judgment."[72]

Grace, then, was God's way of showing his preferences: his inexplicable fondness for some, his inexplicable aversion to others. Augustine's doctrine of grace thus carried with it a dark underside, a fatalistic verdict for those God happened to dislike: a doctrine of predestination harsher than that of any major orthodox thinker since Paul. In the succeeding centuries, though, it was the doctrine of grace alone that was emphasized by the Catholic Church, so that, as Jaroslav Pelikan points out, "normative Augustinism" increasingly became "a position that vindicated Augustine's essential teaching on grace but muffled his views on predestination to punishment."[73] That "muffling" was undone, of course, by the Reformation, which brought predestination to the polemical foreground. It was Augustine the predestinarian, then, that Luther invoked when he shockingly proclaimed that "Augustine has to this day not been accepted by the church of Rome."[74] And it was the same predestinarian that he honored when he declared himself, "I, Martin Luther, Augustinian."[75]

THE LANGUAGE OF PROTESTANT MEMORY

But something else—a different sort of intellectual need, a different sort of emotional compulsion—also seemed to be fueling Luther's renewed emphasis on predestination. "I am saying this," he said, "in order to refute the dangerous doctrine of the sophists and the monks, who taught and believed that no one can know for a certainty whether he is in a state of grace."[76] The key word for Luther was "certainty," and it was this word that he would repeat over twenty times in his commentary on a single verse of Galatians (one that, moreover, does not itself make certainty an issue).[77] "The enemies of Christ," Luther insisted, "teach what is uncertain, because they command their consciences to be in doubt." Good Christians, therefore, must do the opposite, namely, "strive daily to move more and more from uncertainty to certainty." Noting that the "monster of uncertainty is worse than all the other monsters," Luther "thank[ed] God, therefore, that we have been delivered from this monster."[78] That deliverance separated right-thinking Christians once and for all from those doubting papists: "We, by the grace of God, are able to declare and judge with certainty, on the basis of the Word, about the will of God towards us, about all laws and doctrines, about our own lives and those of others. On the other hand, the papists and the fanatical spirits are unable to judge with certainty about anything."[79]

The great boon of predestination was just that: it granted certainty. And for Luther, certainty could come only from what he called the "necessary foreknowledge of God," which, especially in *The Bondage of the Will* (1525),[80] he elevated into the central divine attribute. It is "fundamentally necessary and salutary," Luther said, "for a Christian to know that God foreknows nothing contingently, but that he foresees and purposes and does all things by his immutable, eternal, and infallible will." Luther's God was sometimes wrathful, sometimes merciful, but he was always knowing, or rather, *fore*knowing, his infinite prescience making up for our infinite ignorance. Against Erasmus, then, who argued that it was "irreverent, inquisitive, and vain to say that God foreknows necessarily," Luther countered with due incredulity: "Do you, then, believe that he foreknows without willing or wills without knowing?" Since that was absurd, Luther concluded that it was impossible that anything "should exist or persist contingently," if by "contingent" one means "by chance and without our expecting it." In the end, then, divine foreknowledge turned out to be a *transitive* foreknowledge: human beings could not aspire to partake of its contents, but they could at least partake of its certitude. It was for that reason, indeed, that Luther was able to point to the "necessary foreknowledge of God" as "the one supreme consolation of Christians," one that set them apart from "the greatest minds [who] have stumbled and fallen, denying the existence of God and imagining that all things are moved at random by blind Chance or Fortune."[81]

Luther did not seem particularly concerned with the conceptual relays between divine foreknowledge and human certitude (the latter is not, after all, logically or experientially consequential upon the former, as the American Puritans could easily have told him). Like Calvin, who, in the *Institutes of the Christian Religion* (1536), also spent several pages arguing that there was no such thing as chance,[82] he seemed to have believed that the elimination of the contingent would itself be sufficient ground for human certitude.[83] But what is important here is perhaps not so much the rigor of Luther's reasoning as the way he reanimated a cluster of concepts, deriving from their apparently syllogistic connection a newly authorized mode of being in the world. And so it was that faith (or, more precisely, "justification by faith") would emerge as the central tenet of the Reformation, both as an attitude toward God and as equipment for living. "Faith in God," Luther said, was "the supreme worship, the supreme allegiance, the supreme obedience, and the supreme sacrifice."[84] More than that, it was also the "principal weapon" for Christians, an indispensable weapon, for

> We are engaged in a battle, not with one prince or emperor but with the whole world. Everywhere the devil has spiritual weapons with which he attacks the ministers of the Word on the right and on the left. For this reason we now have so many adversaries—not only the fanatics but the princes, the popes, and the kings of the whole world with all their adherents. Who will overcome all these adversaries? He, says John, who is born of God. This must happen through faith in Christ, which is the victory.[85]

The images of universal belligerency (and, of course, the image of ultimate victory) were hardly incidental here; they made up the very language of faith for Luther: a language that construed the world as "the kingdom of the devil" and construed the Christian as, first and foremost, "a warrior."[86] Over and over again, then, Luther rejoiced that "through faith we kill unbelief, contempt and hatred of God," that "faith slaughters . . . and kills the beast that the whole world and all the creatures cannot kill," that "it killed and sacrificed God's bitterest and most harmful enemy."[87]

A language such as this inevitably suggested political usages. Michael Walzer, in his influential study of the political legacy of Protestantism, has argued for a direct link between the Reformation and the political discipline of the state, although he is also careful to distinguish between Luther's mystical inwardness and Calvin's institutional fanaticism, tracing the "programmatic and organizational" character of the Puritan state primarily to the latter.[88] But there is another sense in which Luther himself, mystical and inward as he so often was,[89] might nonetheless be said to be a willing party (and indeed a major contributor) to a newly emerging language of faith, faith not only spiritual but also temporal, dictating not only political discipline (Walzer's emphasis) but also political belligerency. Here, Walzer's insight should perhaps be supplemented by that of Sacvan Bercovitch, who has emphasized the intimate connection between Puritan religiosity and the geopolitical ambition of the state. It was the continuing vitality of the Puritan rhetoric, its periodic professions of doom, Bercovitch argues, that would sustain a dream of national expansion, a dream of Manifest Destiny, for over two hundred years.[90]

Especially in light of *that* legacy, it is worth noting that faith was singled out by Luther not only as a much-needed weapon against a world teeming with enemies but also as a much-needed corrective to a Catholic theology wallowing in love. The "dangerous and wicked opinion of the papists" was that good work must be "performed in the grace that makes a man pleasing before God, that is, in love"; they had even "attributed formal righteousness to an attitude and form inherent in the soul, namely, to love." Duns Scotus had written (and Luther quoted him with disgust) that "if a man can love a creature, a young man love a girl, or a covetous man love money—all of which are a lesser good—he can also love God, who is a greater good."[91] For Scotus, love of God was not categorically different from love of the world: the two shaded into each other, one drawing sustenance from the other. For Luther, this confusion of the divine and the naturalistic could not be more wrong. But here he seemed to have found an enemy in none other than Augustine himself, who, in his *Confessions*, had celebrated just such a confused love of God and of the world:

> But what is it that I love in loving thee? Not physical beauty, nor the splendor of time, nor the radiance of the light—so pleasant to our eyes—nor the sweet melodies of the various kind of songs, nor the fragrant smell of flowers and ointments and spices; not manna and honey, not the limbs embraced in physical love—it is not these I love when I love my God. Yet it is true that I love a certain kind of light and sound and fragrance and food and embrace in loving my God, who is the light and sound and fragrance and food and embracement of my inner man—where that light shines into my soul which no place can contain, where time does not snatch away the lovely sound, where no breeze disperses the sweet fragrance, where no eating diminishes the food there provided, and where there is an embrace that no satiety comes to sunder. This is what I love when I love my God.[92]

For Augustine, love of God was indeed not the same as love of the world, but it was also not intelligible apart from the latter, because it was our love of the world, our capacity to enjoy it, that enabled us to love God and enjoy *him*. In *On Christian Doctrine*, Augustine wrote,

"To enjoy something is to cling to it with love for its own sake. . . . Those things which are to be enjoyed make us blessed." And though he cautioned against loving the world too much, enjoying it too much, lest we lose sight of "Him who is to be enjoyed," in the long run it was nonetheless "by means of corporal and temporal things [that] we may comprehend the eternal and spiritual."[93]

Luther did not include Augustine in the company of the dangerous and wicked papists,[94] but he might well have, when he accused those papists of believing that "faith is the body, the shell, or the color; but love is the life, the kernel, or the form."[95] Luther did not mince words here:

> Such are the dreams of the scholastics. But where they speak of love, we speak of faith. And while they say that faith is the mere outline but love is its living color and completion, we say in opposition that faith takes hold of Christ and that He is the form that adorns and informs faith as color does the wall. Therefore Christian faith is not an idle quality or an empty husk in the heart, which may exist in a state of mortal sin until love comes along to make it alive.[96]

For Luther, faith was all in all unto itself; it had no need for love and indeed no room for it. "Where they speak of love, we speak of faith": that injunction mapped out a new path for Protestant theology, a new language it would henceforth speak to worship God and to dwell among men.

Still, if the discourse of love was to be officially outlawed in Reformation theology, the language of Christianity itself, with its ancient habit of piety and ecstasy, its inherited capacity for earthly and heavenly delight, might turn out to be less reformable, less observant of the narrow discipline Luther would impose upon it. He could not, in fact, completely reform even his own language, and even his belligerency was not as straightforward as one might have expected: "our hearts will be filled by the Holy Spirit with the love which makes us free, joyful, almighty workers and conquerors over all tribulations, servants of our neighbors, and yet lords of all."[97] And so, in spite of his injunction, in spite of his attempt to turn Christian theology into some austere edifice—some windowless structure, illuminated only by faith—the language of Christianity (and indeed the language of Protestantism itself) would ultimately survive in a manner different from what he would like. It would not (and could not) submit to his reformation, because, historical language that it was, its semantic field would always be a field of accumulated usage, saturated with inherited emotions, inherited meanings, a language not reducible to any theological accent momentarily put upon it, nor exhausted by any political program momentarily sanctified in its name.

Indeed, even in the American colonies, the most obviously Protestant, and most obviously Puritan, commonwealths in the world, the language of Protestantism was sometimes such as would have made Luther turn in his grave. Edward Taylor (1642–1729), minister for fifty-eight years in the frontier town of Westfield, Massachusetts, nonetheless found the occasion, in that "howling wilderness," to write the following lines in his *Preparatory Meditations*:

> My lovely one, I fain would love thee much
>   But all my Love is none at all I see,
> Oh! Let thy Beauty give a glorious tuch
>   Upon my Heart, and melt to Love all mee.
>   Lord melt me all up into Love for thee
>   Whose Loveliness excells what love can bee.[98]

Between the love of the adoring subject and the loveliness of the adored object—the boundaries between the two theologically maintained but rhetorically melting, rhetorically melted into each other— Protestantism is not exactly what it should be, or not exactly what Luther said it should be. The animating sentiment here is not Lutheran certainty but Augustinian delight, an emotion at once older but also more fragile, less useful for military purposes. This poem (and scores of others like it)[99] forcefully reminds us that "faith" is only one possible relation between the finite and the infinite, and that other relations would not cease simply because of the Reformation. It reminds us as well that within the domain of language, Protestantism was not so much a new departure as a variation on an ancient theme. Looming behind Taylor were his beloved Metaphysical poets (especially George Herbert) and, behind them, the shadow of Augustine, with his complex and self-conscious relation to rhetoric, his theology of enjoyment, as well as the entire tradition of biblical tropes and diction, the intellectual and affective styles of Christian worship, in existence for over fifteen hundred years.[100] Not the least interesting feature of Protestantism is thus its historical memory, habits of speech and habits of emotion sedimented over time, sedimented, as David

Hall has suggested, in a "muddied, multilayered process," as "a river full of debris."[101] And, once in a while, it is overcome by that sedimentation—as Taylor is in this poem—so that the Protestant voice would sometimes come across much like a transported voice, redolent of a different place and time. "The United States itself has no medieval period," Sydney Ahlstrom has written, "but in Puritanism we confront more than faint vestiges of that era."[102]

Those vestiges are discernible, not least of all, in the enduring presence of Augustine: not necessarily Luther's Augustine, but a figure that both predated him and survived him, an Augustine less austere, less fiercely channeled, richer with liberalities and delights, an Augustine read and elaborated upon over the centuries, passed down from generation to generation. Perry Miller has written about an "Augustinian strain of piety" in American Puritanism.[103] That Augustinian strain, I want to emphasize, came not only from the Reformation but also from an older Christian tradition. Seen in that light, American Protestantism too would seem to be a more heterogenous, more "multivocal" field than it might sometimes appear.[104] Indeed, alongside what was perhaps its dominant trajectory—one that led to the belligerent nationalism of the nineteenth and twentieth centuries, a secular religion of faith without love—we might want to speculate about a host of incipient alternatives, some more tangential than others, some more clearly articulated than others, but all attesting in any case to the semantic richness of the Protestant rhetoric, to the complexity of its historical memory, and to its ability always to exceed, always to overflow, any of its momentary expressions, whether theological, literary, or political. The language of love, in particular, while not directly opposed to the language of nationalism, was nonetheless not encompassed by it and, in its capacity as *residue*, would not only look forward to a series of residual developments in American theology and American literature but would look backward as well to an affective tradition inherited from a Christianity older than Puritanism itself. In this instance, at least, American Protestantism "does not have its own beginning," as Sydney Ahlstrom has observed. "It is like a conversation being continued by people as they walk into another room."[105]

The Wide, Wide World is one such conversation. Even as it entertains a newfangled language of modern consumerism, as analyzed by Ann Douglas,[106] it also draws its sustenance from a time-honored Christian tradition, alive not only as institutional fact but above all as historical memory, as the intellectual and affective habits which lingered in time. Broadened by that memory but also chastened by it, Warner's novel reminds us, as the church had always done, that "merit" and "desert" are not necessarily self-evident concepts and that throughout much of history, human beings had been inspired and admonished in quite other terms. It reminds us as well that the phenomenon of preference, whether human or divine, is perhaps more deeply arbitrary and more darkly inscrutable than we would like, and so gives us a world tougher and harsher than Whitman's—but one that, in its very toughness and harshness, might also seem more satisfying, or at least more emotionally persuasive. If only implicitly, then, it gestures toward a world more enigmatic than the concept of justice can make of it, a world in which justice appears not only as a more tenuous virtue but also as a smaller one.

MERE AND ARBITRARY GRACE:
JONATHAN EDWARDS

This uneasy, unceasing, and almost involuntary return to the question of justice, haphazard as it might appear, nonetheless represents, to my mind, one of the most interesting claims of Christian theology, a claim it rarely makes now but which perhaps it should: namely, as a corrective to the bloodless placidity of philosophy. Susan Warner is most interesting when seen against this claim, although, needless to say, she is hardly alone here. I want to suggest, indeed, that she is in the company of none other than Jonathan Edwards,[107] her intellectual forebear in numerous ways: not only as a theologian who has something to say to philosophers but also as one who hones his analytic skill on the phenomenon of love, on its positive manifestation and, more vexingly still, on its negative expression, on the problematic justice of dislike, disinclination, sheer aversion, both human and divine.

Going on for pages and pages in *A Treatise Concerning Religious Affections* (1746), Edwards, too, said things that would have made Luther turn in his grave. "The essence of all true religion lies in holy love," Edwards wrote, and not tepid, run-of-the-mill love either, but "earnest desires, thirstings and pantings of soul after God, delight and joy in God, a sweet and melting gratitude to God for his great goodness."[108] Indeed, "in nothing, is vigor in the acting of our inclinations so requisite, as in religion; and in nothing is lukewarmness so odious."[109] "Inclination," far from being a wayward or brutish phenomenon, turns out to be the very "vitals, essence, and soul" of the Christian religion, and, as such, it has a special place in Edwards's lexicon. The sensations of "pleasedness or displeasedness, inclination or disinclination" are native to all of us, Edwards said, for the soul

> does not merely perceive and view things, but is some way inclined with respect to the things it views or considers; either is inclined to 'em, or is disinclined, and averse from 'em. . . . [T]he soul does not behold things, as an indifferent unaffected spectator, but either as liking or disliking, pleased or displeased, approving or rejecting. This faculty is called by various names: it is sometimes called the *inclination*: and, as it has respect to the actions that are determined and governed by it, is called the *will*: and the *mind*, with regard to the exercises of this faculty, is often called the *heart*.[110]

Stuck in a theological treatise, this passage must nonetheless stand as one of the most remarkable moments in the history of Western philosophy. Unlike Locke before him, with his complex and endlessly qualifying distinction between "preference" and "volition,"[111] and unlike Kant after him, with his relatively uncomplex and sharply categoric opposition between "will" and "inclination," Edwards here simply announced that inclination and will are one and the same thing, different names assigned to the selfsame faculty engaged in different activities. There is no ontological distinction between the two, only a nominal distinction. Indeed, not only are "will" and "inclination" here fused into the same substance, but, if anything, it is inclination that is prior to will, inclination that is determinative of will, for it is "our inclination that governs us in our actions," so that in every "act of the will, wherein the soul approves of something present, there is a degree of pleasedness; and that pleasedness, if it be in a considerable degree, is the very same with the affection of joy or delight. And if the will disapproves of what is present, the soul is in some degree displeased, and if that displeasedness be great, 'tis the very same with the affection of grief or sorrow."[112]

Edwards could not have known about the "indifferent unaffected spectator" so important to Kant and, in our own century, to John Rawls, but he seems to be refuting their arguments ahead of time, in suggesting that such a liberty of indifference—such a principle of impartial, dispassionate rationality—is strictly an illusion, a vain and presumptuous dream, since our will does not act outside of our inclination and our reason does not deliberate prior to our affect. What follows, then, from this priority of affect, is thus a radically *preferential* universe, in which rational deliberations are always retroactive, always subsequent to arbitrary inclinations, so that moral judgment itself turns out to be no more than a function of our initial likes and dislikes.[113]

Unfortunately, the priority of affect over reason governs not only human judgment but divine judgment as well. Edwards's God is a God who judges always out of the "disposition of his heart."[114] He "may have a real and proper pleasure or happiness in seeing the happy state of the creature; yet this may not be different from his delight in himself; being a delight in his own infinite goodness . . . and so gratifying the inclination of his own heart."[115] That divine inclination means that there will always be invidious distinctions in the world, for there are things "God reserves only for those who are the objects of his special and peculiar love," just as there are things he "bestows on those for whom he has no love, but whom he hates."[116] And since God "best knows his own heart," and since "it would be relying too much on reason to determine the affair of God's last end,"[117] divine affect must always remain a human mystery, at once in excess of and perhaps even antithetical to human comprehension, forever unaccountable and arbitrary from our human point of view. What does it mean not to be beloved of God? What does it mean to be an object of his dislike, disregard, special aversion? Edwards's theology offers no explanation, just as it offers no consolation. If "love is the key" to his thinking, as Alan Heimert and Norman Fiering have persuasively argued,[118] that fact must be understood to carry its particular curse as well as its particular blessing, its darkness as well as its radiance. It leads not only to the ecstatic but relatively obscure sermon, "Heaven Is a World of Love," but also to the far better known "Sinners in the Hands of an Angry God," both logical expressions for a world permeated by divine preference.

Still, dubious blessing that it was, it was within this language of love—this cruelly arbitrary language of divine preference—that Edwards was able to articulate something like a principle of *tolerable* arbitrariness, an oddly earthbound, oddly nontranscendent perspective that, to my mind, represents the most powerful challenge of eighteenth-century theology, a challenge to political philosophy then and now. This takes the form of some remarkably compressed but also remarkably suggestive passages, in *The Nature of True Virtue* (1765), about the nature and limits of justice. Significantly, those passages occur in a chapter entitled "Concerning the Secondary and Inferior Kind of Beauty," because that is where justice stands in Edwards's ethical thought: among the secondary and the inferior. "This secondary kind of beauty," Edwards said, "consist[s] in uniformity and proportion,"[119] so that

> there is a beauty in the virtue called *justice*, which consists in the agreement of different things that have relation to one another, in nature, manner, and measure: and therefore is the very same sort of beauty with that uniformity and proportion which is observable in those external and material things that are esteemed beautiful. There is a natural agreement and adaptedness of things that have relation one to another, and a harmonious corresponding of one thing to another: that he which from his will *does* evil to others should *receive* evil from the will of others . . . in *proportion* to the evil of his doings.[120]

Justice, as Edwards represents it in this astonishing analysis, turns out to be an *aesthetic* phenomenon: it has to do with our appreciation of beauty, especially the beauty of form, the beauty which comes from "uniformity and proportion." It is this formal aesthetics that underlies our language of desert,[121] our insistence on retribution and recompense, as a guaranteed relation of proportionality between crime and punishment, merit and reward. Our attraction to justice, from this perspective, is no different from our attraction to the "beauty of squares, and cubes, and regular polygons in the regularity of buildings, and the beautiful figures in a piece of embroidery." It is also no different from those other attractions in having no ultimate claim to ethical primacy, for, being no more than "a relish of uniformity and proportion," "this beauty, considered simply and by itself, has nothing of the nature of true virtue."[122]

Justice, the cornerstone of political philosophy, is considerably less than a cornerstone in Edwards's ethics, which, because it is not founded on the morality of reason or even on the aesthetics of form, must face up to its own insufficiency, its lack of an adequate justificatory ground—an inadequacy which, if not exactly reassuring, is perhaps more genuinely humane. And it is on the basis of that constitutive lack of adequation that Edwards defines "true virtue" as a self-consciously asymmetrical relation of the finite to the infinite: as our "consent, propensity and union of heart to Being in general."[123] Consent is not so much an alternative to justice as an intimation that justice is not all, an intimation that its language is only one way (and perhaps an unduly aesthetic way) to think about the world, that it might not fully express or exhaust what it is that we most want for ourselves, and what it is that we are sometimes capable of giving to others. Locating the limits of justice at the limits of human reason, limits that are part concession, part celebration—concession, because our reason does not always prevail, and celebration, because that failure is a tribute to what is in excess of it—Edwards gestures toward a world in which the language of justice must always contend with the unceasing, ungrammatical language of love.

4

Pain and Compensation

"Although the traditional subject of economics is indeed the behavior of individuals and organizations in markets, a moment's reflection," Richard Posner explains, "will suggest the possibility of using economics more broadly."[1] These words, offered at the outset of *The Economics of Justice* (1981), might be taken as a manifesto for one of the most powerful movements in contemporary legal thought, the "Law and Economics" movement.[2] Posner wants to apply economics to law, or, more accurately, he wants to absorb law into economics, as its subset. Law is a subset of economics because the latter discipline is not only more encompassing but also more foundational—more controlling of our behavior and more constitutive of our thought—so much so that all rational choice must issue from its premise and look to it for justification.

This cognitive primacy of the economic, for Posner, is not at all occasional but is absolute. Like Gary Becker[3] (his acknowledged intellectual forebear and winner of the 1992 Nobel Prize in Economics), Posner thinks of human reason itself as fundamentally economic in nature. Human beings are "rational maximizers of their satisfactions," and our thoughts are always calculations, always a form of cost-benefit analysis, guided always by efficiency as their legitimizing end. In short, for Posner as for Becker, economics is coextensive with (and indeed equatable with) human rationality; it makes up the "reason" in any reasoning process. And since "rationality is not confined to explicit market transactions but is a general and dominant characteristic of social behavior," economics too must reign as the governing principle in all areas of life, "not limited to the market." Indeed, given its universal currency, its status as a language common to all, a language that informs every decision-making, "the economics of nonmarket behavior" must encompass the sum total of human experience. It is nothing less than a language of "rational choice," nothing less than a "moral system," nothing less, in fact, than "a concept of justice."[4]

A JUST MEASURE

Like Marx, Posner can figure in this book only as an agent provoca-
teur, only as a style of rationality and a style of explanation the limits
of which I want to test. This chapter is, in many ways, an extended
response to Posner. I take issue not only with the economic reasoning
he exemplifies but also with the theory of justice he expounds. That
theory, broadly speaking a theory about the *quantifiability* of justice
(using cost-benefit analysis as the all-purpose yardstick), can claim a
precursor as remote as Aristotle, but it is Law and Economics that has
secured its current authority and vitality. As is characteristic of the
method throughout this book, my response to Posner is threaded
through a historical argument in which Posner himself will actually
appear as a less than central figure, since the adequating rationality
of which he is so forceful an exponent is also a phenomenon with a
genealogy of its own, one whose ambitions and limits might be historically investigated. In the nineteenth century, for example, such a
rationality would inspire not only a new penal philosophy, and not
only a new tort law (the precursor of Law and Economics), but also,
especially in the contexts of slavery and urban poverty, a new ambition to quantify sentience as the instrumental ground of humanitarian reform, an ambition to come up with something like a calculus
of pain.

These (and other) rationalizing projects might be seen as so many
contextual associates—and so many quarreling neighbors—for the
realist novel, a genre driven, perhaps as much as any literature can
be, by a longing for objective adequation, but also haunted, again as
much as any literature can be, by the futility of such an ideal. In its
very search for commensurability, in its very desire for a just measure of things, the realist novel is darkened, fleetingly but also quite
routinely, by the specter of the incalculable, the noncorresponding,
the unrationalizable. Given such specters, such misgivings of a self-
inflected (not to say self-afflicted) character, I want to make a plea for
a critical practice responsive to what we might call the cognitive residues of a text, responsive to what remains not exhausted, not encompassed by its supposed resolution.

The novels of William Dean Howells readily come to mind—one
thinks of *A Modern Instance* (1882), *The Minister's Charge* (1886), *A
Hazard of New Fortunes* (1890)—novels that, like so many other works

by Howells and so many other works in the realist genre, seem to owe their very existence to a certain adjudicatory crisis. This crisis they dwell upon, fret over, and preserve in memory—not in spite of but because of their endings, endings often so meagre in their proposed satisfaction as to seem a virtual parody of the term. Even *The Rise of Silas Lapham* (1885), a novel that, at first glance, might seem less anguished than the others, manages all the same to have an adjudicatory crisis of its own, which it tries (and fails) to handle as a Posner-like problem, a problem in the economics of justice.

On that fateful occasion, the Laphams, feeling confused and wretched, find themselves seated in front of the Reverend Sewell, desperate for advice. They have just been hit by a terrible disaster, a bizarre new development in their daughters' marital fortunes. The presumptive suitor of one daughter, they discover, is actually courting and indeed has proposed to the other one. What is one to do? Should one opt for an across-the-board suffering for all concerned, or should one settle for damage control? The Laphams have no idea. But the Reverend Sewell knows exactly what to think. The answer seems clear to him, as clear as an arithmetic equation, for what is at stake here is simply a question of numbers:

> "One suffer instead of three, if none is to blame?" suggested Sewell. "That's sense, and that's justice. It's the economy of pain which naturally suggests itself, and which would insist upon itself, if we were not all perverted by traditions which are the figment of the shallowest sentimentality."[5]

Like Richard Posner, the Reverend Sewell is impressed by the rationality of economics: by its ability to quantify and clarify, to provide a just measure of things. "Justice," then, for Sewell as for Posner, is a matter of efficiency, achieved in this case by the minimization of cost. "One suffer instead of three," Sewell says, as he urges upon the Laphams what he calls an "economy of pain." Behind this specific recommendation is a more general proposition, one that locates the cognitive ground of ethics in economics and locates it, furthermore, in something like a quantification of sentience, a calculus of pleasure and pain. Sewell's advice is eminently rational, but, we might add, not altogether new, for his "economy of pain" had a different name and a wider currency long before he proposed it, being immortalized by the phrase "the greatest happiness of the greatest number."

That phrase is, of course, most famously (or infamously) associated with Jeremy Bentham. In the preface to *A Fragment on Government* (1776), an anonymous attack on Blackstone, Bentham had offered up (and emphasized with italics) what he called a "fundamental axiom," namely, that *"it is the greatest happiness of the greatest number that is the measure of right and wrong."*[6] This "Greatest Happiness Principle," as John Stuart Mill glosses it in *Utilitarianism* (1861), is one that "holds that actions are right in proportion as they tend to promote happiness, wrong as they tend to promote the reverse of happiness. By happiness is intended pleasure, and the absence of pain; by unhappiness, pain, and the privation of pleasure."[7] Pleasure and pain are not just physical sensations to the utilitarians. They are important, above all, because they are computable units, because they can be weighed, measured, aggregated, and translated into a commensurate ratio. As such, they make up the very numerical ground upon which ethics itself can become quantified, upon which every act of judgment can become an act of calculation. "Sum up all the values of all the *pleasures* on the one side, and those of all the *pains* on the other," Bentham urges, and "the balance" will yield the measure of right and wrong for any individual action. For communal actions, Bentham says,

> take an account of the *number* of persons whose interests appear to be concerned; and repeat the above process with respect to each. . . . *Sum up* the numbers. . . . Take the balance; which, if on the side of pleasure, will give the general good tendency of the act, with respect to the total number or community of individuals concerned; if on the side of pain, the general evil tendency, with respect to the same community.[8]

This hedonistic calculus—this emphasis on the ethical primacy of pleasure and pain, and on their numerical computability—is usually taken to be the hallmark of utilitarianism. Other eighteenth-century thinkers, notably Locke, Hutcheson, and Hume, had also tried to develop an ethical system from a sensationalist epistemology, but it was Bentham who tried, most indefatigably, to ground that epistemology in arithmetic, claiming for it the quantifiability of a simple equation. Of course, Bentham is a man whose company the Reverend Sewell might not relish. Sewell's successor, Richard Posner, certainly does not relish it. Mindful that the critics of Law and Economics are most likely to "attack it as a version of utilitarianism,"[9] Posner sets out to exorcise the "spongy, nonoperational" ghost of Bentham and to demonstrate, once and for all, how infinitely superior "wealth maximization" is to the "greatest happiness" principle. Even so, as he reluctantly admits, "Bentham plays a prominent, if somewhat sinister, role" in his book.[10]

Yet Posner might have set his mind entirely at ease on this score, for his intellectual genealogy is both longer and more honorable than his attacks on Bentham would suggest. It was Aristotle, after all, in the *Nicomachean Ethics*, who first tried out something like a mathematization of ethics, analyzing distributive justice as a geometrical progression and rectificatory justice as an arithmetical progression.[11] Closer to home, the search for a formalizable ethics—a uniform measure for all human affairs—could also claim its descent from Bacon and Newton, Condorcet and Leibniz, Hutcheson and Hume. In short, an idealized principle of commensurability had dominated Western thought long before Bentham gave it his distinctive expression. It is this principle that Adorno and Horkheimer would single out for critique in *Dialectic of Enlightenment*, their fierce attack on the rule of "equivalence" which they see as the origin as well as the burden of Western thought. Enlightenment rationality, they argue, is nothing less than a "principle of dissolvent rationality." It believes in "universal interchangeability," believes in the "calculability of the world," and so equates everything, "liquidates" everything, and subjects everything to the rule of the "fungible." And, as damning evidence, Adorno and Horkheimer cite a remark by Bacon: "Is not the rule, '*Si inaequalibus aequalia addas, omnia erunt inaequalia*,' an axiom of justice as well as of the mathematics? And is there not a true coincidence between commutative and distributive justice, and arithmetical and geometrical proportion?"[12]

Bacon was, of course, doing no more than echoing Aristotle and refurbishing an ancient dream of adequation, a dream of a rational order at once immanent and objective, at once numerically computable and humanly edifying. In its full flowering in the eighteenth century, this rationality would produce, among other things, William Petty's "political arithmetic," Condorcet's "mathematique sociale," and Chastellux's "indices du bonheur." To these ambitious efforts, we might also add the precedent of Descartes, with his *esprit de geometrie*,[13] as well as that of Hobbes, who, writing at almost exactly the same time as Descartes—in 1642—had looked to "the Geometricians" for moral guidance. ("If the moral philosophers had as happily discharged their duty," Hobbes said, "the nature of human actions [would have been] as distinctly known as the nature of quantity in geometrical figures.")[14] And we might add Spinoza as well, who, as if in response to the very challenge issued by Hobbes, would soon take it upon himself to apply Euclidean geometry to moral philosophy; his major work, *Ethica more geometrico demonstrata*,[15] was published after his death in 1677. Leibniz, meanwhile, announced a project which would include not only geometry and mechanics but also a scheme for settling all political, legal, and moral disputes:

> If controversies were to arise, there would be no more need of disputation between two philosophers than between two accountants. For it would suffice for them to take their pencils in their hands, to sit down to their slates, and to say to each other (with a friend to witness, if they liked), "Let us calculate."[16]

Such supreme faith in "calculations" suggests that at the onset of the Enlightenment, the reign of the numerical was already customary rather than revolutionary. Still, there was something unusual about the computing fervor of the eighteenth century: unusual not only in its many obsessions but also in its many innovations. Through the influence of Locke, for example, psychology was to emerge as a new discipline, indeed as the preeminent science of man, predicated in part on a speculative—but nonetheless enumerable—inventory of the mind. The idea of "Number," Locke wrote, "is the most intimate to our Thoughts, as well as it is, in its Agreement to all other things, the most universal *Idea* we have. For Number applies it self to Men, Angels, Actions, Thoughts, every thing that either doth exist, or can be imagined."[17]

The new philosophy of mind, taking its measure from this "most universal Idea," was therefore also to be a science of numbers. And "upon this ground," Locke said, "I am bold to think, that *Morality is capable of Demonstration*, as well as Mathematicks."[18] This was the ambition of Locke's *Essay Concerning Human Understanding* (1689), and it was the ambition as well of a long line of distinguished successors, from Hutcheson's *Inquiry into the Original of our Ideas of Beauty and Virtue* (1725) to Hume's *Treatise of Human Nature* (1740). In this context, it is not surprising that "happiness" should emerge as one of the key words of the Enlightenment, the pursuit of which would animate not just Jefferson's Declaration of Independence but numerous other declarations similarly inspired by dreams of a rational order. As Garry Wills points out, "happiness was not only a constant preoccupation of the eighteenth century; it was one inextricably linked with the effort to create a science of man based on numerical gauges for all his activity."[19] Happiness had a place in ethics precisely because it was quantifiable, because it could be itemized and distributed, on the one hand, and aggregated, on the other hand, in terms of its sum total both within one individual and within any group of individuals. It was in this quantifying spirit that Beccaria would write, in *On Crimes and Punishments*, of "la massima felicità divisa nel maggior numero," a phrase which would in turn inspire Bentham's English adaptation and from which he was to derive "the principle by which the precision and clearness and incontestableness of mathematical calculations are introduced for the first time into the field of morals."[20]

QUANTIFYING MORALITY

And so, for all his disreputableness, then and now, Bentham would seem to be writing out of a broad intellectual tradition.[21] Even his painstaking (and, to us, seemingly demented) efforts, in *An Introduction to the Principles of Morals and Legislations* (1789), to work out the exact degrees and ratios of pleasures and pains, had a genealogy of sorts.[22] Indeed, even the momentous phrase itself, "the greatest happiness of the greatest number," turns out to have a previous user. As Robert Shackleton has shown in his valuable bit of detective work,[23] it was Francis Hutcheson who first used the phrase, in his *Inquiry into the Original of our Ideas of Beauty and Virtue* (1725). That treatise, an attempt to measure morality by algebraic equations, offered advice that, like Bentham's more celebrated formula, might have been of interest to the nineteenth-century Laphams, stuck in their impasse:

> In comparing the moral qualities of actions, in order to regulate our election among various actions proposed . . . we are led by our moral sense of virtue thus to judge: that in equal degrees of happiness expected to proceed from the action, the virtue is in proportion to the number of persons to whom the happiness shall extend . . . and in equal numbers, the virtue is as the quantity of the happiness or natural good; or that virtue is in a compound ratio of the quantity of good

and number of enjoyers. . . . So that, that action is best which accomplishes the greatest happiness for the greatest numbers.[24]

Except for the memorable phrase at the end, the statement is perhaps not overly striking. Still, it is worth pointing out (and not merely as a matter of antiquarian interest) that it was Hutcheson rather than Bentham who introduced the phrase, and who did so within the framework of a moral philosophy in which the numerical would figure centrally as the arbitrating ground. Unlike Bentham (whose influence in America was relatively negligible),[25] Hutcheson, as a major figure of the Scottish Enlightenment, had an intellectual legacy that was both extensive and well documented. That legacy became increasingly transatlantic in the course of the eighteenth century. Both in his own right and through his influence on David Hume, Adam Ferguson, Lord Kames, Adam Smith, Thomas Reid, and others, Hutcheson had every claim to being the founder of a tradition of moral philosophy in America. This moral philosophy, always priding itself on its numerical clarity, would soon gravitate (especially in the hands of Adam Smith) toward an intellectual as well as institutional alliance with the emerging discipline of economics.[26] Beginning with Hutcheson, then, we can map out a line of descent for a style of rationality characteristic of the Scottish Enlightenment, a rationality in which the moral and the economic would soon become commensurate: commensurate, because they were articulated out of a shared cognitive foundation, a shared assumption about the quantifiability of the world.

Terence Martin has alerted us to this Scottish tradition in American thought.[27] Henry May has characterized its powerful influence as the "conquest" of America.[28] More recently, as revisionist historians try to unseat Locke from his putative centrality in America, the philosophy of the Scottish Enlightenment has emerged (along with classical republicanism) as a major contending force within the volatile intellectual climate that was the eighteenth century.[29] By the late eighteenth century, the Scots had scored a decisive victory in at least one area. Sober, pragmatic, and lucid, their moral philosophy was eminently readable and eminently teachable. The Common Sense popularizers—Thomas Reid, Lord Kames, James Beattie, and Dugald Stewart—all showed up in great numbers on booksellers' lists. To American colleges, charged with the education of a free and virtuous people, this enlightened doctrine must have seemed a gift from heaven. Championed by Francis Alison and William Smith of the College of Philadelphia and by John Witherspoon of Princeton (all transplanted Scots), the Scottish moral philosophy quickly became the backbone of the American college curriculum. Madison studied it at Princeton, Jefferson studied it at William and Mary, and five future signers of the Declaration of Independence applied themselves to it at the College of Philadelphia. Even at the Anglican King's College (later Columbia), the Presbyterian Hutcheson would still claim the pride of place, his text taking up the last two years of study.[30]

The intellectual accessibility of moral philosophy was further enhanced by its disciplinary centrality within the Scottish organization of knowledge. In Scottish universities, moral philosophy had always been defined in the broadest of terms, as an umbrella discipline. Hutcheson, Ferguson, and Reid were all professors of moral philosophy. So was Adam Smith—who wrote not only *The Wealth of Nations* (1776) but also *The Theory of Moral Sentiments* (1759) and who held the Chair of Moral Philosophy at Glasgow for twelve years, from 1752 to 1764, lecturing on political economy only as one of the fourfold divisions of moral philosophy.[31] Inspired by that tradition, American colleges during the first half of the nineteenth century also featured moral philosophy as the centerpiece of the curriculum. The entire senior year was devoted to it. Often taught by the college presidents themselves and using textbooks written by them, this core course provided the standard educational experience for generations of college graduates. Needless to say, moral philosophy so broadly defined was also broadly various in its subject matter. Like its Scottish kindred, it became at many points indistinguishable from political economy, the two being seen as adjacent (or overlapping) disciplines. Thus, the Reverend John McVickar at Columbia, appointed in 1818 to the first chair of political economy in the United States, had actually been appointed the year before as the professor of moral philosophy, rhetoric, and belles lettres. Similarly, Francis Wayland, the energetic president of Brown, not only began as a minister and not only wrote a "phenomenally successful" textbook, *The Elements of Moral Science* (1835), but also felt qualified, in the space of two years, to write another textbook, *The Elements of Political Economy* (1837).[32] As late as 1860, political economy at Harvard was taught by Francis Bowen, the Alford Professor of Natural Religion, Moral Philosophy, and Civil Polity.[33] This arrangement was not as outrageous as it might seem, for Bowen, like McVickar and Wayland, and like Richard Posner in the twentieth century, turned out to be an expert on both morality and economics. Just one year after he collected his Lowell Lectures into the popular *Principles of Metaphysics and Ethical Science Applied to the Evidences of Religion* (1855), he would publish an equally magisterial volume, *The Principles of Political Economy Applied to the Conditions, Resources, and the Institutions of the American People* (1856).

If figures like McVickar, Wayland, and Bowen seem to us unduly interdisciplinary, it is helpful to remind ourselves that what we now take to be clear-cut "disciplines" had not always been so perceived. As Francis Wayland said, "The Principles of Political Economy are so closely analogous to those of Moral Philosophy, that almost every question in one, may be argued on ground belonging to the other."[34] And there was every reason why the "analogy" between moral philosophy and political economy should be regularly enforced, for not only did they share a common foundation, a quantifying foundation, but as Albert O. Hirschman has shown, political economy had always been held up by its early advocates as a much-needed complement and corrective to the unstable field of morality. In David Hume and Adam Smith, and even in Montesquieu, economic "interests" were understood to have a sobering effect, useful in restraining and counteracting the dangerous "passions" afoot in the moral universe.[35] Far from being an enemy to morality (a reputation it later acquired), economics at the outset of its career was looked upon very much as the guardian of morality, as the expression of morality in its strictest and most rational form. It was this commensurability that prompted John McVickar to remark, in his *Outlines of Political Economy* (1825), that "the high principles which this science teaches entitle it to be regarded as the moral instructor of nations."[36]

The Reverend Sewell is in good company, then, when he urges upon the Laphams his moral instructor, his "economy of pain." Such equation of the moral and the economic echoes not only the teachings of Sewell's ecclesiastical forebears, the Reverend Wayland and the Reverend McVickar, it echoes as well the teachings of someone closer to home. Simon Nelson Patten, the Wharton School economist and a contemporary of Howells, was writing about pleasure and pain at almost exactly this time and, like the Reverend Sewell, was also doing a kind of double bookkeeping on these sensory phenomena, counting them up, that is, on two registers at once commensurate and interchangeable: ethics on the one side, economics on the other. A popularizer of "marginal utility analysis"[37] and a pioneering advocate of modern consumerism, Patten gave the utilitarian calculus what amounted to a late-nineteenth-century facelift by turning it into a dual-purpose index, unifying and indeed equalizing both the economics and the morality of consumption. In a series of books published in the 1880s and 1890s, Patten made a case for something like an ethics of spending, arguing that consumer demand was directly translatable into the general well-being of the nation. The private splurges of the consumer led to the common good for all.[38] The effect of that, Patten went on to say (in language strikingly similar to the Reverend Sewell's), was that "we are now in the transition stage from this pain economy to a pleasure economy." "The development of human society has gradually eliminated from the environment the sources of pain," he said. "These changes make a pleasure economy possible and destroy the conditions which made the subjective environment of the old pain economy a necessity."[39]

The open advocacy of a "pleasure economy" by such an economist as Simon Nelson Patten and the confident counsel of an "economy of pain" in such a novel as *The Rise of Silas Lapham* suggest that the intellectual landscape of the late nineteenth century might be more complicated than we have hitherto assumed. Morton White, who has given us the most influential account of that landscape, has characterized it as a revolt against utilitarianism, a revolt against its "abstraction, deduction, mathematics, and mechanics." As White describes it:

> When Dewey first published books on ethics, it was hedonism, and utilitarianism, which he most severely attacked; when Veblen criticized the foundations of classical economics, it was Bentham's calculus of pains and pleasures that he was undermining; when Holmes was advancing his own view of the law, it was the tradition of Bentham that he was fighting against.[40]

We might disagree with White about the three figures he specifically mentions.[41] We might further disagree with his account of a unified revolt—a revolt on one front against one enemy—which, to my mind, does not quite square with the rich brew of philosophical contradictions during this period. White's discretely periodizing model—

marked by the clear banishment of utilitarianism—should perhaps be qualified, then, by analytic concepts more fluid and more subtly evolving. My own candidates here are "uneven development" and "imperfect rationalization"—concepts that, especially in this case, would acknowledge both the persistence of certain cognitive categories and their semantic mutations and permutations over time. The evolution of the utilitarian calculus is especially interesting in this context, for the late-nineteenth-century language of pleasure and pain, as articulated by Patten and Howells, was as much a transformation as it was an inheritance from the language of their eighteenth-century precursors. After all, for all his faith in a future of abundance and for all his impatience with "sufferers who have made an art of wretchedness," Patten was deeply troubled by the psychological implications of a world without pain.[42] Noting that "individuals as well as nations show the deteriorating influence of pleasure as soon as they are freed from the restraints of a pain economy," he was almost consoled by the thought that even in a pleasure economy, pain would still remain—not as physical deprivation but as psychic anguish, brought about by the "defective relations which exist between men or between man and nature." Pain of this sort would always be with us, he predicted, for "no change in the ultimate forms of the universe or of man can alter" this salutary affliction.[43] The Reverend Sewell is not so adamant on this point, but even he, for all his sensible optimism, is strangely unconcerned with the greatest happiness of the greatest number. He speaks only of the economy of pain.

If happiness was the key word of the eighteenth century, pain might well be the key word of the nineteenth. Ideas about pain—about its provenance and consequence, its reality and calculability—have of course evolved throughout the course of history. In the nineteenth century, this "changing ethos of injury" was especially striking, as G. Edward White has noted.[44] That changing ethos, I would argue, had much to do with various emerging forms of nineteenth-century rationality, as they achieved various degrees of institutionalization. Earlier that century, a concern with objective adequation had led to an international venture in penal reform, which, rejecting torture as a corrective instrument, had insisted on applying no more than a "just measure of pain" to the criminal, proportional to the crime committed.[45] Further into the century, the same adequating rationality would manifest itself in a range of practices inspired by a

newborn utilitarianism, a utilitarianism modernized and reinvigorated.[46] These practices, revolving around the quantification, supervision, and utilization of pain, are most readily observable in three
fields institutionalized in the nineteenth century: humanitarianism,
modern tort law, and anesthetics. To their company, I would add a
fourth field, adjacent to and in dialogue with the others, but, I would
also argue, complexly at odds with them, complexly irreducible to
them. I am thinking of the realist novel of the nineteenth century, a
genre in which pain is documented both with judicious precision and
with involuntary obsession, a genre committed to rational solutions
but also haunted by their unsuccess.

RATIONAL BENEVOLENCE

The new visibility of pain (and the rational solutions it called forth)
might be studied in conjunction with a host of historical developments. Here, I begin with the rise of cities, which, especially in the
nineteenth century, would confer on human suffering not only the
status of a "problem" but, happily for all concerned, the status of a
solvable problem.[47] "Why is it, my friends, that we are brought so near
to one another in cities?" William Ellery Channing asked in an 1841
sermon. "It is, that nearness should awake sympathy; that multiplying wants should knit us more closely together; that we should understand one another's perils and sufferings; that we should act perpetually on one another for good."[48]

Nineteenth-century cities were scenes of moral action, in which
nearness translated into sympathy, perils and sufferings into the desire to do good. Between 1800 and 1880, New York grew from a city of
just 60,000 inhabitants to a metropolis of 1,100,000, with 600,000 more
living across the East River in Brooklyn.[49] Other cities across the nation experienced similar rates of growth. By 1900, 60 percent of the
inhabitants of the nation's twelve largest cities were either foreign-
born or of foreign parentage, with the figure approaching and even
exceeding 80 percent in some cities, including St. Louis, Cleveland,
Detroit, Milwaukee, Chicago, and New York.[50] With their miseries
and mysteries of indigence, these new metropolises showcased human suffering as a sign, a symptom, a challenge to the explanatory
powers of the new social sciences, and a challenge to the investigatory zeal of the new philanthropists.

Humanitarianism was thus very much an institutional presence in the nineteenth century, an organized experiment in rational benevolence. And most rational of all was the "Charity Organization Movement," which, first launched by S. Humphreys Gurteen in Buffalo, in 1877, quickly spread across the country in the 1880s. By the 1890s over 100 cities had charity organization societies, equipped with their own journals (*Lend-a-Hand* in Boston, *Charities Review* in New York, *Charities Record* in Baltimore) and convening once a year in the National Conference of Charities and Corrections.[51] Rejecting the traditional practice of public outdoor relief (which they saw as sentimental and haphazard), these new charities emphasized information gathering, the compilation of dossiers, and moral supervision by middle-class "visitors." In short, for these new-style philanthropists, the point was not simply to do good but to do so efficiently, scientifically, wasting no sentiment and no expense.[52] Josephine Shaw Lowell, founder of the New York City Charity Organization Society in 1882 and its guiding spirit for the next twenty-five years, personified this new development. Lowell distinguished between what she called mindless "benevolence" and vigilant "beneficence." Clearly an advocate of the latter, she argued that the proper goal of philanthropy was not to relieve suffering but rather to economize it, which is to say, to dispense it in such a way as to get the maximum result.[53] What was wrong with traditional almsgiving, she said, was that it was "indiscriminate," that it operated without "the intimate knowledge of the suffering people . . . necessary to all efficient help,"[54] and that, far from minimizing suffering, it actually perpetrated it:

> The argument which always has the most weight in favor of continuing public out-door relief is that many deserving poor persons may suffer should it be cut off. It has already been proved by experience, however, that not only many suffer, but *all suffer*, by the continuance of a system which undermines the character of those it pretends to relieve, and at the same time drags down to their level many who never, but for its false allurements, would have been sufferers at all.[55]

With a kind of accusatory compulsion, then, Lowell called attention, over and over again, to the *pain* caused by inefficient philanthropy. "Almsgiving and dolegiving are hurtful," she insisted; they are "injurious act[s]"; they not only "injure" the recipients by destroying their character but "are hurtful even to those who do not receive them," because the "moral harm" they propagate is so "infectious" as to afflict the entire community.

Against such multiplication of injuries, the Charity Organization Society offered itself, by contrast, as a veritable economy of pain: it would "bring less suffering to the innocent and less injury to the community."[56] It would do so, however, not by eliminating pain but by instrumentalizing it, which is to say, by inflicting it and utilizing it in the short run in order to minimize it in the long run. On this point, of course, Lowell was simply echoing Herbert Spencer, her guiding spirit in every respect. Spencer had argued that "the well-being of existing humanity" could only be "secured by that same beneficent, though severe discipline[,] . . . a discipline which is pitiless in the working out of good: a felicity-pursuing law which never swerves for the avoidance of partial and temporary suffering." There was such a thing as "salutary suffering," he insisted, and the challenge was to put it to good use.[57] Following his lead, Lowell too never doubted for a moment that humanity "*must* suffer"; the "only question" was "as to the kind of suffering." On this point she had no doubts either: salutary suffering must be purgative suffering, directed at its cause, for "the process of cure . . . will be painful to all alike." And so, "finding fellow beings in want and suffering, the cause of the want and suffering are [*sic*] to be removed if possible even if the process be as painful as plucking out an eye or cutting off a limb."[58]

Lowell's emphasis on the *cause* of suffering—and her determination to eradicate that cause, even when it means plucking out an eye or cutting off a limb—casts an interesting light on a recent debate among historians about causation and humanitarianism, a debate that has ignited the pages of the *American Historical Review*. What occasioned the debate was an important theoretical essay by Thomas Haskell, "Capitalism and the Origins of the Humanitarian Sensibility." Haskell argues that a particular form of moral sensibility, in this case a capacity for humanitarian action, is most likely to flourish within the causal universe of a particular form of economic life, in this case capitalism. Capitalism rewards those who can think in terms of distant events, who can connect things across space and time, and in doing so it helps to enlarge not only "the range of causal perceptions" but also the range of assumed responsibilities. What capitalism accomplishes is not just an economic revolution but, even more crucially, a cognitive revolution, a drastic broadening of our causal horizons. Out of this revised causality, Haskell suggests, a "new moral universe" is born, where "failing to go to the aid of a suffering stranger might become an unconscionable act." Against the usual assumption that capitalism encourages greed and selfishness, then, Haskell argues that the opposite is just as true. Indeed, according to him, "the emergence of a market-oriented form of life gave rise to new habits of causal attribution that set the stage for humanitarianism."[59]

Haskell's argument is partly designed to outrage his colleagues, but, polemics aside, his remains an intriguing hypothesis. Indeed, we only have to think of the Ford, Rockefeller, and Carnegie Foundations to see that there is in fact a vital link between capitalism and humanitarianism. Haskell's paradigm is invaluable in foregrounding a historical conjunction between a form of economic life and a form of moral action, and in theorizing it as a *cognitive* conjunction, a shared set of assumptions about time and space, about distance and connectedness, about causation and responsibility. And yet, readers of Sophocles must wonder whether remote causation really did begin with capitalism, whether its prospect and terror might not already have cast a large shadow over, say, *Oedipus the King*.[60]

Rather than seeing capitalism as the "origin" of humanitarianism, then, it might be more helpful to think about the relation between the two as one of cognitive affinity (not one of inaugural entailment). Both might be seen, that is, as expressions of a rationality with a longer and more complex genealogy: a rationality predicated on the commensurability between the moral and the economic, a rationality that, in this instance, would underwrite not only the *moral* claims of capitalism but also the *economic* claims of humanitarianism. In short, what seems most striking to me in the historical conjunction of capitalism and humanitarianism is the extent to which morality in the nineteenth century was always understood to be a cognate of the economic, compatible with and translatable into the most exacting standards of bookkeeping. S. Humphreys Gurteen and Josephine Shaw Lowell, vigilant philanthropists that they were, were no less emphatic about the money-saving virtues of their charities. "To cure paupers and make them self-supporting, however costly the process," Lowell said, "must always be economical as compared with a smaller but constantly increasing and continual outlay for their maintenance."[61] Gurteen, meanwhile, even had statistics at his fingertips. "The saving to the city, in out-door relief alone during the first year of the Society's work," he proudly reported, "amounted, in round numbers, to $48,000, and the average saving, during the past three years, has been somewhat over $50,000 per annum."[62]

This supposed commensurability between the moral and the economic—the supposed ease with which one translated into the other—led not only to the peculiar institutional landscape of the nineteenth century, its many projects of rational benevolence, but also to some of its deepest anxieties and bewilderments. What was one to do when the moral and the economic turned out to be less than equatable, when the translation between them turned out to be less than complete, less than recuperative? These were the questions that would come to haunt the realist novel in a rather conspicuous way, just as, less conspicuously but perhaps no less persistently, they would also come to haunt the precincts of tort law and of social theory. It was not altogether fortuitous, perhaps, that the word "responsibility"—a word with resonances in all three fields, and with both moral and economic implications—would emerge as one of the most deeply conflictual words in the nineteenth century, its scope subject to contrary definition, its boundaries and limits being matters of dispute.

In an 1887 essay called "The Shifting of Responsibility," for example, William Graham Sumner complained bitterly about a new concept of responsibility, which he found "immoral to the very last degree." According to this immoral concept,

> the employer becomes responsible for the welfare of the employees. . . . The employee is not held to any new responsibility for the welfare of the employer; the duties are all held to lie on the other side. The employer must assure the employed against the risks of his calling, and even against his own negligence; the employee is not held to assure himself. . . . [H]e is released from responsibility for himself.[63]

Sumner's semantic usage was less than consistent, no doubt because he was choking over the very sound of "responsibility." But his point, at least, was consistent enough. For him, responsibility as a relational concept—responsibility as an obligation to others—was clearly a travesty of the term. The word has only one legitimate usage, a reflexive usage, as in a man's "responsibility for himself."

Such vitriolic outbursts over the definition of responsibility were clearly fueled by more than just a semantic interest. Sumner, as always, did not mince words about what was at stake. He condemned responsibility of the "immoral" sort, he said, because it imposed obligations not only between individual human beings but, more specifically, between different *classes* of human beings: human beings differently endowed, differently situated, and differently entitled. In a short work with a self-explanatory title, *What Social Classes Owe to Each Other* (1883), Sumner took it upon himself "to find out whether there is any class in society which lies under the duty and burden of fighting the battles of life for any other class."[64] The answer, to no one's surprise, was a resounding no. No obligations exist, Sumner concluded, and no obligations ought ever to exist, for, as he explained in "The Forgotten Man," his well-known essay published the same year, society works by "the balance of the account," and the "advantage of some is won by an equivalent loss of others." It follows, then, that "if you give a loaf to a pauper," you are in effect "trampling on the Forgotten Man," that "clean, quiet, virtuous, domestic citizen" who is the "victim" of the "idle, the intemperate, the extravagant," who is "weighted down with the support of all the loafers," who is made to pay "the penalty while our minds were full of the drunkards, spendthrifts, gamblers."[65] In short, all social obligations must be seen as unfair impositions, for, according to Sumner, each of us has only "one big duty," namely, "to take care of his or her own self."[66]

Sumner's recommendations here are only to be expected, given his reputation. It would be a mistake, however, to see his teachings solely as an expression of Social Darwinism. The scope of responsibility was a matter of concern to a much more diverse group of commentators and in a much more diverse set of contexts. As early as 1838, Francis Wayland was already publishing a popular text in moral philosophy entitled *The Limitations of Human Responsibility*. Wayland argued that whereas "our responsibility for the temper of mind is unlimited and universal, our responsibility for the outward act is limited and special."[67] In other words, as far as our intentions are concerned, unlimited responsibility applies; as far as our actions are concerned, however, that responsibility must be set within judicious boundaries.

Wayland was writing in the context of slavery, which for the North made the question of moral responsibility especially thorny. If slavery was indeed an abomination, as most Northerners believed, wasn't one morally obligated to put an end to it? And wouldn't that obligation commit one to abolition, civil war, perhaps even the dissolution of the union? Wayland's answer was exquisitely tempered. "Granting all that may be said of the moral evil of this institution," he reasoned, "the question still remains to be decided, what is our duty in respect to it; and, what are the limitations." It was those "limitations" that he proposed to dwell on. In the end, the only "practical duty" he counseled was that of moral suasion, which is to say, the duty of imparting to our Southern "friends and acquaintances . . . the truth which we believe to be conducive to their happiness."[68] Wayland clearly had a genius for moderation. Even so, that did not prevent his book or its predecessor, *The Elements of Moral Science* (1835), from stirring up a storm of controversy. The sales figures for both books were "phenomenal," according to Joseph Blau.[69] Moral responsibility was a best-selling topic in the nineteenth century.

TORT LAW

The topical interest of moral responsibility did not end with the Civil War, for human suffering was to remain a visible problem all through the nineteenth century. Indeed, beginning in the 1840s, a whole new arena of suffering would open up, fueled by the pace of industrial expansion and the rate of industrial accidents. Injury was an accepted hazard of early industrialization, its liability cost being computed as a standard operational cost.[70] Not surprisingly, it was during this period that a newly consolidated legal field should come into being, drastically expanding its domain to cope with the drastically escalating cases of civil responsibility for injury. Modern tort law (popularly known as "injury law") was very much a creation of the nineteenth century. And among the many injurers brought before it, none was guiltier than the railroad. Still primitive in its safety features, operating without the benefit of the air brake, the early railroads, according to Lawrence Friedman, behaved like "wild beasts; they roared through the countryside, killing livestock, setting fires to houses and crops, smashing wagons at grade crossings, mangling passengers and freight. Boilers exploded; trains hurtled off tracks; bridges collapsed; locomotives collided in a grinding scream of steel."[71]

The nineteenth-century railroad might be said to carry an economy of pain of its own—quite literally so, since judges were increasingly called upon to award money damages for bodily injuries, and thus to work out a numerical equivalent not only for the experience of physical harm but also for the scope of moral responsibility. Here then was a unique juncture of the moral and the economic,[72] one whose resolution would have profound consequences both for legal and nonlegal thinking. What the court adopted was the doctrine of "negligence" (as opposed to the doctrine of strict liability), which made the relation between injury and compensation a mediate relation, contingent upon demonstrable fault on the part of the injurer.[73] In *Farwell v. Boston & Worcester Railroad Corporation* (1842), a landmark case decided by Chief Justice Lemuel Shaw of Massachusetts (better known to literary critics as Melville's father-in-law), a railroad engineer, who had lost his right hand in an accident caused by a switchman, sued the railroad for damages. His claim was rejected. The court ruled that since the engineer had voluntarily taken on a dangerous job, he must also be held to have assumed the ordinary risks of that job. His higher than usual wages had already adjusted for the higher than usual hazard, and any injuries sustained must be considered already compensated for.

The legal reasoning exhibited in this case (and in the tort law that came after it) was a style of reasoning very much predicated on a notion of reflexive compensation and reflexive equilibrium. Even though the employee was hurt, his wages had already rectified that hurt, and so everything ended up being balanced out. This compensatory equilibrium quickly became a standard premise of legal reasoning, and, by the beginning of the Gilded Age, the general drift of the new tort law was unmistakable. Its central features—the fault principle, assumption of risk, contributory negligence, the fellow-servant rule—all helped to limit the grounds for redress and hence the scope of entrepreneurial responsibility. Liability was unquestionably a critical issue in late-nineteenth-century legal thinking, so critical, in fact, that when Oliver Wendell Holmes delivered his famous lectures at the Lowell Institute—collected into his equally famous *The Common Law* (1881)—he was inspired to devote his first lecture to "Early Forms of Liability," followed by others on criminal liability, tort liability, and contractual liability.[74] For Holmes, too, the notion of "universal and unlimited responsibility" was infinitely troubling, because it would "make a defendant responsible for all damage, however remote, of which his act might be called the cause." If such a concept were to prevail, the state would have to act like "a mutual insurance company against accidents, and distribute the burden of its citizens' mishaps among all its members." This was clearly unacceptable to Holmes; it would "offend the sense of justice." To guard against this eventuality, it was the business of tort law "to fix the dividing line" between what was actionable negligence and what was not, and to ensure that the "loss from accident must lie where it falls."[75]

Austerely just, and austerely economical, the modern tort law is now seen by some of its theorists as a "mirror of American society, held up to some of its most difficult moments of private conflict."[76] If so, what that mirror revealed in the late nineteenth century was not only the frequency of injury but also the seeming ability of legal reasoning to localize its effects, to restrict its claims, and to define legal responsibility without moral ambiguities. The emergence of the modern tort law might be seen, in this context, as an especially important moment in the history of American law, consonant with that broad process whose stated goal, in the words of Holmes, was to shape the "law as a business with well understood limits," to "emphasize the difference between law and morals," and to keep "the boundary constantly before our minds."[77] What is further clear is that, in that proposed parting of ways between the legal and the moral, it was the economic that was consistently enlisted as the instrument of separation. The economic, that is to say, was now appealed to as something more basic than morality, subsuming it and replacing it as the cognitive foundation for the law. Economics, and economics alone, would now furnish the rational ground for legal action.

It is logical, then, that in our own time, exponents of Law and Economics—notably Richard Posner—would be quick to commend Holmes on just this point and quick to endorse nineteenth-century tort principles on the ground of efficiency.[78] And yet, to read Law and Economics against Holmes (or against contemporaries of Holmes who also wrote on liability, including Charles Peirce and Nicholas St. John Green),[79] is to be struck by the enormous distance, intellectual as well as stylistic, between the nineteenth-century theorists and their twentieth-century successors. For Holmes, Peirce, and Green, liability was primarily a philosophical (or perhaps even metaphysical) problem. The technicalities of tort law were anchored and broadened, always, within a discourse as wide-ranging as it was conceptually intricate. For them, what had to be circumscribed through a focus on tort liability was the idea of causation itself, for here as elsewhere, this vexed concept, with its radically enlarged operative radius, proved to be both intriguing and intolerable. Indeed, the nineteenth-century debate on tort liability quickly became a debate over what Morton Horwitz has called the "politics of causation."[80]

In a series of important cases, including *Stone v. Boston and Albany Railroad Co.* (1898) and *Central of Georgia Railway Co. v. Price* (1898), the court decided that "the proximate, and not the remote, cause is to be regarded" as responsible for damage and that "a proximate cause must be that which immediately precedes and produces the effect, as distinguished from the remote, mediate, or predisposing cause."[81] Proximate cause—the narrowest range of causal attribution—must be upheld, for it alone could provide an adequate safeguard against the specter of unlimited claims, not only in specific cases of industrial accidents but more generally in any distributive situation: any situation, that is, where a dispute might arise about the proper allocation of pleasures and pains, burdens and benefits. Theories of causation are, at heart, social theories on a grand scale, with broad implications for distributive justice and broad conclusions about the legitimacy of a particular social order. Nineteenth-century theorists of causation were very much aware of this. Indeed, for Francis Wharton, the influential treatise writer, the seemingly arcane question of "whether a railroad company is to be liable for all fires of which its locomotives are the occasion" turned out to be the central question for "the industrial interests of the land," so central that what hinged upon it was nothing other than the life of capitalism itself.[82]

Wharton reprimanded those who acted on the assumption that "when we are seeking for a responsible cause, we are allowed to go back until we hit, in the line of antecedents, upon wealth that is without immediate friends." Such a mistake is all too common, he said, because we "are accustomed to look with apathy at the ruin of great corporations, and to say, 'Well enough, they have no souls, they can bear it without pain, for they have nothing in them by which pain can be felt.'" For Wharton, this was not at all the right way to think about causation, or about corporations, or about pain. It would lead to "communism," which "makes wealth the basis of liability."[83] It would encourage us to blame our sufferings on an unlimited range of causal antecedents and to say:

> "Here is a capitalist among these antecedents; he shall be forced to pay." The capitalist, therefore, becomes liable for all disasters of which

he is in any sense the condition, and the fact that he thus is held liable, multiplies these disasters. Men become prudent and diligent by the consciousness that they will be made to suffer if they are not prudent and diligent. If they know they will not be made to suffer for their neglects; if they know that though the true cause of a disaster, they will be passed over in order to reach the capitalist who is a remote condition, then they will cease to be prudent.[84]

For Wharton, pain, in all its undesirability, was nonetheless an economic resource and as such must be *instrumentally* distributed. It must be distributed, that is, as a corrective mechanism, a hard lesson to those who needed it. In the case of industrial accidents, this lesson must fall on those who were "mediately or immediately employed,"[85] those who were injured by the accidents, and who, for that reason, must also be designated the cause of those accidents. Wharton thus insisted that "one of the chief offices of society was to discriminate between the antecedents by which an event is conditioned," to "single out one only of the antecedents under the denomination of cause, calling the others merely conditions."[86] That being done, the employer, as a "remote condition," would be excused from the scene, leaving behind only the workers, the real causes of the disaster and therefore the rightful sufferers—which, for Wharton, was all to the good. Pain would teach the lesson of prudence.

In localizing the distribution of suffering, Wharton offered one way to think about time and space, about distance and nearness, about causation and responsibility. In converting suffering into a resource, a usable resource, he offered as well an example (perhaps the most striking we have seen thus far) of the rationalization of pain: a rationalization openly economic, grounded in the trade-off between the brute fact of suffering and the moral it could be counted on to deliver. Nineteenth-century tort law thus stood as one of the boldest experiments in commensurability, one of the boldest attempts to create a symmetrical order out of its designated problem and solution. It did so, we might add, primarily by instrumentalizing pain, turning it into what Spencer would call "salutary suffering." Chastened by it, workers would become so prudent as to make any further suffering unlikely. The cause of pain and the effect of pain were understood, then, both to emanate from and to descend upon the same party. Mutually entailed and inversely corresponding, they would work to neutralize and cancel out each other. Tort law thus brought about an adaptive equilibrium in the workforce, even as it achieved an operative equilibrium within itself, by a method of damage control that contained the damage within the narrowest possible compass. The problem of pain was not at all a problem here: not a problem, because it could be counted on to take care of itself, to work toward its own cure and its own end.

FUNCTIONAL ADAPTATION

For Wharton specifically, as for tort law more generally, suffering thus carried with it a rationality of its own, a rationality that made it necessary, useful, and, in the end, happily self-regulating. This was the hope, I have argued, of the philanthropists, and it was also the hope, I would further argue, of an entire age fascinated by the phenomena of pleasure and pain and predisposed to see an instrumental reason behind their occurrence. Pleasure and pain were understood, that is, to be *purposive* phenomena: they came into the world for a certain reason, they functioned in a certain way, and they produced a certain result. For Herbert Spencer, for example, it was through the agency of pleasure and pain that human evolution could take place at all. If it were not for our sentience, our ability to register those hard lessons taught by the environment, we would not have been made to adapt functionally to that environment.

Since pleasure and pain were instruments of adaptation, since there were evolutionary reasons for them to be felt in a particular way, Spencer also argued that human sentience must vary—vary in degrees of acuity as well as thresholds of susceptibility—in different environments, which is to say, they must vary from one human population to another. "There is no kind of activity which will not become a source of pleasure if continued," he said, for, by the doctrine of evolution, "there will be evolved, in adaptation to any new sets of conditions that may be established, appropriate structures of which the functions will yield their respective gratifications." And so "the common assumption that equal bodily injuries excite equal pains" could not be more of "a mistake." Indeed, "after contemplating the wide divergences of sentiency accompanying the wide divergences of organization which evolution in general has brought about," one cannot doubt "the divergences of sentiency to be expected from the further evolution of humanity."[87]

The medical profession, staking its faith on this "divergence of sentiency," was quick to develop a procedure rejecting "the common assumption that equal bodily injuries excite equal pains." Between 1840 and 1880, it became common for doctors to administer anesthetics to some patients and not to others, not only because they believed that "different types of people differed in their sensitivity to pain" but also because they believed there was a reason behind this difference, a reason medical science ought to respect. Doctors seemed to be guided by "a calculus of suffering," the historian Martin Pernick has observed, a calculus which, in making pain a measure of the functional disparities among human beings, and therefore a measure of the functional rationality of the world, obviously had "implications reach[ing] far beyond anesthesia."[88]

And indeed, Spencer was by no means the first to see in pain the differential effects of adaptation. Throughout much of the nineteenth century, medical doctors experimented with the idea that pain was a variable phenomenon, that those who were refined and civilized were also more susceptible. As early as 1806, Thomas Trotter, surgeon to the British fleet, began to worry that the march of civilization would result in a "general effeminacy," since it "never fail[s] to induce a delicacy of feeling, that disposes alike to more acute pain, as to more exquisite pleasure."[89] Other physicians, sharing his concern, lamented that "civilized life" had sharpened the sensitivity to pain, and that childbirth had become "exceedingly painful[,] . . . especially in the upper walks of life."[90] As late as 1892, Dr. S. Weir Mitchell, the founder of American neurology, would make the same argument, in an essay entitled "Civilization and Pain." "In our process of being civilized we have won an intensified capacity to suffer," he wrote. "The savage does not feel pain as we do."[91]

The "savage [who] does not feel pain" included Indians, who, according to Benjamin Rush (the most prominent physician of the late eighteenth century), could "inure themselves to burning part of their bodies with fire."[92] It also included blacks, who, having a "greater insensibility to pain," could "submit to and bear the infliction of the rod with a surprising degree of resignation, and even cheerfulness."[93] But cheerfulness in the face of bodily affliction was by no means limited to these two groups of savages, hardened by experience into insentience. "Savagery" was a remarkably elastic category in the nineteenth century—it was understood to exist, for instance, also in urban slums, whose population, according to Horace Mann, was rapidly "falling back into the conditions of half-barbarous or of savage life."[94] These born-again savages, adapting functionally to their new environment, were also now becoming immunized to pain, much in the manner of Indians and blacks—a fact attested to by John William De Forest, a wealthy Connecticut citizen and an occasional social commentator. "We waste unnecessary sympathy on poor people," he said. "A man is not necessarily wretched because he is cold & hungry and unsheltered; provided these circumstances usually attend him, he gets along very well with them."[95]

By a feat of adaptation, insensitivity to pain turned out to be proportional to the incidence of pain. Those who had the most to suffer were least hurt by it. The functional correlation between pain and insentience thus became for De Forest the ultimate proof of the rationality of the world, for here too injury was dispensed with minimal damage, dispensed, that is, literally as an economy, the frequency of pain being compensated by a corresponding immunity. Such faith in a compensatory structure might sound like the sentiment of some arch-antihumanitarian, but (and the point is worth emphasizing) that was precisely what De Forest was *not*. A Civil War veteran and an agent of the Freedmen's Bureau in Greenville, South Carolina, from 1866 to 1867, his credentials revealed quite a different profile, not at all what one would expect from his seemingly callous statement about the painlessness of pain.

The paradox deepens when we turn from John William De Forest to Lydia Maria Child. A staunch abolitionist, loyal friend of Harriet Jacobs, and the author not only of the popular *Appeal in Favor of That Class of Americans Called Africans* (1833) but also of the controversial 1824 *Hobomok* (with its daring depiction of an interracial marriage between an Indian man and a white woman), Child would seem to personify the very spirit of nineteenth-century humanitarianism. Yet she too believed in a differential scale in pain, seeing a functional correlation between the necessary hardships of blacks and their necessary insentience. For her, it was a "merciful arrangement of Divine Providence, by which the acuteness of sensibility is lessened when it becomes merely a source of suffering."[96] Like De Forest, then, Child also envisioned a principle of compensatory equilibrium in every living organism. Indeed, her abolitionism rested on just this point. For her, the slaves' insentience was evidence in itself, proving that slavery was atrocious and that abolition was imperative.

It might seem odd that those who made pain a political issue should also argue for its endurability among the habitually afflicted. But the oddity here is perhaps no more than a dramatic example of the adequating rationality we have been examining, a rationality that imaged forth the world as a commensurate order, so that problem and solution were not only reflexively generated but also instrumentally corresponding. Adaptation to pain turned out to be nature's solution to the problem of pain. It was Herbert Spencer, of course, who gave this functional rationality its grandest expression, making it the centerpiece of his "Doctrine of Evolution," which saw adaptation itself as a cosmic drive toward compensatory equilibrium, toward a "conciliation of individual natures with social requirements," so that at the end of the process "pleasure will eventually accompany every mode of action demanded by social conditions."[97] Spencer found such an adaptative equilibrium "in the balanced functions of organic bodies that have reached their adult forms, and in the acting and reacting processes of fully-developed societies," both of which were "characterized by compensating oscillations." Indeed, according to him, "the evolution of every aggregate must go on until" all imbalances are eliminated, for "an excess of force which the aggregate possesses in any direction, must eventually be expended in overcoming resistances to change in that direction: leaving behind only those movements which compensate each other, and so form a moving equilibrium."[98] It was this compensatory structure that made it possible for Spencer to speak of a "rational ethics" in which "men themselves are answerable" to themselves, justice here being simply a reflexive equilibrium, simply "a definite balance, achieved by measure."[99]

In making "compensation" and "equilibrium" the overarching terms under which pain is both instrumentalized and neutralized, Spencer dramatizes the functionalist logic of the nineteenth century, a logic at work, as we have seen, not only in tort law, perhaps its most salient expression, but also in the practice of selective anesthesia, and in the rational beneficence of the new-style philanthropists. It is against that logic, against its claim to being a universal form of reason, that I want to bring to the foreground a different cognitive style, a different way of thinking about pain. Here, over and against any proposed solution, any proposed equilibrium, there remains the untidy fact of residues: residues unutilized, uncompensated, unspoken for. The phenomenon I have in mind is something like "incomplete rationalization,"[100] a phenomenon I associate most especially with the realist novel of the nineteenth century. Committed as it is to a dream of commensurate order, the novel is also haunted, fleetingly but also quite routinely, by the obverse of such a dream: by the failure of the world to conduct itself symmetrically, its failure to resolve itself into a perfect fit, a self-regulating circuit of pain and compensation.

A COGNITIVE HISTORY OF THE NOVEL

Incomplete rationalization—understood as an analytic postulate about structural *non*totality, about what is not integrated, not instrumentalized—thus seems to me to one of the most fruitful ways to think about the form of the novel, about its messiness, its ample proportions, and sometimes its lack of proportions. In chapter 1, I examined the signifying latitude in the novel, generated by its figurations, a latitude I see as residual especially in relation to the increasingly strict constructions in criminal law. In this chapter, I examine the novel's narrative latitude, generated by its complex plot, a latitude residual perhaps along a different axis: residual in relation to the instrumental reason of the nineteenth century. Against the latter's compensatory equilibrium, it is hard not to be struck by the imbalanced form of the novel. There is no symmetry of resolution here, and no symmetry of compensation. That lack of symmetry is most striking when the novel interweaves, as it so often does, a narrative epistemology about the bounds of time and space with a moral epistemology about the bounds of causation and responsibility. This interlocking epistemology—with its ethical imperatives and embarrassments— calls for a form of criticism attentive to the cognitive mapping[101] of the fictional domain, attentive, that is, to the landscape generated by the narrative sequence and associative radius, the length of antecedence and breadth of concurrence. The designation of a length of time understood as meaningful duration and the designation of a width of space understood as meaningful vicinity—these are matters not only of the novel's form but also of its vexed relation to the prevailing rationality of the nineteenth century. I call this a cognitive history of the novel.

From *The Pioneers* (1823, in which the revelation of a past secret restores Oliver Effingham to his rightful estate), to *The Blithedale Romance* (1852, in which a similar revelation disinherits Zenobia), to

Pierre (1852, in which yet another revelation literally destroys everyone), the American novel of the mid-nineteenth century might be called the novel of remote causation. In its richly involved (and sometimes richly improbable) plots, in its far-flung attribution of cause and consequence, it gives voice to a deep fascination, and perhaps a deep discomfort, with the bounds of pertinent time and pertinent space, with the range of human connectedness, and with the scope of assumable responsibility.

Howells himself would write explicitly about this problem in *The Minister's Charge* (1886), published just one year after *The Rise of Silas Lapham*. In this book, it is once again the Reverend Sewell who is made to deliver the book's central statement. "Everybody's mixed up with everybody else," he observes with admirable succinctness, in a sermon entitled "Complicity."[102] Complicity, the condition of being all mixed up, is indeed an inescapable fact in Howells and in virtually all realist fiction. The ethical entanglements it creates—and the imperfect disentanglements that follow—dramatize not only the need for rational order in the world but also a sharp and sharply unsettling sense of where such an order might not suffice. A cognitive history of the novel, then, might want to focus on those very lapses in its instrumental logic, those very qualities of dissatisfaction and inefficacy which afflict its reasoning. And to the extent that these afflictions are seen to be especially endemic in the novel, this cognitive history will imagine human reason itself not as a unified principle but as a field of uneven development, giving rise to different domains of thought, different shapes of causation and compensation, different shapes of pertinence and answerability.

Paradoxically, then, to approach the novel as a cognitive phenomenon is to destabilize the very idea of cognition itself. It is to acknowledge, within the seemingly integral idea of "reason," something like a constitutive ground for incommensurability.[103] Nineteenth-century humanitarianism[104] and tort law are "cognitive associates" for the novel, then, not only in the sense that they jointly inhabit a universe of thought but also in the sense that they jointly attest to the differentiations within that universe. Even the most ordinary cognitive coordinates—for example, the length and breadth of pertinent connections, longer and broader in some domains than in others, and longest and broadest of all in the novel—will suggest to us some intriguing lines of inquiry both about the contrary claims of reason and about its contrary institutionalizations over time. "Incomplete rationalization" thus seems to me one of the most helpful concepts, both to think about the imperfect integration of a literary text and to think about the unconcluded dynamics of historical process. Confronting us with what is imperfectly aligned, imperfectly adapted, imperfectly utilized, such a concept restores every naturalized given to a state of underdeterminacy, in which the nontotality of effect also marks the limits of instrumental reason itself.[105]

It is the limits of instrumental reason—its inability to resolve the world in its own image, its inability to translate the world into a functional blueprint—which suggest that human history is perhaps also not a story of functional integration but a story considerably less streamlined, a story of losses unrecovered and residues unassimilated. By the same token, the literary text, too, is not a perfectly working unit, not a feat of engineering, but something less efficient, less goal oriented, less instrumentally assignable, and, because of that, perhaps also less exhausted by its rational purpose, its strategic end.[106] Proceeding from this premise of "incomplete rationalization," what I hope to explore, then, is not a "logic" of the novel,[107] but something like its obverse, an *illogic*, which is to say, a lapse in its ability to instrumentalize its narrative universe, to make that universe serve one particular end. From the standpoint of practical criticism, what this suggests is a retreat from the functionalist premise which has long dominated our thinking about the novel and which, in its current emphasis on the novel as "cultural work," would seem to align it unproblematically with the reign of instrumental reason. Qualifying that premise, we might want to think of the novel instead as something less seamlessly at work, less seamlessly integrated, something not necessarily unifiable under the category of "function," something that might suggest a limit to that concept.

RADIUS OF PERTINENCE

That lapse in seamlessness is perhaps most noticeable in the novel's radius of pertinence, which, linking each episode to yet another antecedent or adjacent episode, making it contingent upon yet another eventuality, must attest at every turn to the infinitude of causal horizons and the infinitude of perceptual limits. More than any other American author, William Dean Howells champions the realist novel, and champions it for just that radius of pertinence. The novel has the ability to give the world its broadest representation, to "widen the bounds of sympathy." Nothing is extraneous for the realist: "In life he finds nothing insignificant. . . . He cannot look upon human life and declare this thing or that thing unworthy of notice."[108] But the realist novel is not only inclusive, it also dwells on the connectedness among all that it sees fit to include. Giving primacy to those threads "which unite rather than sever humanity," it everywhere proclaims the "equality of things and the unity of men."[109] Howells himself was so taken with the idea that he even suggested that, as a writer, he was "merely a working-man," "allied to the great mass of wage-workers." He urged other writers to forge the same alliance, "to feel the tie that binds us to all the toilers of the shop and field, not as a galling chain, but as a mystic bond."[110]

It was these mystic bonds that made for the abiding sympathies (and the abiding sense of guilt) in a novel like *A Hazard of New Fortunes* (1890). And it was the same mystic bonds that, just three years earlier, had prompted Howells (virtually alone among his generation of writers) to come to the defense of the Haymarket anarchists, whose trial and conviction he protested not as an abstract problem of justice but as a matter deeply affecting to himself. "The justice or injustice of their sentence was not before the highest tribunal of our law, and unhappily could not be got there. That question must remain for history, which judges the judgment of courts," Howells warned.[111] Meanwhile, "for many weeks, for months," he had been living with a "heavy heart," for the "impending tragedy" of the anarchists had not "been for one hour out of my waking thoughts; it is the last thing when I lie down, and the first thing when I rise up; it blackens my life."[112]

Howells's sense of human connectedness has been accepted as one of the central attributes of the realist novel.[113] But it is important, too, I think, to treat that attribute not simply as an isolated phenomenon but as one cognitive style, one among others, fashioned in a cultural environment in which the question of pertinence is almost always linked to the question of responsibility. Within that context, the novel must be seen as an exceptionally intriguing document, in that its temporal and spatial boundaries are so amorphous, its connections so thick and intricate, its threshold of extraneousness so nearly nonexisting. The boundaries of the novel are everywhere expandable, and, in placing the scope of responsibility within those uncertain boundaries, it offers a striking counterpoint to the "rational ethics" so endlessly celebrated in the nineteenth century, upsetting its forms of resolution and grounds for redress.

In *The Rise of Silas Lapham*, the radius of pertinence is so broad as to appear at times to be outside the bounds of plausibility. The book is what Henry James would definitely call a "loose baggy monster." And as loose baggy monsters go, this one is worse than most—primarily because of two subplots, one only marginally related to the main story and the other apparently not related at all.[114] The first has to do with Milton K. Rogers, a former partner of Lapham's, squeezed out by him when the business began to prosper, who returns to feed on his guilt and to borrow money from him. This borrowing helps to bring about Lapham's downfall, and Rogers in that regard has something to contribute to the plot. His contribution is not strictly necessary, however, since bad investments alone could have ruined Lapham, and the plot hardly depends on this extra help. Even so, Rogers is more integral to the story than Miss Dewey, a typist in Lapham's office and the center of the other subplot. *Her* only contribution to the story is to provoke Mrs. Lapham into a fit of unfounded jealousy, but otherwise she seems completely superfluous.

In their semidetached state, Rogers and Miss Dewey would seem to confirm our usual view of the novel as an unruly concoction of plot and subplot, intrigues and entanglements. Here, I want to propose a somewhat different account of this phenomenon, beginning with a conception of the plot and subplot as competing lengths of pertinent time, competing widths of pertinent space. The thickly multiplying subplots, in their unwieldy, unwarranted extension, mark the furthest reach of the novel's causal radius, its most thoroughgoing adventure in connectedness. And since that adventure is ultimately not only far-flung but also far-fetched, each subplot represents as well something of an epistemological crisis, which the main plot must try to rectify, contain, counteract. On this view, plot and subplot would seem to be related, not in thematic collaboration but in cognitive contestation. The novel is thus internally divided, propelled by conflicting narrative coordinates, conflicting grounds of intelligibility, conflicting senses of the extraneous. If it ever achieves a structural equilibrium, that is not so much an effortless given as a precarious effect, a generic crisis confronted and averted. And where that equilibrium falls short, that too is not so much an aberration as a constitutive failing, a return to what appears to be a generic disposition, a return to the claims of the incommensurate.

The tenuous ties linking Rogers and Miss Dewey are important, then, precisely because they *are* tenuous, because they define a radius of pertinence so wide as to be virtually untenable. In such a world of causal infinitude, human responsibility becomes infinitely problematic. Is Lapham still responsible for the fate of Rogers, after all these years? How long should he keep on making amends, and how far must he go? That is the very question Mrs. Lapham asks, and her answer is unequivocal. "I want you should ask yourself," she urges her husband, "whether Rogers would ever have gone wrong, or got into these ways of his, if it hadn't been for your forcing him out of the business when you did. I want you should think whether you're not responsible for everything he's done since" (262).

Mrs. Lapham has "a woman's passion for fixing responsibility" (277), Howells tells us, and she certainly seems to be indulging it on this occasion. Still, her passion turns out to be not uniform but strategic and sporadic. She has no desire to "fix responsibility," for instance, when the responsibility involves taking care of the widow and child of a dead army buddy. In fact, she is as vehemently opposed, on this point, as she is vehemently insistent on the other. "One of the things she had to fight [Lapham] about was that idea of his that he was bound to take care of Jim Millon's worthless wife and her child because Millon had got the bullet that was meant for him" (340). As far as she is concerned, this is just "willful, wrong-headed kind-heartedness" (341) on Lapham's part, for he has no moral responsibility to speak of in this case and no reason to "look after a couple of worthless women who had no earthly claim on him" (362). Fight as she does, however, she cannot "beat [the idea] out of" his stubborn head, because, on this occasion at least, Lapham is committed to a wider causal circumference than her own. Seeing himself as the cause of Jim Millon's death, he voluntarily puts himself under what seems to be a lifelong obligation toward the dead man's family. That is why Miss Dewey is in his office to begin with: she is Jim Millon's daughter, and Lapham feels "bound to take care of" her and her mother. The subplot revolving around the typist, then, turns out to be exactly analogous to the one revolving around Rogers. In both cases, a distant event generates a network of complications and entanglements, giving rise to a universe of ever-receding and ever-expanding causation: a universe of unlimited pertinence and unlimited responsibility.

It is the unlimited responsibility, of course, that precipitates Lapham's downfall. The causal universe he inhabits is not only fatally expansive but also fatally expensive. Moral obligations have a way of becoming financial liabilities here, because both Rogers and Miss Dewey (as well as her mother) use their moral claims to exact money: a fact disturbing not only in its own right, but also in the havoc that it wreaks on the very principle of commensurability which elsewhere had seemed so reassuring to the jurists and philanthropists of the nineteenth century. Lapham is speaking both too prophetically and too soon, then, when he says, "I don't think I ever did Rogers any wrong . . . but if I *did* do it—if I did—I'm willing to call it square, if I never see a cent of my money back again" (132). The money that he will "never see a cent of back again" turns out to be the sum total of his fortune, for Milton K. Rogers, Lapham later discovers, has a way of "let[ting] me in for this thing, and that thing, and [has] bled me every time" (274).

What is striking here, in Howells's narrative universe, a universe of infinite antecedence, is the degree to which the moral and the economic are here not commensurate—or rather, are commensurate only in the most ironic sense, only through the cruellest inversion of their joint agency. Structured as it is by an almost boundless radius of pertinence, Lapham's moral universe is economically disastrous for just that reason. Far from being self-regulating, self-compensating, it has no rational checks and balances to speak of, nothing to save it from utter collapse, utter disaster. Lapham himself suggests as much. All his trouble began with "Rogers in the first place," he says. "It was just like starting a row of bricks. I tried to catch up, and stop 'em from going, but they all tumbled, one after another. It wasn't in the nature of things that they could be stopped till the last brick went" (364).

A morality given over to excess—a radius of pertinence extended beyond prudential limits—can lead only to the worst case predicted by domino theory. But if so, the very nature of the problem already suggests a solution of sorts. For if the trouble here is a morality gone awry, a morality at odds with its economic foundation, the logical thing to do would simply be to repair that breach, to reconstitute the moral domain once again as a balanced proposition, a self-regulating circuit of gains and losses. It is here, I think, that the category of moral "character" is especially important—important to the novel's attempt to harness its erring morality, to restore it to the fold of the economic—for the "rise" of Silas Lapham, the moral ascent which the novel advertises, is of course purchased by the corresponding financial downfall he is made to endure. The very category of "character," in other words, is based on a kind of internal bookkeeping, which in effect transforms the radius of pertinence into a circumscribed radius, turning Lapham's life itself into a compensatory structure, a trade-off between suffering and edification.

From this perspective, Lapham's beginnings—the assets that initially grace his person—are especially worthy of notice. And "assets" is the right word because, in the first part of the book, Lapham is noticeably well endowed: endowed with bodily parts that are not only conspicuous but downright obtrusive. Over and over again, we hear about his "bulk" (4), his "huge foot" (3), his "No. 10 boots" (6). He is in the habit of "pound[ing] with his great hairy fist" (3), and, instead of closing the door with his hands, he uses "his huge foot" (3). When he talks to Bartley Hubbard, he puts "his huge foot close to Bartley's thigh" (14). Lapham's body is prominently on display in the opening scene, and in the succeeding chapters we continue to hear about his "hairy paws" (84), his "ponderous fore-arms" (202), and his "large fists hang[ing] down . . . like canvased hams" (188).

In short, Lapham comes with a body, a body grossly physical and grossly animal, and that is the sum and measure of who he is. Such a body, not surprisingly, is often linked with his failures to "rise"—failures first literal and then not so literal. When Bartley Hubbard shows up at the office, for instance, Lapham "did not rise from the desk at which he was writing, but he gave Bartley his left hand for welcome, and he rolled his large head in the direction of a vacant chair" (3). Similarly, when he needs to close the door, he does not rise, but "put[s] out his huge foot" to push it shut (4). So far, Lapham's failure to rise is literally just that: he does not get up from his chair, his body stays put. Things become more worrisome, however, when this bodily inertia becomes metaphorical: Lapham's head, we are told, rests on "a short neck, which does not trouble itself to rise far" (4). Some tyranny of physique seems to be keeping him down, and perhaps it is only to be expected that he should have failed to rise on another occasion as well, when it would have behooved his moral character to do so. Years ago, when he had to decide whether to keep Rogers on or to force him out, Lapham found that he could not "choose the ideal, the unselfish part in such an exigency," he "could not rise to it" (50). This is a fatal mistake, of course, although with a body like his, it is all but a foregone conclusion.

But Lapham does eventually rise and indeed is destined to do so, as the title promises. Between the unrisen Lapham at the beginning of the book and the risen Lapham at the end, some momentous change has taken place. Or perhaps we should say momentous *ex*change, for Lapham is able to rise only insofar as he is destined to fall in equal measure, only insofar as his fictive career narrativizes a principle of economy into an edifying trajectory. What he possesses at the end is no longer the bodily vitality he once flaunted, but rather "a sort of pensive dignity that . . . sometimes comes to such natures after long sickness, when the animal strength has been taxed and lowered" (349). In short, a gain and a loss seem to have occurred somewhere, "taxing" Lapham's animal strength to raise his moral capital. Suffering ennobles then precisely because, by virtue of the loss that it entails, it is able to bring about a new ratio in one's composition of character, a new balance of attributes, and a gain commensurate with the loss.

Here, then, is Howells's attempt at a compensatory equilibrium, one that puts the realist novel directly in the company of Herbert Spencer and directly in the company of nineteenth-century humanitarianism and tort law. Like these advocates of a functionalist ethics, the novel too tries to imagine a morality within bounds: a morality commensurate with economic reason, a morality premised on internal regulation and internal adequacy. Such a morality is, of course, the sine qua non of a twentieth-century theorist such as Richard Posner. In *The Rise of Silas Lapham*, it is the Reverend Sewell who is its chief advocate and who, in proposing an "economy of pain," would seem to be gesturing toward just such a rationalized universe, in which every misfortune carries its organic benefit and every suffering its organic anodyne.

And yet—such is the radius of pertinence in the novel, and such its messy complications—it is not Lapham, after all, who would furnish the human illustration to this economy, nor is he even the occasion for its pronouncement. Sewell, in his recommendation, actually has in mind an entirely different problem: not the economy of a pain that compensates for itself, but the economy of a pain that must be rationed out, a pain that, because it must fall on some particular person, must turn every act of distribution into a crisis of allocation. What Sewell is doing, after all, is to try to single out one recipient of pain, when there are three equally eligible candidates: Tom, Penelope, and Irene. It is this sense of economy—economy as differential distribution rather than adequate compensation—that would emerge as the obsessive concern not only of *The Rise of Silas Lapham* but of the realist novel as a genre. Since there is no possibility (and indeed no pretense) that this distribution would ever be fully self-justifying, fully equitable to all concerned, "satisfaction" as a novelistic category is not so much realized as it is ironized, not so much affirmed as renounced. And to the extent that there remains a residue—a character uncompensated, an injury unaccounted for—the novel would seem to have smuggled, into the very heart of its crisis of allocation, something like a generic question mark, a generic ground for disagreement. For all its deference toward a rational order that settles everything and amends everything, the novel's narrative medium is not quite a neutralizing agency, not quite an all-purpose solvent. And so, even though the Reverend Sewell is emphatic about the "economy of pain," even though he is emphatic that "one suffer instead of three," the novel nonetheless finds itself perversely asking a question that it is not supposed to ask, namely, "Why this particular one?"

INCOMPLETE RATIONALIZATION

In its less than convincing answer to that question, its less than convincing attempts to justify its distributive effects, the novel is less of an "economy" than we may think, less fortified by that long tradition of presumptive and indeed prescriptive commensurability. To honor the novel in its dissent from that tradition, to honor the persistent sense of injury that it manages to keep alive, we need a theory, I think, about its structures of failed resolution, about the range of satisfactions it refuses to claim, let alone to grant. We need a theory, that is, about the "incomplete rationalization" of the novel, about the narrative form itself as an imperfect form of closure, an imperfect form of justification. Along those lines the novel would appear to be less summarizable by any single line of reasoning and less exhausted by any single adducible logic. By the same token, its distributive relations too might turn out to fall only partially within the domain of rational explanation, which is to say, they might turn out simply to obtain, but might not necessarily be justified as such, and might not even claim justification as a premise.

Some such distributive relation, in any case, is what Tom Corey notices as *The Rise of Silas Lapham* draws to a close. And, whether justified or not, it certainly gives him hope, as he watches the synchronized gain and loss being meted out to himself and to the man who, he hopes, will one day be his father-in-law. "Lapham's potential ruin," for Tom, is nothing short of a windfall, because this is a case where "another's disaster would befriend him, and give him the opportunity to prove the unselfishness of his constancy" (272). This is not just wishful thinking either. It actually comes to pass: Lapham's trouble does indeed "befriend" Tom, and his marriage to Penelope does indeed take place, to the tune of his father-in-law's financial downfall. In some mysterious fashion, the two events seem to have compensated for each other in a kind of cosmic trade-off, a cosmic exchange of fortunes. Here then, once again, are the familiar motions of a compensatory equilibrium. And yet the terms of the equilibrium are such as to provoke questions in turn. In what sense, and by what calculus, is the marital bliss of Tom and Penelope a fit compensation for Lapham's financial disaster (not to mention the elder Coreys's afflicted sensibility)? What rate of exchange—to put the question most crudely—measures these occurrences and certifies their commensurability?

That such questions can be asked, that some of them can even be answered, is a tribute to the economized ethics of the novel, its dream of a rational order resolvable into matching terms. This is its hoped-for foundation, its hoped-for justificatory ground, from which it derives a sequence, a circumference, a principle of economy doubling as a principle of narration. And yet the shakiness of such a foundation—its lapses not only in coverage but also in guarantee—suggests that the novel is, after all, both more complex and more vulnerable than the concept of an "economy" would make of it. There can be no full adequation here. Instead, what the novel registers, over and over again, is something like the traces of an insoluble residue: a residue offered up to us, unhappily but also quite unsparingly, as the limits of commensurability and the limits of any justice founded upon its image.

In *The Rise of Silas Lapham*, the limits of justice begin with a troubling mismatch, a troubling lack of commensurability, among the characters. Unexplained but also quite unmistakable, it manifests itself not only in a disparity of intelligence but also in a nonreciprocity of affections. This creates a headache for all concerned, and none is more aware of it than Mrs. Lapham. "She isn't really equal to him" (109), she announces with palpable misgivings, when she first toys with the idea of a romance between Tom and Irene. Many pages later, when that romance has become no more than a monstrous illusion, this is the theme she comes back to: "But she never was equal to him. I saw that from the start" (226). Against that brute fact of inequality, Penelope's marriage to Tom, an equal match in all respects, would seem to stand both in contrast and in remedy. But if so, that remedial equality turns out to be a kind of differential effect, generated out of inequalities and rendered intelligible only by that contrary phenomenon. It is this mind-boggling logic—and the mind-boggling "justice" predicated on its terms—that Howells would wrestle with, not only in *The Rise of Silas Lapham* but also in an essay entitled "Equality as the Basis of Good Society" (1895), published ten years later.

"Humanity is always seeking equality," Howells writes. "The patrician wishes to be with his equals because his inferiors make him uneasy; the plebeian wishes to be with his equals because his superiors make him unhappy. This fact accounts for inequality itself, for classes." The desire for equality turns out, in short, to be the basis for inequality. This is certainly a discouraging prospect, although (if it is any consolation) the inverse turns out to be true as well. Equality, as it happens, can also be born out of a desire for its antithesis. "People often wish to get into good society because they hope to be the superiors of those who remain out of it; but when they are once in it, the ideal of their behavior is equality." This is so because "if you are asked to a house, the theory is that you are the equal of every person you meet there, and if you behave otherwise, you are vulgar." Such behavior can be kept up "only on a very partial and restricted scale, and of course the result is an effect of equality, and not equality itself, or equality merely for the moment." Still, this is better than nothing, and Howells offers the dubious advice that "good society," "though it is the stronghold of the prejudices which foster inequality, yet it is the very home of equality."[115]

In its self-confounding logic, "Equality as the Basis of Good Society" stands as a kind of remote coda to *The Rise of Silas Lapham*. In the dubiousness of its advice (not to say the dubiousness of its consolation), it also echoes the novel's curious reluctance to claim for itself anything like full satisfaction. "The marriage came after so much sorrow and trouble," Howells tells us, "and the fact was received with so much misgiving for the past and future, that it brought Lapham none of the triumph" (358–359). As for the Coreys, "the differences remained uneffaced, if not uneffaceable, between [them] and Tom Corey's wife" (359). "That was the end of their son and brother for them; they felt that"; and, with so much "blank misgiving," such a "recurring sense of disappointment," all Mrs. Corey could do was to "say bravely that she was sure they all got on very pleasantly as it was, and that she was perfectly satisfied if Tom was" (360–361).

By the force of convention, the marriage between Penelope and Tom counts as a happy ending; and yet what Howells chooses to dwell on is the manifest *un*happiness it occasions, to which the supposedly happy ending attaches itself almost as an afterthought. The intrusive shades of disappointment certainly seem striking in *The Rise of Silas Lapham*. But the same might also be said of numerous other nineteenth-century novels as well. To cite only the most obvious examples, the best-known (and most-lamented) marriages in the novels of George Eliot—between Dinah Morris and Adam Bede, between Dorothea Brooke and Will Ladislaw, between Daniel Deronda and Mirah Lapidoth—are "happy endings" only in name; in every other respect they bring a disconcerting inflection to that label. Within this context, the famous last line of *The Bostonians* (1886) might serve as an epigraph for the entire genre. When Verena goes off with Basil Ransom, she is discovered, James tells us, to be "in tears." And he goes on, "It is to be feared that with the union, so far from brilliant, into which she was about to enter, these were not the last she was destined to shed."[116]

Howells does not say that about Penelope, of course, and we have every hope that she will fare better than Verena Tarrant. Still, even in *The Rise of Silas Lapham*, a book that otherwise has little in common with *The Bostonians*, the happily married heroine is not allowed to go off without shedding some tears of her own.[117] When Penelope finally departs with Tom, she too is seen "cry[ing] on his shoulder" (361). That activity is perhaps more appropriate to Verena, but it is not entirely out of place even here, for Penelope's marriage too carries with it something like a generic signature of the novel, a generic

sense of the unappeased. The ending, then, is not so much a full resolution as a problematization of that very concept. Inadequate to all
that has gone on before and inadequate, above all, to the phenomenon of pain which the novel foregrounds as its subject, the ending
marks not the passing of its crisis of allocation, but the rewriting of
that crisis into a generic condition for residue.

It is Irene, of course, who stands out, as the most unyielding and
most inconvenient of residues, in the crisis of allocation which ani-
mates and confounds *The Rise of Silas Lapham*. Significantly, Howells
does not choose to supply Irene with a suitor, a figure of commensurability, someone who would have rectified her mismatch with
Tom, even though there are certainly available candidates, including
her cousin Will and the young West Virginian who has taken over her
father's business. Irene is uncompensated in her marital fortunes,
and she is uncompensated, as well, in her moral bookkeeping. For
even though she is indeed educated by her suffering—"toughened
and hardened" by it, as a host of nineteenth-century scientists and
philanthropists would have predicted—it is not at all clear that her
account is truly balanced, that her pain is truly its own reward. If
anything, the emphasis here is on the discrepancy between suffering
and edification, between the injury sustained and the recompense
received. Irene has "necessarily lost much," Howells writes. "Perhaps what she had lost was not worth keeping; but at any rate she
had lost it" (347). At the end of the book, we see her treating "both
Corey and Penelope with the justice which their innocence of voluntary offense deserved. It was a difficult part, and she kept away from
them as much as she could" (347).

The transformation of sister and lover into recipients of "justice"—
recipients of some generalized "desert"—marks the logical outcome
as well as the logical limit of an economized ethics, an ethics respect-
fully invoked in *The Rise of Silas Lapham* but, I would argue, also re-
spectfully contested, if not quite rejected out of hand. For Irene as for
Howells, justice is defensible (and indeed practicable) only when it is
recognized for what it is, which is to say, an attempt to map our reason onto the world, an attempt which in the end can be no more than
that, an attempt. Irene is just to Tom and Penelope; she cannot stay far
enough away from them. In the necessary proximity—and necessary
dissonance—of those two attitudes, we see the shadows haunting the
cognitive domain of the novel, a domain that, while informed by the

dream of a commensurate order, is nonetheless not fully integrated into it. In all those moments (and they are numerous) when things refuse to tally, when injuries go uncompensated, when resolutions fall short, the novel offers itself as the most eloquent of failures: a failure in the economics of justice.

5

Rights and Reason

"A strident language of rights," Mary Ann Glendon argues, has come to dominate—and to impoverish—our current political discourse. This language of rights, a legal language first and last and itself impervious to the more nuanced languages circulating in other cultural domains, has nonetheless "seeped" into all spheres of life, saturating their expressive channels and blocking out their "nonlegal tributaries." In so doing, it has hardened into a distinctive "dialect," an American dialect, notable for "its starkness and simplicity, its prodigality in bestowing the rights label, its legalistic character, its exaggerated absoluteness, its hyperindividualism, its insularity, and its silence with respect to personal, civic, and collective responsibilities."[1]

This statement, prefacing Glendon's recent (and much-discussed) book, *Rights Talk* (1991), serves as a lucid summary for the "critique of rights" that, since the late 1970s, has been gathering force from three directions: from Critical Legal Studies in law,[2] from exponents of "classical republicanism" in history,[3] and from communitarian philosophers in political theory.[4] All three see themselves as challengers to liberalism, challenging its procedural neutrality, its historical primacy, its moral ontology. And, though coming from different intellectual traditions and often gesturing toward different political ends, all three share the conviction that rights are not only central to liberalism but also symptomatic of it, symptomatic of its conceptual contradiction as well as its operative predicament.

Glendon herself (a professor at the Harvard Law School and a popular spokeswoman for communitarianism) thus fashions her critique on broadly cognitive and institutional grounds: namely, that an undue emphasis on rights unduly privileges the judiciary, making public policy as well as private settlement dependent on litigation; that this centrality of jurisprudence comes at the expense of legislative and electoral processes; and that its strident legalism impedes "a grammar of cooperative living."[5] In short, what flows from the language of rights is an absolute principle of justice, one that extends to

all areas of life, and one that knows neither compromises nor conces-
sions. Describing the world (and dividing the world) always in categorical terms, always in terms of those with "right" and those with
"no right," such a language can render only a categorical verdict: an
unconditional victory for one party and an unconditional defeat for
the other. As Glendon succinctly puts it, the language of rights en-
sures that "the winner takes all and the loser has to get out of town."[6]
Such a language—inscribing an absolutism at once cognitive and consequential—clearly has implications for the shape of our public life,
for the shape of liberal society.[7]

MORAL SUBJECTIVISM: HOBBES AND LOCKE

Glendon (as noted) is not the only one to have taken on this formidable target. Still, to gauge the force of her critique, it is helpful to recall
the tremendous ethical weight that has coalesced around the concept
of rights since the seventeenth century, an ethical weight that in turn
has helped to anchor something like the moral ontology of liberal justice. The work of Ronald Dworkin is representative here. For Dworkin, any theory of justice worth its name—any theory of justice that
aspires to be a general principle—must be based on an antecedent
"deep theory" of rights. Rights are foundational to justice, Dworkin
argues: foundational, because they "are not simply the product of
deliberate legislation or explicit social custom, but are independent
grounds for judging legislation and custom."[8] Rights, in other words,
belong to a moral order at once higher and deeper than positive law,
higher and deeper than customary practice. Themselves underived
from human institutions, they define a more basic sphere of sanctity, at once predating the social order and overriding it if necessary.
Dworkin thus insists that rights are "*natural*," that they are rooted in
humanity rather than society, and that to infringe upon a right is to
infringe upon the humanness of that person: it "means treating a
man as less than a man."[9]

   This moral priority of rights—the sense that they are humanly immanent rather than socially designated—is even more striking in the
work of Joel Feinberg. Our very conception of humanity, our idea
about "what it is to be a human being," Feinberg argues, would have
been unintelligible without an antecedent concept of rights. Indeed,
according to him, "our respect for persons may simply be respect

for their rights."[10] Feinberg is speaking for himself, of course, in his strong claim, his belief in a perfect fit, a perfect coextension or correspondence between rights and humanness. His weaker claim, however—about the immanence of rights—has been an important feature of English political thought since the seventeenth century. What follows from this immanence is what we might call a sequential ordering of two domains, the moral and the political, the former being understood not only as ontologically prior but prior in such a way as to be vested exclusively in the private subject, vested in him in contradistinction to his political obligations. The claim of rights, in other words, is understood to issue from the natural man. Growing out of his humanness, and out of the morality immanent in that humanness, it puts the moral subject at the origin of any polity.

In Hobbes, this presumption about an antecedent moral domain—and its antecedent placement within the natural man—thus made it possible to think of politics as a secondary, auxiliary order, founded on contractual obligation, and founded very much as a sequel to the phenomenon of natural rights. The monarchical despotism that Hobbes championed was thus eminently amoral. Its justification must be derived, then, from a prior morality, a morality inhering in the consent of those who voluntarily agreed to its terms, those who voluntarily entered into contract. Hobbesian morality thus had its home not in the realm of politics but in the realm of private judgment, private volition. What was "moral" was what was judged moral by those who consented to it; it had meaning only for those consenting judges.

Morality, then, was not only individually vested in Hobbes, it was also individually constructed. This individual construction, in turn, gave rise to a radically subjectivized definition of the good. "Aristotle hath well defined *good* as that which all men desire," Hobbes said. "But, since different men desire and shun different things, there must need be many things that are *good* to some and *evil* to others. . . . Therefore one cannot speak of something as being *simply good*; since whatsoever is good, is good for someone or other. . . . For the nature of good and evil follows from the nature of circumstances."[11] Hobbes's syntax of morality—"whatever is good, is good for someone or other"—thus constructed the moral predicate as a conditional predicate: appended to, dependent on, and limited by a "someone" who validated it and gave it meaning. And, since it was this "someone" who was vested with the Hobbesian natural right—a right not only individually held but also individually interpreted—the claim of rights was necessarily a subjective claim, a claim constituted by the judgment of some particular person. Its primacy signaled "the incorporation of a subjectivist ethos" into political theory and "open[ed] the way for the emotivist revolution in ethics," as Ian Shapiro has persuasively argued.[12]

In Locke, this moral subjectivism became nothing less than an epistemology: a highly elaborate (and highly influential) theory about the grounds for private knowledge, the grounds for private judgment. Fashioned out of the Protestant theology of voluntarism, this subjectivist epistemology would in turn lay the groundwork for some of the most enduring features of modern liberalism.[13] What followed from it, in fact, was nothing less than the central tenets of liberalism, toleration and consent. Since Locke believed that moral knowledge was autonomously achievable by every individual, that every private judgment reflected this knowledge, he also accorded political priority to such judgment, arguing that it should always be given institutional sanction.[14] Each of us has the capacity for reflexive knowledge, Locke said, and, through it, each of us becomes the best judge of our own actions:

> We have a power to . . . examine, view, and judge, of the good or evil of what we are going to do; and when, upon due *Examination*, we have judg'd, we have done our duty, all that can, or ought to do, in pursuit of our happiness; and 'tis not a fault, but a perfection of our nature to desire, will, and act according to the last result of a fair *Examination*.[15]

Moral knowledge, for Locke, was subjectively attainable and subjectively demonstrable. It was this subjective ground for knowledge which made "liberty of conscience" not just a psychological theory, and not just a religious doctrine, but above all a political credo, the founding tenet of liberalism. "Every man is put under a necessity, by his constitution as an intelligent being, to be determined in willing by his own thought and judgment what is best for him to do," Locke said.[16] And, since each man is the best judge of his own welfare, the "consent" of each must be the sole ground for the legitimacy of any political order.

It was this epistemology—this presumption about the private

grounds for knowledge, private grounds for judgment—that lay at the heart of *A Letter Concerning Toleration* (1689). "The care of Souls cannot belong to the Civil Magistrate," Locke wrote, for "true religion consists in the inward and full perswasion of the mind," and no one should be "put under a necessity to quit the Light of their own Reason, and oppose the Dictates of their own Consciences." As for the church, Locke thought that it should be treated as no more than a secular institution, which is to say, as "a voluntary Society of Men, joining themselves together of their own accord." As such, the church should be granted the "fundamental and immutable Right of a spontaneous society," but not the right to compel any belief, not the right to coerce the conscience of any citizen, so that "all the Rights and Franchises that belong to him as a Man, or as a Denison, are inviolably to be preserved for him."[17]

A Letter Concerning Toleration was not strictly about rights, but its epistemology, its cognitive environment, was one in which the concept of rights was entirely at home.[18] Indeed, as its repeated appearance here suggests, "rights" was crucial to Locke as a kind of notational point of transit: a word which would allow him to inscribe both his key tenets, toleration and consent, and to stipulate a reciprocal relation between the two. Toleration was understood, that is, as a species of right, a right of immunity extended by the state to its citizen, while consent was understood as a right reciprocating it, a right of legitimacy extended by the citizen to the state. The concept of rights thus institutionalized the moral claim of the subjective, guaranteeing its political expression, even as it individualized the ground of consent, moralizing its operative term.

And yet, to the extent that moral judgment and political consent were not fully symmetrical—to the extent that the "Light of one's own Reason" might not shine equally brightly as a reason of state—the concept of rights was also haunted from the outset by a kind of epistemological predicament, a dangerous lack of fit between its two operating terms. Committed, on the one hand, to the moral priority of private judgment, and, on the other hand, to the political need for consensual legitimacy, the idea of "rights" would seem to be torn by a divided allegiance from its very inception. Locke himself recognized the problem, and, in his cautious endorsement of "majority rule," he would seem to be suggesting a solution of sorts, a way to circumvent that divided allegiance:

For when any number of men have, by the consent of every individual, made a community, they have thereby made that community one body, with a power to act as one body, which is only by the will and determination of the majority[,] . . . and so every one is bound by that consent to be concluded by the majority. . . . [T]he act of the majority passes for the act of the whole and, of course, determines, as having by the law of nature and reason the power of the whole.[19]

Majority rule was one way by which the subjective could be conditionally bound to the collective, one way by which the moral claim of private judgment could be honored even in its breach. And yet the very need for such a concept would also suggest that the "Light of one's own Reason" had ceased to be a foundational concept, had ceased to be the adequate ground for a political community. Indeed, at the heart of Lockean liberalism is an epistemological crisis, a wavering definition of "Reason," wavering, we might say, between two operating agencies and two operating locales: between Reason as it is individually embodied and Reason as it is collectively manifested, between Reason as it inheres in the judgment of particular individuals and Reason as it inheres in the political will of a community.

the tension between individual + collective (communal) reason.

With no guarantee of universality, no guarantee of a rational ground for agreement, moral subjectivism is thus always in danger of becoming a "mere" subjectivism, a subjectivism with no referential ground other than what is apprehended by itself. Indeed, to the extent that toleration is premised on the legitimate existence of rational *disagreement*—the legitimate noncoincidence between one's own reason and the reason of others—Lockean reason itself would seem to be infinitely divisible and infinitely relativized by those divisions, to the point where one's own reason might turn out to bear no resemblance to the reason of others. Reason, so divided and so relativized, must seem an argument against itself: an argument against its presumed transcendence, its supposed status as the ground of commensurability, its much-lauded ability to settle disputes. Seen not as an integral entity or unifier, but as something possibly fractured and possibly incomplete, reason would seem to constitute human beings not as consensual subjects, but as contending ones. And human differences, issuing from such a divided constitution, might turn out never to be reconcilable, never to fall within the domain of rational settlement. Reason, for Locke then, would seem always to be hovering on the verge of a principled concession: a concession to the limits of its adjudicative scope, a concession to the limits of its integrity, instrumentality, absoluteness.

In the three hundred years following Locke, it is the language of rights which makes this concession unnecessary and, to some extent, unthinkable. For if rights begin as a conflictual mode, it is simultaneously a mode of conflict resolution, one which operates, we might add, not only by awarding one side with an undisputed victory, but also by awarding it with an undisputed claim to reason. The universe of rights is thus a "concessionless" universe, in which conflict is understood only to be a kind of epiphenomenon, resolvable by reason— and resolvable above all by imagining reason as a discrete, absolute entity, discretely and absolutely assignable to one side, the side with "rights." If the concept of rights grew out of an epistemology of moral subjectivism, as I have tried to argue, it is also compelled by the very terms of its operation to disavow that genesis, or rather, to rewrite it and to rename it, so that the triumph of the right holder is never anything other than the triumph of sole and objective truth. And so, the adversarial language so crucial to rights turns out to be a language incapable of anything other than a categorical verdict, one that divides the adversaries into those with "reason" and those with "no reason," absolute winners and absolute losers. It is perhaps inevitable then that in the recent debate over liberalism, it is the concept of "rights" that is once again being adduced by both sides, adduced as the trumping claim, the most invincible of forensic weapons. A defender of the welfare state like John Rawls, for example, can do so by invoking rights as a "deontological" (that is, nonutilitarian) order of justification.[20] Conversely, a defender of the minimal state like Robert Nozick can invoke the same concept, only to argue that, because "individuals have rights" that are absolute, an "extensive state will violate persons' rights not to be forced to do certain things, and is unjustified."[21]

The language of rights has indeed "saturated" our public life, as Mary Ann Glendon charges, so much so that its invocation in most political debates now seems as reflexive as it is obligatory. And yet, as Alasdair MacIntyre has reminded us, the availability of such a language (let alone its preeminence) is a relatively recent phenomenon. The concept of rights, according to him, had no means of expression in Hebrew, Greek, Latin, Old English, classical and medieval Arabic, or in Japanese even as late as the mid-nineteenth century.[22] And indeed, even in a political culture increasingly defining itself through the concept of rights, there has always existed a countertradition whose exponents have tried, under various banners, to uncover the contradictions (or predicaments) of this concept.

Writing in 1640, Hobbes's infamous but not altogether undiscerning critic, Sir Robert Filmer, argued that the natural rights theory was untenable because it imagined human beings to be free, to be unencumbered and unobligated, in a way that no actual human beings could ever be. "I cannot understand," he wrote, "how this right of nature can be conceived without imagining a company of men at the very first to have been all created together without any dependency one of another, or as mushroom (*fungorum more*) they all on a sudden were sprung out of the earth without any obligation one to another."[23] Filmer was speaking, of course, from the vantage point of monarchical absolutism, but his objection to Hobbes's mushroomlike individuals would be echoed, two and a half centuries later and from quite a different place on the political spectrum, by none other than Emile Durkheim. "One can exercise a real right," Durkheim said, "only by thinking one is alone in the world, without reference to other men." Rights do "not lead wills to move toward common ends, but merely [make] things gravitate around wills in orderly fashion." For that reason, a society founded upon rights "will resemble an immense constellation where each star moves in its orbit without concern for the movements of neighboring stars."[24] Still more recently, J. G. A. Pocock, in his sponsorship of classical republicanism, has linked the concept of rights to the "law-centered paradigm" of liberal culture, an adversarial culture. In such a culture, the citizen is "defined not by his actions and virtues, but by his rights to and in things," a "negative citizenship" which can lead only to an "extra-civic" and "ego-centered" form of life.[25] Meanwhile, for Roberto Unger and others associated with Critical Legal Studies, the language of rights is chiefly responsible for the "antinomies" in "liberal psychology" as well as in "liberal political theory," antinomies not only "fatal to its hope of solving the problems of freedom and public order" but also generative of "basic and insoluble paradoxes" in its "accounts of experience."[26]

And so, the language of rights, as natural and immanent as it has now become, can appear quite otherwise to its critics. My own argument is very much inspired by these critics. Like them, I am skeptical about the foundationalist claim made on behalf of rights, skeptical about the alleged fit between rights and humanness. I am skeptical, most of all, about its epistemology, skeptical about its description of the world through an adversarial grammar that constructs its subjects not only as opponents, but as opponents bearing discretely judgeable sets of claims and having discretely judgeable relations to Reason. Such a grammar can resolve conflict only by a verdict of "total justice,"[27] only by resolving the world into a residueless language: a syntax of uncompromising and all-liquidating absolutes. Airtight and all too legible, such a syntax virtually invites its own abuse. And, at its most abused, it will lend itself to a moral subjectivism which, triumphant under its dispensation, will also rewrite its victory as objective truth, rewrite its name as the name of Reason.

Still, as troubling as that syntax is, what concerns me here is not so much its formal properties, but rather the circumstances which set it into motion: the circumstances which enlist its descriptive and adjudicative capacities and stretch those capacities, either to the point of illegibility or, as is more often the case, to the point of *super*legibility. In reconstructing those circumstances, I hope to fashion something other than a purely logical critique based solely on the internal consistency or adequacy of its object. I want to acknowledge, rather, both the historical need for the language of rights and some of the abuses it has historically authorized. To take both into account, the language of rights is most fruitfully studied, I argue, as a *historical semantics*, a language invoked always within a genealogy of conflict, an inherited web of tyrannies and injuries, and a language whose human meanings must matter as much as its logical coherence.

This is what Patricia Williams has in mind when, against the inherited tyrannies and injuries of black history, she makes a case for the continual vitality, and indeed the continual necessity, of the language of rights:

> For the historically disempowered, the conferring of rights is symbolic of all the denied aspects of their humanity: rights imply a respect that places one in the referential range of self and others, that elevates one's status from human body to social being. For blacks, then, the attainment of rights signifies the respectful behavior, the collective responsibility, properly owed by a society to one of its own.[28]

Williams's emphasis on the special relation of rights to black history forcefully reminds us that the language of rights is above all a semantic structure, sedimented into being by its many invocations, given meaning by its many contexts of use. At the same time, this semantic particularity—its construction by a particular social group, with meanings unique to that group—must remind us as well of its non-foundational character and the danger of any foundationalist claims made on its behalf. In what follows, I want to keep this double perspective alive, paying attention both to the experiential need for rights and to the possible dangers of their deployment. The language of rights, then, will appear both as an inflected structure of meaning and as a vexed negotiation with a syntactic form. It will both speak in its own voice, on its own terms, and speak in its own despite, in a theater too large to be entirely its own and in full view of the consequences—intended or not, foreseen or not—of its grammar of justice.

While this double perspective is, to some degree, my own experiment within this chapter, it is also an experiment—carried out with great aplomb, if not always with the happiest conclusion—within the nineteenth-century novel itself. For it is here that the language of rights is most often seen from both inside and out: as an inflected structure of meaning and as a vexed negotiation with a syntactic form. Here, on the one hand, the language of rights is intimately rehearsed: as a way of life, a set of felt necessities and compulsions, and a set of meanings subjectively elaborated and subjectively ascertained. But here too, on the other hand, this language is cruelly put on display: its descriptive and adjudicative properties sharply tested, tested in their operative effect and in the shape of the world they prescribe and project. Moral subjectivism is both reality and "reality" in the novel, both naturalized in its self-evidence and exhibited in quotation marks. The image of justice that emerges, then, out of this simultaneous immersion and perspective, is also an image less than perfectly rationalized, one that invites, if nothing else, a reading that supplements it, a reading that ponders its "reality" as well as the losses and residues entailed by its naturalization.

AN ADVERSARIAL LANGUAGE: *THE AWAKENING*

I want to try out some of these propositions in Kate Chopin's *The Awakening* (1899), a novel that in its complex play of personal grievance and personal indulgence, in its portrayal of moral subjectivism and delineation of its excess, would seem not only to exemplify a rights-based model of justice but also, in light of its outcome, to serve as that model's most devastating, if most cherishing, critic.[29] Published just nine years after the landmark essay by Samuel D. Warren and Louis D. Brandeis, "The Right to Privacy" (an essay arguing for the "right of the individual to be let alone"),[30] and written moreover during a period when the substantive rights of the Fourteenth Amendment had become an interpretive minefield, *The Awakening* is a salient example of what I have tried to call a "historical semantics," a textual field rich with accumulated resonances. Certainly, the language of rights is everywhere observable in the book. Indeed, in the very opening scene, we see a rather bizarre instance of its usage, a usage occasioned by a dispute between a man and two birds.

The man in question is Mr. Pontellier, who is trying to read the newspaper. He is prevented from doing so by a talking parrot and a whistling mockingbird, who are making nuisances of themselves. What follows is an account of the respective claims of the man and the birds, couched in the language of jurisprudence with the rights and privileges of each party specified and enumerated: "The parrot and the mocking bird were the property of Madame Lebrun, and they had the right to make all the noise they wished. Mr. Pontellier had the privilege of quitting their society when they ceased to be entertaining."[31]

The parrot and the mockingbird would be surprised to learn that they have a "right" to make noise, and Mr. Pontellier, on his part, would be equally surprised to learn that it is a "privilege" to escape from birds that are dinning into his ears. If the language of rights is conspicuously present here, it is also conspicuously present in quotation marks, a dubious honor that, I might add, will not be its last in this novel. Indeed, the concluding pages of *The Awakening*, like the opening scene, also bring the language of rights into a kind of dubious prominence, for this is the very language Edna Pontellier invokes the night before she drowns herself, when she tries to make sense of her life and justify her behavior.

"I'm not going to be forced into doing things," Edna tells Dr. Mandelet, her well-intentioned but largely unhelpful counselor. "I don't want to go abroad. I want to be left alone. Nobody has any right—except children, perhaps—and even then, it seems to me—or it did seem—" The sentence is left tantalizingly unfinished, for Edna, sensing the "incoherency of her thoughts, [has] stopped abruptly" (147). Perhaps, given the claim she is making, this is not a sentence she can afford to finish. Like Warren and Brandeis, Edna wants privacy, she "want[s] to be left alone." And, for her as for them, it seems natural that this desire should be expressed in terms of a fundamental entitlement, in terms of a "right" which is not to be denied her. What is striking about Edna's language of rights, however, and what makes it immediately problematic, is that in her particular syntax, the right holder turns out to be a nonsubject, a nonentity, a "nobody [who] has any right."

Seen in isolation, Edna's statement must seem more than a little puzzling, because, far from being something that "nobody" has, rights are usually thought of as something that *everybody* has. Still, the construction is not as strange as it might appear, for Edna, true to the language of rights, is operating here out of an adversarial grammar, one that, in assuming a constitutive opposition between persons, must assume as well a constitutive opposition between two kinds of rights: rights possessed by oneself and rights possessed by others. Since the latter is necessarily a threat to the former, its consignment to a "nobody" is likewise necessary, the negative attribution here being a syntactic effect (and a necessary effect) of Edna's language of rights.

And so it is not exactly a contradiction that Edna should believe "nobody has any right," while she fills her head with thoughts "concerning the eternal rights of women" (86), as her husband complains. Mr. Pontellier is exaggerating, of course, because what Edna wants is actually something more personal: not eternal rights for women but a particular right for herself, a right to be "left alone" and to "harbor thoughts and emotions" which "belonged to her and were her own, and [which] she entertained the conviction that she had a right to" (62).

Such a preoccupation with "rights" is not altogether fortuitous. For even though the novel does not elaborate on this point, living as Edna did (and as Chopin herself did), as a married woman in turn-of-the-century Louisiana, the catalog of rights denied her was indeed staggering. Not only was she denied the right to vote, but under the laws of Louisiana (based upon the Napoleonic Code) she was also denied the right to contract without her husband's consent, the right to public office, the right to legal residence, the right to institute a lawsuit, the right to equal partnership in the family's "community property," and the right to equal guardianship of her children.[32] Unlike Mr. Pontellier, whose rights are extensive and absolute, and who, moreover, has just been caught looking at his wife "as one looks at a valuable piece of personal property" (3), Edna's rights are highly limited, highly conditional. It is against that unspoken deprivation that we must see her attempt to imagine for herself one ultimate sphere of entitlement, a space rightfully her own, claimable by "nobody" else. And it is a further sign of that deprivation that she can do so only by retreating into herself, only by taking up residence inside her own "thoughts and emotions," a kind of mental property which "belonged to her and were her own" (62).

For Edna, then, the exercise of rights can come only from a particular account of herself, an account of her inviolate personhood, imagined as a sphere of exclusive possession. She is on good authority here. Warren and Brandeis, in "The Right to Privacy" (1890), had offered a theory about just such inviolate personhood, defined as exclusive possession and defined, most specifically, by invoking the language of rights. Human progress, Warren and Brandeis argued, had enlarged the ranks of existing rights, adding to their numbers an important newcomer, the "right to one's personality," the "right to be let alone." This new right bore some resemblance to traditional property rights, Warren and Brandeis said, for in it there "inheres the quality of being owned or possessed." But in order to acknowledge the unprecedented scope of this new right, it must be defined as a right that exceeded the traditional "narrow grounds of protection to property," a right whose jurisdiction must now extend to all "thoughts, emotions, and sensations." In short, the right to an "inviolate personality" must be seen as the broadest and most inclusive of property rights; it must "comprise every form of possession—intangible as well as tangible," so that its sphere of protection would be equally broad and inclusive:[33] "The right of property in its widest sense, including all possession, including all rights and privileges, and hence embracing the right to an inviolate personality, affords alone that broad basis upon which the protection which the individual demands can be rested."[34]

In defining the "right to one's personality" as a property right—a right whose protectability is vested in the exclusivity of its possession—Warren and Brandeis not only looked forward to a crucial development in twentieth-century constitutional law,[35] they also brought to the fore a long-standing presumption in the theory of rights. In the *Second Treatise*, for example, Locke had also understood the citizen's political right to be a property right, a property right so broadly defined as to afford the broadest scope for immunity:

> the supreme power cannot take from any man part of his property without his own consent; for the preservation of property being the end of government and that for which men enter into society, it necessarily supposes and requires that the people should have property. . . . Men, therefore, in society having property, they have such right to the goods which by the law of the community are theirs, that nobody has a right to take their substance or any part of it from them without their own consent.[36]

Property rights, then, were the most basic of rights. And since Locke also defined "property" to comprise things both tangible and intangible—since he had famously declared that "every man has a property in his own person; this nobody has any right to but himself"[37]—for him, property rights ended up encompassing the full spectrum of rights. This Lockean "proprietary" thinking not only imagined all rights as ownable objects, it also put a special emphasis on their exclusiveness, on their possession by "nobody but himself."[38] In the twentieth century, this line of thinking would lead Joel Feinberg to come up with a striking metaphor for the ownability (as well as utility) of rights. Rights, he says, "are especially sturdy objects to 'stand upon,' a most useful sort of moral furniture."[39]

But if rights are a kind of furniture, the possession of such furniture, even the moral variety, would seem to take some work. Furniture is not something one is born with, it is something one has to acquire. And so, even though in theory rights are supposed to be humanly immanent, native and universal to all of us, in practice they turn out to be things one has to seize from others: they have to be "claimed, demanded, affirmed, insisted upon."[40] The acquisition is strenuous, as Richard Flathman has humorously pointed out: "It is not only common but generally thought unexceptionable for [rightholders] to claim, maintain, assert, demand, and insist upon their rights. It is rarely taken amiss, indeed often applauded, if they do so forcefully, staunchly, resolutely, boldly, and even zealously."[41]

A right so forcefully, staunchly, resolutely, boldly, and zealously claimed must be felt, from the other side, as a highly unsubtle pressure. Theorists from Bentham to Hohfeld thus speak of a "correlativity" activated by the concepts of rights, the complementary genesis of a positive and a negative term, so that whenever there exists a right holder entitled to a benefit, there must also exist a complying party obligated to yield that benefit.[42] Between the one with something to claim and the one with something to surrender, there would seem to be an antagonism at once structural and inevitable.

Indeed, given the proprietary conception of rights—given its imagined status not only as something owned but as something owned in defiance of others and to the exclusion of others—it is hardly surprising that the language of rights should be an adversarial language, haunted by a Hobbesian vision, "a condition of Warre of every one against every one." "In such a condition," Hobbes said, "every one is governed by his own Reason," and "every man has a Right to every thing; even to one anothers body. And therefore, as long as this naturall Right of every man to every thing endureth, there can be no security to any man, (how strong or wise soever he be), of living out the time, which Nature alloweth men to live."[43] It is this natural "Warre of every one against every one" that led Warren and Brandeis to speak of privacy rights as more fundamental than those rights "arising from contract or from special trust," because privacy rights alone can protect us, they are *rights as against the world.*"[44] And it is the same "Warre of every one against every one" that leads political philosophers now to speak routinely not just of a right *to* something but also of a "right *against* someone."[45]

"Right against someone": the phrase hardly sounds idiomatic, but, for that reason, it is also especially telling. We don't tend to use such a phrase, but perhaps it structures our lives more than we think. In any case, I want to suggest that this is the phrase that structures *The Awakening*, when, toward the end of the novel, we are shown a vision of Edna's children—those who do have a right, a right against her—appearing "like antagonists who had overcome her; who had overpowered and sought to drag her into the soul's slavery" (151). Such antagonism is by and large imagined by Edna, but it is also logical that she should so imagine, because within the adversarial grammar which is hers—within the adversarial grammar which is the grammar of rights—"against" is neither incidental nor even circumstantial, but constitutive. The concept of rights is syntactically a combative mode. Its "most natural use," Ronald Dworkin says, arises when a "society is divided, [when] appeals to cooperation or a common goal are pointless."[46]

CONFLICT DISSOLUTION

And yet, while the concept of rights grows out of conflict, it is simultaneously a mode of conflict resolution. Rights are, after all, the primary means by which a victory is claimed, claimed as the absolute subordination of the loser to the winner. "The function of a legal right," Carl Wellman has written, is to give "legal priority to the desires and decisions of one party over those of the other."[47] What allows the concept of rights to resolve conflict, then, is an adversarial grammar that not only divides the world but also expunges it in that division, dispelling its shadows and nuances in the light of two blindingly unambiguous terms: "reason" and "unreason," "right" and "no right." Such a grammar brings together two contending parties only to demolish one of them, hollowing out its features and emptying out its contents, in order to grant full justification, full validity, to the claim of the victor. Rights flourish on an "illusion of absoluteness," Mary Ann Glendon suggests.[48] And what they render most absolute of all is the concept of justice, affirmed now in its dream of objective adequation, its dream of a world exactly equal to the verdict it sees fit to pronounce. So the particular brand of "conflict resolution" achieved by rights might more accurately be called "conflict dissolution," for the world being described, the world being instituted through their agency is a world in which the losing claim does not even amount to a claim, in which the triumph of the winner is the triumph of Reason itself, the fit between the two being perfect, leaving behind no regret and no residue.

This conflict dissolution, the reduction of every conflict into a nonconflict, the reduction of every opposing claim into a nonclaim, thus confers on the concept of rights not just a *coercive* authority but what appears to be a *moral* authority, making it "morally legitimate for one human being to determine by his choice how another should act."[49] The triumph of rights is, above all, an epistemological triumph, one that confers reality on one claim, one body of evidence and one line of reasoning, over that of its opponent. And the undoing of the losing claim, the erasure of its evidence and the dismissal of its reasoning, is perhaps the necessary basis for the authority granted the right holder, an authority which, to be seen as moral authority, must appear to issue not from the successful demolition of its opponent, but from a Reason immanent in the nature of things.

It is this conflict dissolution—the most bitterly partisan, most bitterly divisive use of it—that we are witnessing now on both sides of that most partisan, most divisive of debates, the debate over abortion: a debate conducted, predictably, in the language of rights, with each side claiming full moral authority for itself, full validity on its side, as if what is at stake is solely and exclusively the woman's right to choose, solely and exclusively the fetus's right to life. That absolute claim of reason must entail, again on both sides, an absolute attribution of unreason to the claim of one's opponents, preempting their very contestatory ground, to the point where the debate itself might begin to look like a nondebate, a debate whose verdict is nothing if not objectively self-evident. This is why, for those who are pro-life, the fetus's mother is so often a nonissue, and why, for those who are pro-choice, the fetus is so often a nonbeing. It is this preemptive dissolution of conflict which troubles Laurence Tribe, who, in spite of his staunch support for abortion, cannot nonetheless agree with the Court's decision in *Roe v. Wade* to "rank the rights of the mother categorically over those of the fetus, and to deny the humanity of the fetus."[50] And it is this preemptive dissolution of conflict which troubles Catherine MacKinnon, who has argued, emphatically and courageously, that "the abortion choice must be legally available and must be women's, *but not because the fetus is not a form of life.*"[51]

In any case, the preemptive logic of rights is such that even philosophers who are their advocates have been struck by their ability to make and unmake the world, their ability to sanction not only an adversarial map of reality but also an absolute verdict, an absolute assignment of reason, and an absolute allocation of freedom. As Joel Feinberg puts it, "If Nip has a claim-right against Tuck, Tuck is bound and Nip is free. Nip not only has a right, but he can choose whether or not to exercise it, whether to claim it, whether to register complaints upon its infringement, even whether to release Tuck from his duty, and forget the whole thing."[52] Focusing even more tellingly on this absolutism of rights, H. L. A. Hart suggests that a right is best expressed through "the figure of a bond," a bond which, significantly, is "not that of two persons bound by a chain, but of *one* person bound, the other end of the chain lying in the hands of another to use if he chooses."[53]

If only to protect herself, then, if only to free herself from the "chain" which others will use absolutely, and use absolutely to bind her, Edna must insist that "nobody has any right," that the enthralling chain lies in no other hands but her own. The propositions "Edna has a right" and "nobody has any right" operate, then, not as a contradiction, and not even as two alternative accounts of rights, but as the two faces of a single principle. What is crucial for the right holder, it seems, is not so much self-fashioning as negative attribution, the refashioning of one's adversary from a potential right holder into a nonclaimant, perhaps even a nonentity. Still, this making of a "nobody," while psychologically understandable and perhaps even pragmatically enforceable, is not so rationally justifiable. How does one explain the nonexistence of rights in others, when one does claim a right for oneself? How can one stand up for the integrity of one right rather than that of another, when their domains of entitlement overlap and neither can enjoy a discrete identity? Or, to put the question even more broadly, how can one turn the concept of rights from an *absolute* concept, whose authority rests on a premise of universal applicability, into a *relative* concept, whose claim is conditional, presumptive, and therefore disputable?

This contradiction—between a universalist premise and a particularist enforcement—is one that has haunted the concept of rights since the seventeenth century, one that, according to Roberto Unger, resulted from the synthesis of a "theology of transcendence" and an "interest group pluralism" which attended the genesis of the concept, and one that "had vitiated it from the start."[54] There are conflicting grammars at work here, conflicting grammars sedimented out of a historically divided genealogy. The Critical Legal Studies movement, not surprisingly, has seized upon this uneasy synthesis as a focal point in its critique of rights. More tradition-minded thinkers, too, have struggled to cope with the contradiction. For some of them, the notion of "*prima facie* rights" seems initially to be the answer. These are rights which are more or less provisional, which remain sovereign while left to themselves but can be overridden should a superior right intervene. Clearly, this is one way to acknowledge the possible conflict among rights, invalidating some without abandoning the concept wholesale. However, as we might imagine, such a solution is not without its hazards. Indeed, the very notion of *prima facie* rights is vexing to some theorists, who see in it more damage than benefit. For Herbert Morris, *prima facie* rights amount to a kind of epistemological lie, a denial of rights under the pretense that no rights exist. Such a lie, such a summary transformation of a right holder into a nonclaimant, must end up undermining the very moral ontology which makes rights intelligible:

> It is seriously misleading to turn all justifiable infringements into non-infringements by saying that the right is only *prima facie*, as if we have, in concluding that we should not accord a man his rights, made out a case that he had none. To use the language of *prima facie* rights misleads, for it suggests that a presumption of the existence of a right has been overcome in these cases where all that can be said is that the presumption in favor of according a man his rights has been overcome.[55]

Joel Feinberg, finding *prima facie* rights equally objectionable, has also argued against the concept, on the ground that rights "are not something that one has only at specific moments, only to lose, regain, and lose again as circumstances shift. Rights are themselves *property*, things we own, and from which we may not even temporarily be dispossessed."[56] True to his conception of rights as "moral furniture," Feinberg is mostly worried here about the sanctity of property, worried that a single instance of infraction might make all infractions justifiable. In any case, for both him and Morris, *prima facie* rights threaten the very integrity of rights, because in making rights provisional rather than absolute, situational rather than universal, they also eliminate any hope for a foundational authority, any hope for a transcendent arbiter. To make all rights *prima facie* is to recognize that their domain is a domain of overlapping entitlement rather than a domain of discrete proprietorship. It is also to recognize that commensurability is a judicial hope rather than a natural order, that two legitimate claims might fall on the same object, and that there might not be anything like full adequation in the settlement of disputes, anything like an integral Reason disclosable through adjudication. One might argue, with Martha Minow and others, that this qualified approach to rights is probably the best way to salvage the concept.[57] But, understandably, it is not an intellectual price everyone is willing to pay.

Against this background, *The Awakening* might be seen as an attempt—wonderfully audacious, but perhaps also self-mocking from the outset—not to pay that intellectual price. Indeed, this seems to me to be the very burden of its subjectivist discourse, a discourse so impervious to the claims of others that it might even be said to have resolved, however momentarily, the vexing contradiction between the moral absolutism that the concept of rights inherits and the operative relativism that it dictates. What Chopin experiments with is a strategy of conflict dissolution that, I suggest, is something like the cognitive obverse of *prima facie* rights. For if *prima facie* rights arise out of the reluctant acknowledgment on the part of political philosophers that the domain of rights is the domain of incommensurate claims—and therefore the domain of imperfect resolutions—*The Awakening* labors to dispense with that acknowledgment, to ward off its unwelcome shadow. What the novel offers, then, at its most exhilarating and most utopian, is thus an image of rights-without-conflict, an image of rights as blissfully freestanding, blissfully free from any danger of overlap and any danger of fuzzy entitlement.

It is this fantasy of discreteness which suspends that fearful preposition, the preposition "against," making Edna (if only for a brief moment) simply a *holder* of rights, a holder rather than a claimant. Imagining rights as being somehow intransitive, somehow divorced from the "chain" which usually accompanies them, the novel also imagines Edna as intransitive, as divorced from the recipients of her actions, so that those actions now seem pertinent only to herself, without consequence for others and apparently not directed against others. Because her rights by definition do not interfere with anyone else's, because "nobody has any right" whenever and wherever she does, there is no danger that her exercise of rights might infringe on the rights of anyone and no danger that her actions might hurt anyone. The positive and the negative correlatives of rights are here symmetrical only by inversion, only by virtue of what the symmetry represses. The assumption of rights empties out the possibility of infringement, so that the very substance of rights might be said to reside in the latter's absence.

What *The Awakening* asks us to imagine, then, however briefly and however abortively, is a world in which the moral agent can indeed live by "the Light of [her] own Reason" and honor "the dictates of [her] own conscience," as Locke counsels, and can do so without abuse to others, without infringing upon their rights, without violating the contours of their being. Such a fantasy does not last, for in Edna we see, with fatal clarity, the danger that the "Light of one's own Reason" can run into, its inadequacy as the ground of commensurability with others and indeed its inadequacy as the ground of continuity within itself. Since Edna's reason is indistinguishable from whim, a self such as hers

> can have no rational history in its transitions from one state of moral commitment to another. Inner conflicts are for it necessarily . . . the confrontation of one contingent arbitrariness by another. It is a self with no given continuities, save those of the body which is its bearer and of the memory which to the best of its ability gathers in its past.[58]

I take this passage from Alasdair MacIntyre, from his account of the "emotivist self," not only because it uncannily describes the corporeal and mnemonic life that makes up Edna Pontellier but also because, in highlighting the frailty of that self as the seat of reason, it dramatizes what I take to be the central problem of moral subjectivism: namely, the contradiction between *one's own* reason and a reason not so heavily personalized, the contradiction between a reason possessed by oneself and a reason shareable with others. Taking Edna as a not so remote descendent of the Lockean moral subject, I want to explore not her comfortable sojourn in "bureaucratic individualism" (MacIntyre's emphasis), but her disturbing placement in any theory of justice, both in the larger political sense of what constitutes a legitimate ground for entitlement and in the narrower legal sense of what constitutes a legitimate basis for adjudication. In a world where private judgment is morally prior, how might that judgment be itself adjudged? To what extent can such judgments be taken as the ontological ground for rights, the ontological ground for claims against others? Can a foundation for justice ever be derived from the light of one's own Reason? What epistemology can suffice as the epistemology for a human community?

Living by the light of her own reason, Edna decides one Tuesday, her weekly reception day, not to stay at home to receive callers. Living by the light of her own reason, she decides not to entertain the wives and daughters of her husband's business associates, not to put herself among the human furniture assembled for that purpose: "a light-colored mulatto boy, in dress coat and bearing a diminutive silver tray for the reception of cards," and a "maid, in white fluted cap, offer[ing] the callers liqueur, coffee, or chocolate, as they might desire" (66). There is something exhilarating about Edna's decision, but there is also something troubling about her rationale. "I simply felt like going out, and I went out" (66), she tells her husband. Edna does not meet her husband in confrontation, but neither does she meet him in apology. Indeed, it is her ability to sidestep both—her ability to sidestep any possibility of conflict by sidestepping any acknowledgment of conflict—that marks her new beginning as a discrete holder of rights, someone whose actions have reference only to herself. It is not entirely fortuitous that a few chapters later Edna should be found reading Emerson, reading him until "she grew sleepy" (96), for it is Emerson, of course, who has prescribed, in "Self-Reliance," just such a course of action as Edna would eventually adopt: "I shun father and mother and wife and brother when my genius calls me. I would write on the lintels of the door-post, *Whim.* I hope it is somewhat better than whim at last, but we cannot spend the day in explanation. Expect me not to show cause why I seek or why I exclude company."[59]

Emerson is the most immediate authority for Edna, but a more general authority might be said to be the entire liberal tradition itself, a tradition of moral subjectivism, as I have tried to argue. If *The Awakening* is any indication, that tradition, so strikingly exemplified here, would also seem to be caught in a profound sense of crisis, a profound unease about its relation to anything that might be called a commensurate (or at least communicable) Reason, a reason not uniquely one's own but intelligible to others. Chopin, from that perspective, must be seen not only as an heir to Emerson but as a deeply troubled one. For Emerson had used the word "whim" with confidence, confident that "it is somewhat better than whim," confident, as he also said in "Self-Reliance," that "to believe your own thought, to believe that what is true for you in your private heart is true for all men."[60] That confidence is starkly absent in Chopin. Indeed, Edna's whim is just that and no better than that: whim. It speaks only of her impulse, her caprice, her desire to be unencumbered, but opens outward to no broader frame of reference. The light of one's own reason has become what "I simply felt like." And so, what is true for Edna in her private heart is not and cannot be true for anyone else. It is certainly not true for her husband, who, bewildered by her new conduct, can think of no reason for it except possibly that her mind has gone momentarily astray. "I don't know what ails her," he complains when he goes so far as to consult Dr. Mandelet, the family doctor. "She doesn't act well. She's odd, she's not like herself. I can't make her out" (86).

Nor does Edna want to be "made out" by anyone. Her thoughts and actions are indeed private to her now, but private in a way that would have horrified not only Emerson but Warren and Brandeis as well. For her privacy here is not at all a designated sphere of immunity, not at all the legal recognition of a protected right, but an ontological condition inhering in the very fact of her being, making her oblique to others, unintelligible to others, the light of her reason offering no illumination to theirs. If moral subjectivism ever since the seventeenth century has been in danger of disintegrating into a "mere" subjectivism, in Edna we see that danger materialized with a vengeance. What is dramatized in *The Awakening*, then, what erupts not in spite of but because of its dissolution of conflict, is something like an epistemological crisis, in which the voice of subjectivism is allowed to speak both on behalf of its heroine and in testimony against her, its language of rights being intoned both as a felt necessity and as a relational hazard, both as an ontological given and, in the end, as an ontological nightmare.

EVIDENTIARY GRAMMARS

I want to link this epistemological crisis, this unhappy career of the "Light of one's own Reason," to what I take to be a more widespread problem of subjectivity at the turn of the century. What one "felt like," I have tried to argue, had since the seventeenth century been part of a larger moral and political argument, and so was never strictly a private phenomenon, never strictly private in its ramifications, in the institutional edicts it permitted and sustained. In nineteenth-century America, the primacy of the subjective was especially important in institutional terms, important in a broad range of evidentiary and adjudicative contexts. Indeed, as Morton Horwitz has argued, the entire legal history of the nineteenth century might be said to revolve around this fateful concept. As Horwitz describes it, the rise of modern contract law marked a movement away from an eighteenth-century "doctrine of consideration" (which imposed public regulation on the terms of transaction) to a nineteenth-century "will theory of contract" (which regarded the voluntary agreement, the proverbial "meeting of minds," of the transacting parties as proof of fairness). Evidence was progressively localized and personalized in the nineteenth century, we might say,[61] and by mid-century, Horwitz argues, the transformation was more or less complete: a doctrine of regulated exchange had been replaced by a "subjective theory of contract."[62]

From this perspective, the primacy of the subjective in *The Awakening* is neither accidental nor idiosyncratic, but long heralded, amply instantiated, and indeed utterly predictable. What is not so predictable, however—at least within Horwitz's model—is the extent to which subjectivity is invoked here not in preparation for its famed "meeting" with another subjectivity, in their mutual entry into contract, but to make such a meeting impossible in the first place. After all, when Edna says, "I simply felt like going out," she is not proposing to meet anyone—not her many callers and emphatically not her husband; not on any earthly terrain and not in any mental space. Contract, its structure of agreement and structure of validation, would seem then only to be part of the legal edifice which subjectivity is called upon to uphold. Another part of the edifice, which it upholds with equal facility, is something like the obverse of contract, something like the *non*meeting of minds.

Indeed, what Horwitz seems to have overlooked is the extent to which subjectivity is a reversible category: the extent to which it lends itself both to the honoring of certain claims and to the discounting of others. For subjectivity carries both a positive and a negative evidentiary weight: it comes alternatively stamped with a seal of authority and a badge of disrepute. Authoritatively, it emanates from "the Light of one's own Reason," whose private judgment is ratified, sanctified, legitimated. Disreputably, however, it can turn that reason into its own ground of refutation. Like the concept of rights, which derives from it and formalizes its juridical expression, the subjective too underwrites a structure of correlativity, the complementary genesis of a positive and a negative term, mutually defined and mutually obliterating. In short, just as rights speak to a "Warre of every one against every one" in the realm of entitlement, the subjective speaks to a "Warre of every one against every one" in the realm of evidence.

It is helpful, then, to speak of two evidentiary grammars, both centered on subjectivity, though putting it to two contrary uses. We find, on the one hand, an indicative grammar, where what one "feels like," offered as a kind of descriptive fact, constitutes the basis for asserting claims. Complementing it, on the other hand, is an attributive grammar, where subjectivity imputed to someone else, imputed as a matter of mere perception, makes the claims of that person fanciful and suspect. This evidentiary discrimination is crucial to any moral subjectivism, crucial if private reason is to have any claim to being universal reason, for the integrity of such a claim must rest on its ability to banish all contrary reasons under a provision of dismissibility. It is that provision of dismissibility that we are witnessing in *The Awakening*, in its handling of competing bodies of evidence and competing claims to reason, although what is dismissed here, being made to appear so different from what is affirmed, is perhaps not even recognizable as its counterpart.

In any case, as far as subjectivism is concerned, Edna can hardly be said to have a monopoly. She is the most dramatic example, of course, being the one who, in the course of the book, "began to do as she liked and to feel as she liked" (74). But her husband, as it turns out, is not without subjective doings and feelings of his own. He has feelings concerning his children, for example, which he exhibits late one night when he gets back from Klein's hotel:

> Mr. Pontellier returned to his wife with the information that Raoul had a high fever and needed looking after. Then he lit a cigar and went and sat near the open door to smoke it.
> Mrs. Pontellier was quite sure Raoul had no fever. He had gone to bed perfectly well, she said, and nothing had ailed him all day. Mr. Pontellier was too well acquainted with fever symptoms to be mistaken. He assured her the child was consuming at that moment in the next room.
> He reproached his wife with her inattention, her habitual neglect of the children. If it was not a mother's place to look after children, whose on earth was it? He himself had his hands full with his brokerage business. He could not be in two places at once; making a living for his family on the street, and staying at home to see that no harm befell them. He talked in a monotonous, insistent way. (7)

In a book so subtly nuanced and so evanescent in tone, this portrait of Mr. Pontellier is interesting not because it is ironic, but because the irony is so heavy-handed, so gratuitously close to the surface. In the detail about the cigar and in the blunt verdict that concludes the portrait, Chopin seems to be supplying quotation marks for an incident whose rhetorical status really needs no elucidation. She supplies those quotation marks, I argue, because Mr. Pontellier's subjectivity, presented here as a bad example—as self-indulgent, egoistical, and obviously wrong—is otherwise not so readily, or at least not categorically, distinguishable from its more privileged counterpart: his wife's subjectivity, which, for much of the book, is given a voice only intermittently ironized, only intermittently inflected with its own critique. The quotation marks are firmly in place for Mr. Pontellier, then, not to indicate a difference that preexists but to secure a difference precariously maintained.

Central to the portrayal of subjectivity in *The Awakening* is a practice of selective validation, by which contrary perceptions are sorted out, distributed into separate categories, assigned different evidentiary weight. Seen in this light, the novel offers an important supplement to the Horwitz thesis. Where Horwitz describes a categoric endorsement of the subjective in contractual processes, what we see in Chopin is instead a selective endorsement, an internal differentiation within what Horwitz takes to be a unitary term. The modification is worth noting, I think, not only because it points to a certain unevenness here between law and literature, but also because it helps to highlight a rather surprising outcome from that uneven development. For in the course of the nineteenth century, it was the more complex, more "literary," configuration of the subjective that would emerge as a broad cultural understanding, so that what one "feels like" would come to figure in more and more complex ways, bear more and more complex kinds of witness. In that process, the subjective would also be fitted out for a broader operating theater, moving from its home in contract to a newfound centrality in constitutional law and opening up new venues for the absolutization of justice.

Indeed, given the images of antagonism in *The Awakening*, it is tempting to speculate on a larger shift in the conception of the subjective before and after the Civil War: from one that presupposes a rational common ground to one that envisions the breakdown of that common ground, from one partial to commercial agreement to one mindful of civil dispute.[63] For if the subjective in antebellum America was invoked for the "meeting of minds" in contract, as Horwitz argues, the very possibility of contract would seem to rest on the possibility of such a meeting. According to the canon of commercial law, one's own reason was also the reason of one's contracting partner.

And so the harmony between these two, and between these and others, was extolled in every conceivable guise, by jurists, politicians, economists, and spiritualists. According to Eric Foner, harmony was one of the most important tenets of antebellum republican ideology.[64] The advent of the Civil War made such a presumption highly untenable. Indeed, disharmony seemed the order of the day. As Northerners and Southerners each clung to the light of their own reason, and as each of them offered that as universal Reason, subjectivity itself became the site of sectional conflict: the fault line along which the seemingly unitary fact of slavery was fractured into two mutually unrecognizable accounts.

From this perspective, the Civil War might be seen as a crisis of moral subjectivism itself: a crisis brought about by the violent foregrounding and violent juxtaposition of human reason as the source of antagonism, the source of mutually conflicting and confounding versions of reality. The crisis of subjectivity in the work of the classic authors—in Hawthorne and Melville, for example—would seem to bear a striking relation to the historical crisis which, in one sense at least, was literally a civil war, a war internal, perceptual, and evidentiary, fueled by contrasting representations of slavery and mutual accusations of falsehood. That crisis of subjectivity would reappear in *The Awakening* both as an enduring legacy and as an attempt at erasure, an attempt—as urgent as it was unsuccessful—to put to rest the epistemological anxieties that plagued the American Renaissance and, possibly, the historical conflict that inspired them. We need only compare *The Awakening* with a novel like *Pierre*, or a story like "Young Goodman Brown," to see how far Chopin has traveled. In her hands, the ambiguous evidence that permeated the fiction of the mid-nineteenth century is recomposed into a privileged center, a heroine who colors much of the book in her own hue, until the spectral appearance of infantile antagonists pushes her to her fateful decision.

Subjectivity in *The Awakening*, then, is not just a psychology but also an epistemology and, as such, an adjudicative practice as well. Here, questions of rightness, questions of entitlement, and questions of reality are all subject to an evidentiary weighing, and all subject to a consequential verdict. The legal language that figures so prominently in the opening scene is not at all decorative here; it makes up the very ground rules of the novel, its structure of affect as well as structure of representation. In this sense, *The Awakening* is very much a tribute to the primacy of jurisprudence in American life: a tribute to its adversarial language, its tendency to saturate other domains of discourse, not the least of which being the discourse of subjectivity. It is this "legalization" of the subjective—its definition and permeation by the concept of rights, its definition and sometimes demolition by the "against" which correlates rights—that transforms its seemingly inward domain into a kind of adjudicative battlefield, the scene of evidentiary accrediting and discrediting. And to the extent that this inward domain has traditionally been the domain of the novel, it is through *its* depictions that we might begin to reconstruct the circumstances and consequences of that battle of evidence. Here, in keeping with the novel's double perspective, its habitual play of distance and proximity, we might expect to find not only the experiential fact of moral subjectivism but also its deadly excess, not only the space of freedom it helps to underwrite but also the style of segregation enacted in its name.

The complex inflections activated by the novel—the nuanced perspectives it weaves and unweaves—suggest that the relation between law and literature is perhaps not strictly analyzable as a logic, a formal analogy. We need a more supple vocabulary, more fine-tuned as well as more densely analytic, in order to capture not only the broad principles of commensurability between these two domains but also a few crucial shades of difference. I want to experiment with such a model by looking at the dual career of the subjective—in law and in literature—in the late nineteenth century, a period usually known as the golden age of "laissez-faire philosophy in constitutional law"[65] and one that virtually invites a kind of analogical thinking about law and literature.

It is tempting, indeed, to collapse *The Awakening*, with its search for a personal sphere free of obligation, into the broad outlines of laissez-faire constitutionalism, with its search for an economic sphere free of regulation.[66] In what follows, I want to resist this collapsibility and to maintain an analytic space between the two, in order to study not the linear translatability of a single term, but the positional and appositional network that inflects it and gives it its particular resonance. What interests me, then, is not the category of the "subjective" seen in isolation, but rather the semantic universe revolving around it. In the late nineteenth century, the meaning of this word—and its special importance to the languages of rights—cannot be fathomed without looking at the parallel emergence of a new legal term, a term that, at first glance, might seem its antithesis. I am thinking of the term "substantive," as expounded by the doctrine of "substantive due process," a doctrine which conferred on the concept of rights a definitional solidity and which, by putting these rights under the jurisdiction of the Supreme Court, would drastically expand the role of the judiciary, ushering in the "substantive jurisprudence" of the "*Lochner* era."[67]

SUBSTANTIVE JURISPRUDENCE: *LOCHNER* TO *PLESSY*

Beginning with the *Slaughterhouse Cases* of 1873[68] and moving with increasing speed and unanimity thereafter, the Supreme Court worked out a "substantive" interpretation of the Fourteenth Amendment, which in the succeeding decades would be regularly used to challenge federal and state regulations, subjecting them to judicial review. In *Allgeyer v. Louisiana* (1897), in the now notorious *Lochner v. New York* (1905), and in a host of other cases, including *Adair v. United States* (1908), *Coppage v. Kansas* (1915), and *Adkins v. Children's Hospital* (1923), the Court struck down laws that prohibited "yellow dog" contracts and laws that established minimum wages and maximum hours. Such laws were unconstitutional, the Court explained, because they were a "palpable invasion of rights secured by the fundamental law"—especially the "rights of private property" and the "right of free contract."[69] It is this substantive jurisprudence—this insistence on substantive rights, especially the right to contract—which transformed the Fourteenth Amendment from a guarantee of civil rights into the centerpiece of laissez-faire constitutionalism.[70]

The period between 1897 and 1937,[71] known to legal historians as "the *Lochner* era," might also be called the era of the substantive, during which a particular set of rights would come to appear as solid, as self-evident, and as objective as things, as if they literally had materialized into moral furniture. Although this substantive jurisprudence might seem directly contrary to the weightlessness of moral subjectivism, we should not forget that the substantive is itself a judicial designation, itself a form of attribution, proceeding from an epistemology which, even as it names as "substantive" that which is accorded evidentiary weight, must consign to insubstantiality that which is not.

After all, when the Court struck down a New York statute setting a ten-hour daily maximum for bakers, on the ground that it violated the "right of free contract," it was discounting the bakers' demand for physical and mental well-being.[72] And when it struck down a District of Columbia law setting minimum wages for women, on the similar ground that it violated "the right to contract about one's affairs [which] is a part of the liberty of the individual," it was discounting the women workers' demand for satisfactory pay.[73]

Within the Court's epistemology—not only adjudicating but also affixing reality—the distinction between the "substantive" and the "subjective" was nothing if not self-evident. Dissenting from that epistemology, however, we might point out that the distinction here was only a kind of semantic effect, the effect, that is, of a particular evidentiary grammar, a particular form of judicial designation, which as the very basis for its verdict must assign to the winning and losing sides two discretely opposing names: solid facts versus shaky perceptions, utter validity versus utter groundlessness. Like the language of rights which is its natural language, substantive jurisprudence selectively endorses the world, selectively credits and discredits, emptying out the claim of its opponent in order to give itself full validity, conceding to its opponent no shred of evidence in order to equate itself with the sum total of Truth. In its epistemological absolutism, its impulse always to spell its name as the name of Reason, substantive jurisprudence must stand as one of the most troubling episodes in the history of moral subjectivism. It is certainly one of the most troubling episodes in the history of rights, a history marked not only by moral certitudes but equally by moral erasures.[74] With Roberto Unger, then, we might say that "substantive justice is the political equivalent of the morality of desire,"[75] the former being not so much a check to the latter as a mirror of it; for within the adversarial language of rights, the substantive is the requisite name for the triumphantly subjective, the requisite name for the claim that has won out, that has beaten its opponent into insubstantiality.

The intense subjectivism in such a novel as *The Awakening*, then, is not so much an isolated phenomenon as a cultural disposition, not so much a challenge to substantive jurisprudence as a dramatization of its epistemology. Of course, within the pages of the novel, the embodiment of subjectivism is eventually destroyed—surely a nontrivial detail when we ponder the relation between law and literature, their concurrence as well as their dissonance. In any case, it is perhaps unavoidable that the novel should share with the law a common language, the language of rights, which, in the novel no less than in the law, must make and unmake the world, crystallize and nullify reality. It is within this context that we might take stock of the "groundless" claims of a figure like Mr. Pontellier. Also within this context, we should perhaps take stock as well of another character, whose claims are still more groundless than Edna's husband's. This is the children's quadroon nurse: "a huge encumbrance, only good to button up waists and panties and to brush and part hair; since it seemed to be a law of society that hair must be parted and brushed" (10).

Here the quadroon is not so much an actual person as an abstract device, seen strictly from the standpoint of the children, the targets of that device. She is "a huge encumbrance," a fixture and a nuisance, though also grudgingly a utility of sorts, good for tidying up one's appearance. In that capacity, as the mechanism by which hair is parted and brushed, she is presented, moreover, as an agent of the "law of society." It is inconceivable that any antebellum quadroon would have been portrayed in such a light or within such a cluster of associations. The quadroon is, after all, the quintessential (as well as most glamorous) victim of slavery, and, through the popularizing efforts of authors like Lydia Maria Child, Henry Wadsworth Longfellow, and, of course, Harriet Beecher Stowe, this tragic figure has long been seen not as an agent of the "law of society" but as a human challenge to that "law."

Even in postbellum literature, especially in literature about Creole life, the quadroon remains a significant presence: at once fascinating, enigmatic, and treacherous. Lafcadio Hearn, for example, devotes one of his "Creole Sketches" to quadroon servants, who, according to him, are "absolutely heartless, without a particle of affection or real respect for an employer or his children, yet simulating love and respect so well that no possible fault can be found with them." Such servants "see everything, and hear everything, and say nothing." "They can tell a lie with the prettiest grace imaginable, or tell a truth in such a manner that it appears to be a lie." Not surprisingly, they are "dangerous enemies—and there is no denying that their enmity is to be dreaded."[76] George Washington Cable similarly dwells on two quadroon characters in his 1879 novel, *The Grandissimes*. One of these is the black Honoré Grandissime, who bears the same name as the white hero of the story, and the other one is the slave woman Palmyre, whose "concealed cunning" and "noiseless but visible strength of will" sometimes "startled the beholder like an unexpected drawing out of a jewelled sword."[77]

Clearly, what intrigues both Hearn and Cable is the opaque subjectivity of the quadroons: not so much their proven capacity for mischief as their unknown potential. At once highly developed and highly illegible, their fascination is simultaneously their threat. The quadroon in *The Awakening*, by contrast, is neither fascinating nor threatening.[78] Indeed, in being so unremarkable and so much taken for granted, she might even be said to have inaugurated an entirely new chapter in the career of this well-worn literary type. She is still advertised as a quadroon, of course, and in fact is never referred to by any other term. The repetition of the word, however, inscribes her not as a racial but as a textual phenomenon: she enters the scene routinely only as part of a compositional tableau. She is either heard as background noise (a "pursuing voice . . . lifted in mild protest and entreaty" [66]) or seen as background commotion ("little quick steps" following the children [70]). And in both cases, the spatial mapping of her person is such as to put her at once in sight but out of focus, within earshot but out of our range of attention. Like the lady in black and the pair of young lovers, who are not so much characters as a kind of human stage prop, the quadroon too seems to have no life other than what we might call a compositional life.[79] It is almost as if her center of gravity were somewhere else, as if her natural habitat were a different sort of narrative, whose ghostly lineaments here mark both its separateness and its irrelevance. Unlike Mr. Pontellier, whose subjectivity is accommodated but discredited, the quadroon's subjectivity is unaccommodated and immaterial.[80]

An uneven mapping—a deliberate play of light and shadows—makes subjectivity in *The Awakening* a highly composed phenomenon, which is to say, highly centralized, highly circumscribed, and highly differentiated. The quadroon's "off-centeredness" complements the centered subjectivity that is Edna's. She complements Mr. Pontellier as well, whose subjectivity, though admitted into the narrative, is nonetheless not accorded any evidentiary weight. The fate of these two characters bespeaks the fate of humanity itself in a world organized into substantive claims and groundless claims, a world in which each and every one, living by the light of his or her reason, must try to blot out the light of others. And so Mr. Pontellier turns out not to be the only one (and certainly not the best-known one) whose subjectivity is rendered shadowy after a due weighing of evidence. Indeed, on May 18, 1896, just three years before his fictive case in *The Awakening* was thrown out of court, so to speak, a real case was thrown out of a real court—and on the same ground, that of fallible subjectivity.

I am being coy here, so let me hasten to add that the case I have in mind is *Plessy v. Ferguson*, a case that, as we know, has to do with racial accommodation and discrimination in railroad cars. I would like to argue, however, that it also has to do with the crediting and discrediting of evidentiary authority, the making and unmaking of moral subjects, and thus the granting and withholding of the title of "reason." Not altogether accidentally, *Plessy v. Ferguson*, like *The Awakening*, also unfolded in New Orleans, a city with a prosperous black middle class as well as a long history of racial discrimination.[81] In 1860, for example, a segregated streetcar system was established in New Orleans, blacks being allowed only in cars marked with a star. After the Civil War, white supremacy was maintained by the Black Codes, the 1866 New Orleans riot, and the 1876 Battle of Liberty Place (in which Oscar Chopin, Kate's husband, took part as a member of the White League).[82] In 1890 the Louisiana legislature passed a Jim Crow railroad car bill. It was this segregation law that Homer Plessy set out to challenge when, on June 7, 1892, he took a seat in a white coach. He was arrested and bound over to the Criminal District Court for the Parish of Orleans, where Judge John H. Ferguson ruled against him. That decision was upheld by the state supreme court, and, upon appeal to the United States Supreme Court, it was similarly upheld on May 18, 1896, with a single dissenting vote from Justice John Marshall Harlan.

The *Plessy* case, long considered pivotal (and infamous) by legal historians, has recently also attracted the attention of literary critics, who see it as a dramatic example of the binary construction of race.[83] Enlarging upon these readings, I want to suggest that *Plessy* has to do, still more broadly, with the binary construction of moral subjects— labeling them as either "reasonable" or "subjective," "having rights" or "not having rights"—in one of the most extreme attempts to make the language of rights commensurate with the world, and commensurate with a putatively discrete, putatively unified canon of reason.

Indeed, it is the appeal to this canon of reason that enabled the Court majority to interpret the establishment of Jim Crow cars not as a constitutional violation of the Fourteenth Amendment but as a local "police measure," the reasonableness of which was to be decided by the state legislature and the reasonableness of which the Court was quite ready to affirm:

> So far, then, as a conflict with the Fourteenth Amendment is concerned, the case reduces itself to the question whether the statute of Louisiana is a reasonable regulation, and with respect to this there must necessarily be a large discretion on the part of the legislature. In determining the question of reasonableness it is at liberty to act with reference to the established usages, customs and traditions of the people, and with a view to the promotion of their comfort, and the preservation of the public peace and good order. Gauged by this standard, we cannot say that a law which authorizes or even requires the separation of the races is unreasonable.[84]

Such a claim of reason should alert us, if nothing else, to its constitutive abuse. It should remind us of the danger (as alive today as it was one hundred years ago) of any conception of reason that imagines its object to be integral and undivided, any conception of reason that takes self-evidence to be its predicate and "unreason" to be its partner.

In the immediate case of *Plessy*, since "reasonableness" was to be defined with reference to "established usages, customs and traditions"—and since the Court had also made it clear that no reasonable laws would "conflict with the general sentiment of the community"[85]—it was not surprising that the community in question should lose no time in making its sentiment heard. The *New Orleans Times-Democrat* summed it up: "A man that would be horrified at the idea of his wife or daughter seated by the side of a burly negro in the parlor of a hotel or at a restaurant cannot see her occupying a crowded seat in a car next to a negro without the same feeling of disgust."[86] It was this feeling of disgust that the Court deferred to. According moral authority to the private judgment of its citizens, it must also—by the very terms of its epistemology—generalize that judgment from a particular view into a universal view, generalizing it, in effect, into an objective reason, a judicial reason. Jim Crow laws were not unreasonable because the community had endowed them with the light of its own reason, a reason the Court adopted as its own.

In the semantic universe of *Plessy v. Ferguson*, "reason" turned out to be the judicial name for that "feeling of disgust" that had triumphed, a feeling that was no longer called a feeling now, no longer seen as subjective. But even as the Court sided with one feeling, giving it the dignified name of "reason" and giving it the legal right to keep segregated cars, it must turn the opposing claim into a nonclaim, a "mere" sentiment with no objective ground beneath it. Here as elsewhere, selective discrediting is the necessary complement to the granting of an absolute right, the crediting of an absolute reason, and so in *Plessy*, too, we will find not only a subjectivity that is honored but also one that is dismissed, as we can see in the penultimate paragraph of the ruling:

> We consider the underlying fallacy of the plaintiff's argument to consist in the assumption that the enforced separation of the two races stamps the colored race with a badge of inferiority. If this be so, it is not by reason of anything found in the act, but solely because the colored race chooses to put that construction upon it.[87]

In the opinion of Justice Henry Billings Brown (who wrote for the Court majority), Jim Crow cars are not really discriminatory. There is no good "reason" why one should feel discriminated against. But if one does, it is only because one chooses to put a subjective "construction" upon something that is actually quite neutral. Subjectivity, in this usage, is clearly not something one would want to confess to, but something one must try to uncover in others. Within this attributive grammar, subjectivity is not only itself stripped of any evidentiary weight, but in its newly acquired hollowness it would also become a highly serviceable, highly absorbent category, something like a cognitive black hole, by which another concept—the concept of "injury"—is further dissolved, further relieved of any substantive contents.

Injury here turns out to be a matter of one's private perception, not "anything found in the act" but existing only in the eye of the beholder. The eye of the beholder is a sphere surprisingly commodious, and indeed surprisingly accommodating, but what it accommodates it also discredits. What *Plessy v. Ferguson* upholds, then, is not just separate accommodations for blacks and whites in railroad cars, but also separate accommodations (and separate legal designations) for two versions of the subjective. In this landmark Supreme Court ruling, the crisis of subjectivity that had afflicted the nation for over half a century was finally brought to an end, finally recomposed into a more perfect union, a union of subjects no longer subjective, just plain reasonable.

For those left out of that union, those who perversely clung to their own view of things, the Court also had a handy epithet. Still, in putting the subjective to such good use, in deriving from its alleged groundlessness an entire provision for dismissibility, *Plessy v. Ferguson* might be doing no more than putting a legal mandate on what had long been established as a social practice. It is worth noting that as early as 1867, thirty years before the *Plessy* decision, New Orleans newspaper editorials were already availing themselves of the category of the subjective, which they also used as the ground for dismissal, the ground on which to squelch any protest against the city's segregated "star cars":

> Touching the question of conveyance in the city railroad cars, the negroes have no well grounded cause of complaint. A sufficient number of cars have been set apart for their accommodation, and between the star cars and the others there are no distinctions in make or general appearance. How is it then that they clamor for shadows when their substantial rights are already granted? Simply, because vindictive and avaricious adventurers have poured the leprous distilment of dissatisfaction into their ears, and they are ready to do what in their sober moments they would themselves condemn. What real difference can it make to a negro whether he rides in a car ornamented by a star, or one which is not thus ornamented?[88]

In a language worthy of *Lochner*, the *New Orleans Times* also claimed to know something about "substantial rights" and "real difference." It knew, for a fact, that there were no objective distinctions between the regular cars and the star cars and that, if anything, the latter were somewhat better ornamented. Any black protest against the star cars must be a mere "clamor[ing] for shadows": utterly preposterous and utterly groundless, something no "sober" person would ever do. If this contrary designation of substance and shadow, reason and unreason, seemed almost ritualistic, perhaps it was also a necessary ritual, necessary to an epistemology that, ceaselessly trying to solidify its own claim, must ceaselessly trump the rest of the world into groundlessness.

THE ABSOLUTIZATION OF JUSTICE

After the decision against Homer Plessy in the Criminal District Court, the *New Orleans Times-Democrat* commended Judge Ferguson, "who has completely disposed of the African claim, and shown how little there is in it." It should be clear from now on, the editorial went on to say, that the Louisiana legislature "has the undoubted right to compel negroes to occupy separate cars from the whites." As for those "silly negroes who are trying to fight this law," the sooner they "stop wasting their money in combatting so well-established a principle— the right to separate the races in cars and elsewhere—the better for them."[89]

It might come as a surprise that those who championed segregation should choose to speak in the language of rights, when one would have thought (as Plessy's attorneys did) that the only rights involved here were civil rights, the "rights secured by the 13th and 14th Amendments."[90] And yet it is finally neither illogical nor even ironic that the *Times-Democrat* should insist on its "undoubted right" to segregate blacks and whites, because the language of rights, as we have seen, is the very language by which one can achieve "undoubted" victory, the very language by which one can "completely dispose of the [opposing] claim, and show how little there is in it." What is being worked out here, then, in this unhesitant language, is something like the "absolutization" of justice, a phenomenon still very much with us in the late twentieth century, but whose features were already traceable in the nineteenth—traceable not least of all in its discourse of moral subjectivism, a discourse at home not only in the novel but also in constitutional law, and instituting, in its wake, not only the figure of a right holder but also the figure of a nonentity, someone who has "no well grounded cause of complaint."

And so, even though the *New Orleans Times-Democrat* did not forthrightly declare, as Edna Pontellier does, that "nobody has any right," the logical correlative to its "undoubted right to compel negroes to occupy separate cars" is of course a variant of her statement. I make this observation not to show that Edna is a champion of segregation, or that *The Awakening* is a "racist" book, but to suggest that within a rights-based model of justice, a model entertained, elaborated, but eventually also shattered within its pages, segregation is a possible (and indeed historically proven) outcome. Even in *The Awakening* we can still point to the quadroon as a casualty of sorts: not a casualty of racism but a casualty of the novel's subjectivist discourse, which, to the extent that it is centered on Edna, and to the extent that it coincides with her epistemology, must also be bounded by the representational limits of that epistemology, bounded by its texture, its circumference, its sense of the real. Such a discourse can put Edna at the emotional center of the novel only by marginalizing the emotions of others; it can affirm the substance of her grievance only by consigning to insubstantiality any grievance other than her own.

It is not surprising, then, that the quadroon is a shadowy figure in *The Awakening*. How can she be otherwise? This is a book, after all, where the grievance of the main character is itself shadowy, experienced only by Edna herself and not accessible to anyone else. As Chopin depicts it, "An indescribable oppression, which seemed to generate in some unfamiliar part of her consciousness, filled her whole being with a vague anguish. It was like a shadow, like a mist passing across her soul's summer day. It was strange and unfamiliar; it was a mood" (8). It is a tribute to *The Awakening* that this shadowy oppression is not dismissed out of hand, that, for all its immateriality and undemonstrability, it is nonetheless given a voice, given substance through the very agency of representation. And yet "oppression" defined through this evidentiary grammar must make any alternative ground for grievance not so much nonexistent as unintelligible, so far beyond its pale as to be unrecognizable within its terms. Concentrating on the "shadow" of Edna's unhappiness, the novel can enlist only such an evidentiary grammar, only such a representational scale, as will accentuate that shadow into substance. To address the quadroon's grievance would have meant a different grammar, a different scale, a different relation between shadow and substance. No wonder she is assigned separate accommodations.

It is the segregation of the quadroon, her off-centeredness within the story, that enables Edna to see herself, with almost no irony, as being "dragged into the soul's slavery" (151). True to her compositional utility throughout the novel, the quadroon has once again made herself available, available in this case as a metaphor, which, reflecting upon Edna's condition and substantiating it in kinship, would also give a name to her "indescribable oppression." Appropriating that name, Edna can see herself as a slave, a sister to the quadroon, indeed figuratively to be equated with her.[91] This sisterly equivalence can be asserted, however, only by draining the quadroon of her substance and turning her into an abstract category, a category of injury, which Edna can symbolically try on, symbolically claim as her own. The quadroon is doubly desubstantialized, then, rendered shadowy both by the novel's discourse of moral subjectivism and by a metaphoric structure which translates her onto a different scale, using Edna as her measure. It is this metaphoric translation which gives the quadroon her peculiar weightlessness, just as it is the weight of the metaphor which lends substance to the "shadow" of Edna's grievance. By the force of the metaphor, mistress and servant are now commensurate, although that commensurability, we now see, can be secured only at the quadroon's expense. If Edna is a slave, the quadroon can only be a nonentity.

Edna's identity is thus very much the effect of a symbolic exchange. It is this exchange, in fact, which rationalizes her world, giving her a grievance answerable to her complaint, underwriting both her feat of semantic equation and her feat of subjective adequation. Unlike many of the female characters we have encountered in the course of this book—unlike Judith in *The Deerslayer*, Deborah in *Life in the Iron Mills*, and Irene in *The Rise of Silas Lapham*, none of whom can be said to inhabit a fully matching universe—Edna, to her credit but also to her misfortune, has indeed achieved full rationalization by the end of her story. Thanks to the book's evidentiary grammar, she has found a name for her condition, matched herself with an identity which equals her sense of being. But having thus made herself equatable with a slave, Edna would seem also to be subsumed by that identity, exhausted by it, so that, again unlike the other characters we have studied, she alone lends herself to an integral verdict, a verdict that admits of no qualification, no margin of discrepancy, and thus no possibility of residue. She is a slave, no more and no less, and it is the absoluteness of that equation that now renders her life "complete," in the most chilling sense of that word, in a way that the lives of Judith, Deborah, and Irene will never be. Not altogether accidentally, then, it is at this juncture that Edna is visited with an apparition, a haunting image of those who, she thinks, are on their way to enslave her: "The children appeared before her like antagonists who had overcome her; who had overpowered and sought to drag her into the soul's slavery for the rest of her days" (151).

The children, who have been insubstantial throughout the book—

in much the same manner as the quadroon—now materialize before her. Of course, their appearance here is in one sense only a phantom appearance, a trick in the eye of the beholder. (The actual children are in Iberville, being taken care of by their grandmother.) But that apparition is in another sense a necessary apparition for Edna, a necessary corollary to her newfound identity as a slave. In a completely integrated world, as Edna's world has now become, the making of the slave must be matched by the making of her masters, and it is to fit that bill that the phantom children are now summoned forth. They are her "antagonists"; they have "overcome" and "overpowered" her. And so, what H. L. A. Hart calls "the figure of a bond" is once again at work, except that, of course, it is Edna who is now in bondage, the chain of enslavement being firmly lodged (or so she imagines) in the hands of her children.

Edna is a slave, then, nothing but a slave, just as her children are slave masters and nothing but slave masters. In that residueless description, in the numbing completeness of its all-or-nothing verdict, the epistemology of moral subjectivism has come full circle. Having metaphorically turned herself into a slave, Edna can only see herself now as absolutely powerless, absolutely tyrannized, absolutely without rights. This language, the language of absolutism, is the only language Edna speaks, and she is a slave to it in more senses than one. A slave to that language, there is nothing left for her to do but to claim for herself the only freedom legible in its terms, and to head out toward that realm which is as absolute as her enslavement is imagined to be absolute: a realm where her right to herself can indeed be undisputed, where her husband and children "need not have thought that they could possess her" (152).

If *The Awakening* begins with an ambiguous gesture toward the language of rights, it ends, in the death of Edna Pontellier, with a gesture no less ambiguous. But a rights-based model of justice is perhaps always about endings, always about a verdict that dissolves all conflict, clearing away all lingering doubt, all lingering messiness. *The Awakening*, in giving its ending that summarizing and crystallizing weight, would seem to embody the language of rights up to the last. Embodying that language, it must remain a discourse of subjectivism even as it chronicles the demise of its moral subject. And indeed that demise, unfolding in its luminous detail, its sense of ceaseless yearning and ceaseless endeavor, its sense, in short, of being anything but a suicide, is a fate reserved only for Edna. The quadroon would have been an unimaginable candidate.

Because it is so unimaginable, however, it is also helpful, for a brief moment, to entertain this unlikely candidacy. What might have prompted the quadroon to kill herself? What would have been the circumstances of her heroic (or not so heroic) decision? And what sort of response might it have elicited? These questions cannot be answered under the auspices of *The Awakening*, under its too closely guarded emotional center of gravity, its too tightly knit fabric of the world. But some indirect answer, some intimation of an answer, is perhaps suggested by another exemplary "suicide" which would also unfold in New Orleans, only one year after the publication of *The Awakening*. Unlike Edna's idyllic demise, however, this act of self-destruction brought with it no "hum of bees" or "musky odor of pinks" (153). It took place, rather, on the unidyllic Saratoga Street, in the midst of the most fanatic manhunt New Orleans had ever known.

On the night of July 23, 1900, a black man named Robert Charles got into a scuffle with the police while sitting with a friend on the doorstep of a house that belonged to a white family. When more officers were dispatched to arrest him, he killed two of them. And before he was himself shot and trampled into the ground four days later, on July 27, he would kill five more people, including two more officers, and leave eight others seriously wounded. A race riot, meanwhile, quickly spread across New Orleans.[92]

Anticipating *Native Son* by some forty years, Robert Charles might be seen as a precursor of Bigger Thomas, especially in Richard Wright's generic description of that figure: "The Bigger Thomases were the only Negroes I know of who consistently violated the Jim Crow laws of the South and got away with it, at least for a sweet brief spell . . . [before they were] made to pay a terrible price."[93] Robert Charles was, of course, more deliberate and deadlier in his plan of execution and, in that regard, also more resolutely suicidal. He was universally branded as a "demon," a "devil in embryo," and a "lawless brute, only in the form of human."[94] Amid this denunciatory fervor, however, it occurred to the *New Orleans Daily States* that some sobriety might be advisable after all. "If the wild and heroic stories of his bloody triumphs are continued," that journal warned, "some Yankee scoundrel will write his life and depict him as the negro

Coeur de Lion."[95] But the bloody triumphs of Charles were so riveting that hardly anyone (least of all the *Daily States* itself) was able to heed that warning. In an editorial called "Making of a Monster," the *New Orleans Times-Democrat* tried to put the monster into perspective and ended up conceding that it "involv[ed] one of the most remarkable psychological problems of modern times":

> It is only natural that the deepest interest should attach to the personality of Robert Charles. What manner of man was this fiend incarnate? What conditions developed him? Who were his preceptors? From what ancestral strain, if any, did he derive his ferocious hatred of the whites, his cunning, his brute courage, the apostolic zeal which he displayed in spreading the propaganda of African equality?[96]

Whatever it was, the subjectivity of Robert Charles was at least not dismissible. Still, for all its fascination, his life would not be written for many years: not by the journalists of New Orleans and not by Kate Chopin. Indeed, a subjectivity such as his is not so much repugnant as unintelligible within their language of rights, a language in which the likes of him will never find accommodation, because its evidentiary grammar, its map of shadow and substance, will give credence only to one sort of feelings, one set of claims, one image of Reason. But even though that language refuses to make room for Robert Charles, even though it refuses to grant him substance in its account of the world, his response to that erasure is, all the same, a response strictly within its terms. For his attempt to do justice, in all its violent absolutism, is perhaps no more than an exaggerated mirror image of that violent absolutism which, then as now, has cast such a large shadow over the idea of justice. This instance of commensurability, at once grotesque and grotesquely recognizable, is itself a plea for an alternate language, a language that, responsive to the many shades and meanings of reason, will perhaps bring to our awareness not only the absolute claim of rights, not only the absolute claim of justice, but also what is not resolved by these concepts.

Notes

INTRODUCTION

1. Aristophanes, *The Frogs*, in *The Complete Plays of Aristophanes*, trans. R. H. Webb, ed. Moses Hadas (New York: Bantam, 1962), 394.

2. Ibid., 412.

3. Aristotle, *Nicomachean Ethics*, trans. David Ross (New York: Oxford University Press, 1980), Book 5, 1131a27 (p. 113).

4. Ibid., 1131a6–1133b20 (pp. 112–121). Aristotle's position on commensurability is of course a matter of much dispute, a dispute sharpened, perhaps, by many inconsistencies on his part. While his arguments here would seem to suggest that he is not entirely opposed to the idea of commensurability, his statements elsewhere (for example, in *Politics* 1282b15–1283a15) would seem to suggest otherwise. Martha Nussbaum and David Wiggins have both emphasized this latter aspect of Aristotle. See Nussbaum, *The Fragility of Goodness: Luck and Ethics in Greek Tragedy and Philosophy* (New York: Cambridge University Press, 1986), esp. chapter 10, "Non-scientific Deliberation," 290–317; Wiggins, "Weakness of Will, Commensurability, and the Objects of Deliberation and Desire," in *Essays on Aristotle's Ethics*, ed. Amelie Oksenberg Rorty (Berkeley: University of California Press, 1980), 241–266.

5. *Nicomachean Ethics*, Book 5, 1129b13–1130b6 (pp. 108–109).

6. Ibid., 1130b26–1131a6 (pp. 110–111), italics in original.

7. Aristotle thus speaks of "particular" justice and "particular" injustice, which he distinguishes from justice and injustice "in the wide sense," his ethics dealing only with the former, not with the latter. See especially *Nicomachean Ethics*, 1130a6–1131a6 (pp. 109–111).

8. In that ascendancy, St. Thomas Aquinas might be said already to mark a departure from Aristotle. Pondering the question whether "justice as a general virtue [was] essentially the same as every virtue," Aquinas suggested, on the one hand, that "legal justice, if general by power, is a special virtue in essence," and, on the other hand, that "legal justice is one in essence with all virtue though notionally distinct." He concluded, "Hence the need for one sovereign moral virtue, essentially distinct from the rest of the moral virtues, which order them to the common good: this is legal justice." See "Justice," question 58, article 6 (2a2æ. 57–62) in volume XXXVII of the *Summa Theologiae*, trans. Thomas Gilby (London: Blackfriars, 1975), 37.

9. John Rawls, *A Theory of Justice* (Cambridge: Harvard University Press, 1971), 3, 12, 4, 11. I should point out that more recently, in response to his critics, Rawls has offered a much more delimited conception of justice, locat-

ing it strictly within the political sphere. As the rest of my book will make clear, this movement away from Kant (toward a conception of justice closer to Aristotle's) is one I entirely agree with. See Rawls, *Political Liberalism* (New York: Columbia University Press, 1993).

10. One notable exception is Judith Shklar, and here I can do no better than to quote her on the celebrated case of *Bardell v. Pickwick*:

> Indeed, can any court do justice to Mrs. Bardell's grievances? She was humili-ated in front of a lot of people and nothing can make Pickwick marry her. At most he can be made to pay a sum to the lawyers. Dodson and Fogg no doubt played on Mrs. Bardell's natural desire for revenge, but judicial proceedings cannot satisfy that urge fully. Had Mrs. Bardell been the heroine of a Gothic romance, she would have put a stiletto through Pickwick's heart and gone mad. And if the story had been set in Corsica, the male members of her clan would have been obliged to avenge her honor by killing Pickwick and his friends who witnessed her disgrace.

See Shklar, *The Faces of Injustice* (New Haven: Yale University Press, 1990), 11. See also her suggestive discussion of justice in *Legalism: Law, Morals, and Po-litical Trials* (Cambridge: Harvard University Press, 1986), 113–123.

11. John Stuart Mill, *Utilitarianism*, in *Essential Works of John Stuart Mill*, ed. Max Lerner (New York: Bantam, 1961), 227.

12. Ibid., 227.

13. As Aristotle says: "justice exists only between men whose mutual re-lations are governed by law" (*Nicomachean Ethics*, 1134a12–32 [p. 122]). The description of justice as the "most legal of the virtues" is from H. L. A. Hart, *The Conception of Law* (Oxford: Clarendon Press, 1961), 7.

14. Mill, *Utilitarianism*, 232.

15. Ibid., 241, 245.

16. See, for example, Isaiah Berlin, "Empirical Propositions and Hypo-thetical Statements" and "Logical Translation," both in his *Concepts and Cate-gories: Philosophical Essays*, ed. Henry Hardy (New York: Penguin, 1981), 32–55, 56–80; Bernard Williams, "Conflict of Values," in his *Moral Luck* (New York: Cambridge University Press, 1981), 71–82.

17. Michael J. Sandel, *Liberalism and the Limits of Justice* (New York: Cam-bridge University Press, 1982), quotation from 1.

18. Carol Gilligan, *In a Different Voice: Psychological Theory and Women's Development* (Cambridge: Harvard University Press, 1982), 73, 74, 160, 172. For an important extension and qualification of Gilligan, see Robin West, "Jurisprudence and Gender," *University of Chicago Law Review* 55 (1988): 1–72.

19. For an exemplary study highlighting the phenomenon of uneven-ness, see Mary Poovey, *Uneven Developments: The Ideological Work of Gender in Mid-Victorian England* (Chicago: University of Chicago Press, 1988).

20. John Burt has made this point eloquently. "We think of reason as set-tling disagreements," he writes. "But reason is itself a rich source of disagree-ment, since it raises new questions in the process of settling old ones, unsettles old answers as it puzzles out their implications, introduces new distinctions

which divide those who thought themselves to be in agreement with each other, or discovers inner unities which put previously distinct views in each other's company." See Burt, "John Rawls and the Moral Vocation of Liberalism," *Raritan* 14 (Summer 1994): 136. For an important argument about the nonsingular relation between justice and reason, see Alasdair MacIntyre, *Whose Justice? Which Rationality?* (Notre Dame: University of Notre Dame Press, 1988).

1. CRIME AND PUNISHMENT

1. Immanuel Kant, *The Philosophy of Law*, trans. W. Hastie (Edinburgh: T. and T. Clark, 1887), 196–198, italics in original text. This is the Edinburgh edition of Kant's *Metaphysische Anfangsgrunde der Rechslehre* (1796). The Hastie translation is more complete than the 1965 Ladd translation, which appeared under the title of *The Metaphysical Elements of Justice.*

2. Ibid., 197.

3. It is the transcendent end of the death penalty—an end uncontaminated by any thought of social utility—that makes Kant insist, "Even if a Civil Society resolved to dissolve itself with the consent of all its members—as might be supposed in the case of a People inhabiting an island resolving to separate and scatter themselves throughout the whole world—the last Murderer lying in the prison ought to be executed before the resolution was carried out" (*The Philosophy of Law*, 198).

4. John Rawls, for example, has stated emphatically that "to think of distributive and retributive justice as converses of one another is completely misleading." See *A Theory of Justice* (Cambridge: Harvard University Press, 1971), 315. Michael Sandel has seized upon this as a point of inconsistency in Rawls. See *Liberalism and the Limits of Justice* (New York: Cambridge University Press, 1982), 89–92.

5. Friedrich Nietzsche, *The Genealogy of Morals*, in *The Birth of Tragedy and The Genealogy of Morals*, trans. Francis Golffing (Garden City, N.Y.: Doubleday Anchor Books, 1956), 197, 202, 203, 202.

6. Ibid., 195.

7. Peter Gay, *The Enlightenment: The Science of Freedom* (New York: Norton, 1977), 437–447, quotation from 438.

8. On Beccaria's immense popularity, see Coleman Phillipson, *Three Criminal Law Reformers* (London: J. M. Dent and Sons, 1923), 83–106.

9. See, for example, Book 6, chapters 1 and 18 of *Commentaries on the Laws of England: A Facsimile of the First Edition of 1765–1769* (Chicago: University of Chicago Press, 1979). Beccaria is mentioned by name in chapter 17 (p. 237). Blackstone's own view of criminal justice clearly echoes Beccaria's: "*preventive* justice is upon every principle, of reason, of humanity, and of sound policy, preferable in all respects to *punishing* justice" (p. 237), italics in original text. Bentham's reference to Beccaria is cited in Elie Halévy, *The Growth of Philosophical Radicalism* (London: Faber and Gwyer, 1928), 21.

10. John Adams, *The Works of John Adams* (Boston: Little, Brown, 1856),

2:238, quoted in Henry Paolucci, "Translator's Introduction" to Cesare Beccaria, *On Crimes and Punishments* (Indianapolis: Bobbs-Merrill, 1963), xxi.

11. Garry Wills, *Inventing America: Jefferson's Declaration of Independence* (New York: Vintage, 1978), 152.

12. Beccaria, *On Crimes and Punishments*, 45, 65, 47–48.

13. Ibid., 47.

14. Ibid., 47.

15. Ibid., 48.

16. Kant, *The Philosophy of Law*, 202, 201.

17. Marcello Maestro, *Cesare Beccaria and the Origins of Penal Reform* (Philadelphia: Temple University Press, 1973); Leon Radzinowicz, *Ideology and Crime* (New York: Columbia University Press, 1966), 1–28.

18. David Rothman, *The Discovery of the Asylum: Social Order and Disorder in the New Republic* (Boston: Little, Brown, 1971); Michael Ignatieff, *A Just Measure of Pain: The Penitentiary in the Industrial Revolution, 1750–1850* (New York: Pantheon, 1978). See also an important critique of Foucault, Rothman, and Ignatieff, by Ignatieff himself, "State, Civil Society, and Total Institutions: A Critique of Recent Social Histories of Punishment," in *Crime and Justice: An Annual Review of Research*, ed. Michael Tonry and Norval Morris (Chicago: University of Chicago Press, 1981), 3:153–192.

19. Beccaria, *On Crimes and Punishments*, 64.

20. Ibid., 62–64.

21. This position is most influentially argued in James Willard Hurst, *Law and the Conditions of Freedom in the Nineteenth-Century United States* (Madison: University of Wisconsin Press, 1956), and Morton Horwitz, *The Transformation of American Law, 1780–1860* (Cambridge: Harvard University Press, 1977).

22. Lawrence Friedman, "Notes Toward a History of American Justice," *Buffalo Law Review* 24 (1974): 111–125, quotation from 125.

23. *Court Records of Kent County, Delaware, 1680–1705*, ed. Leon deValinger, Jr. (Washington, D.C.: American Historical Association, 1959), 234–235, 270–271, recounted in Friedman, "Notes Toward a History of American Justice," 111.

24. Lawrence H. Gipson, *Crime and Its Punishment in Provincial Pennsylvania* (Bethlehem, Pa.: Lehigh University Press, 1935), 7.

25. *The Laws and Liberties of Massachusetts, 1641–1691*, ed. John D. Cushing (Wilmington, Del.: Scholarly Resources, 1976), 1:12.

26. *The Colonial Laws of New York from the Year 1664 to the Revolution* (Albany: J. B. Lyon, 1894), 1:21. Cited in David H. Flaherty, "Law and the Enforcement of Morals in Early America," *Perspectives in American History* 5 (1971): 213.

27. Flaherty, "Law and the Enforcement of Morals," 203–253.

28. William E. Nelson, *The Americanization of the Common Law: The Impact of Legal Change on Massachusetts Society, 1760–1830* (Cambridge: Harvard University Press, 1975), 37. For a discussion of Nelson (along with Morton Horwitz and J. P. Reed) in the context of the new legal history, see Hendrik Hartog, "Distancing Oneself from the Eighteenth Century: A Commentary

on Changing Pictures of American Legal History," in *Law in the American Revolution and the Revolution in the Law*, ed. Hendrik Hartog (New York: New York University Press, 1981), 229–257.

29. For findings that support Flaherty's and Nelson's, see Michael S. Hindus, *Prison and Plantation: Crime, Justice, and Authority in Massachusetts and South Carolina, 1767–1878* (Chapel Hill: University of North Carolina Press, 1980), 48–51; George Dargo, *Law in the New Republic* (New York: Knopf, 1983), 25–27.

30. Christopher Hill, *Society and Puritanism in Pre-Revolutionary England* (New York: Penguin, 1964), 343.

31. Douglas Hay has argued, for example, that a margin of discretion in eighteenth-century English law enabled the ruling classes to demonstrate magnanimity and to exact deference from the lower orders. See his "Property, Authority, and the Criminal Law," in *Albion's Fatal Tree: Crime and Society in Eighteenth-Century England*, ed. Douglas Hay et al. (New York: Pantheon, 1975), 17–54. But see also John H. Langbein's critique of such a concept, in "*Albion's* Fatal Flaw," *Past and Present* 98 (1983): 96–120. For the uses of discretion in the late nineteenth and early twentieth centuries, see Lawrence Friedman, "History, Social Policy, and Criminal Justice," in *Social History and Social Policy*, ed. David Rothman and Stanton Wheeler (New York: Academic Press, 1981), 204–215.

32. *The Colonial Laws of Massachusetts, reprinted from the edition of 1672*, ed. William H. Whitmore (Boston: City Council, 1887), 54–55. Quoted in Flaherty, "Law and the Enforcement of Morals," 209.

33. Patrick Lord Devlin, *The Enforcement of Morals* (London: Oxford University Press, 1959), 2. This was originally delivered as the Maccabaean Lecture in Jurisprudence at the British Academy.

34. *The Wolfenden Report; Report of the Committee on Homosexual Offenses and Prostitution* (New York: Stein and Day, 1963), quoted in Devlin, *Enforcement*, 3.

35. Devlin, *Enforcement*, 3, 5.

36. H. L. A. Hart, *Law, Liberty, and Morality* (Stanford: Stanford University Press, 1963), 16–19, 28–70; for a weaker claim, see Ronald Dworkin, "Lord Devlin and the Enforcement of Morals," *Yale Law Journal* 75 (1966): 986–1005. The relation between law and morality is important not just for criminal law but also for constitutional law. See "Symposium: Law, Community, and Moral Reasoning," *California Law Review* 77 (1989): 475–594, for a discussion occasioned by *Bowers v. Hardwick*, 478 U.S. 186 (1986) (i.e., the constitutional right of privacy not extended to homosexual practices).

37. John Austin, *The Province of Jurisprudence Determined, and The Uses of the Study of Jurisprudence*, ed. H. L. A. Hart (1832; rpt. New York: Weidenfeld and Nicolson, 1954), 371. For a twentieth-century elaboration of Bentham's and Austin's position, see H. L. A. Hart, "Positivism and the Separation of Law and Morals," *Harvard Law Review* 71 (1958): 593–629; for a response to Hart, see Lon Fuller, "Positivism and Fidelity to Law—A Reply to Professor Hart," *Harvard Law Review* 71 (1958): 630–672. For a Kantian (as opposed to

utilitarian) argument for the separation of law and morals, see George P. Fletcher, "Law and Morality: A Kantian Perspective," *Columbia Law Review* 87 (1987): 533–558.

38. Oliver Wendell Holmes, "The Path of the Law," *Harvard Law Review* 10 (1897): 459, 464, 460.

39. Nelson, *Americanization of the Common Law*, 110.

40. Lawrence Friedman, *A History of American Law*, 2nd ed. (New York: Simon and Schuster, 1985), 291.

41. Holmes, "The Path of the Law," 459.

42. D. A. Miller, "The Novel and the Police," *Glyph* 8 (1981): 127–147, and *The Novel and the Police* (Berkeley: University of California Press, 1987); John Bender, *Imagining the Penitentiary* (Chicago: University of Chicago Press, 1987); Richard Brodhead, "Sparing the Rod: Discipline and Fiction in Antebellum America," *Representations*, no. 21 (1988): 67–96.

43. William Hazlitt, *Lectures on the English Comic Writers* (1819; rpt. New York: Wiley and Putnam, 1845), 138; Charles Lamb, letter to Walter Wilson, December 16, 1822, in the latter's *Memoirs of the Life and Times of Daniel Defoe* (London: Hurst, Chance, 1830), 3:428. Both quoted in Ian Watt, *The Rise of the Novel* (Berkeley: University of California Press, 1957), 34.

44. Friedman, *A History of American Law*, 291.

45. For an extended argument along those lines, see chapters 2 and 4.

46. Nancy Armstrong, *Desire and Domestic Fiction: A Political History of the Novel* (New York: Oxford University Press, 1987).

47. James Fenimore Cooper, *The Deerslayer* (1841; rpt. New York: Signet Books, 1963), 534. All subsequent citations to this edition will appear in the text.

48. See, for example, Jay Fliegelman, *Prodigals and Pilgrims: The American Revolution against Patriarchal Authority, 1750–1800* (New York: Cambridge University Press, 1982); Jan Lewis, *The Pursuit of Happiness: Family and Values in Jefferson's Virginia* (New York: Cambridge University Press, 1983), 169–187; Gordon Wood, *The Radicalness of the American Revolution* (New York: Vintage, 1991).

49. Eve Kosofsky Sedgwick, *Between Men: English Literature and Male Homosocial Desire* (New York: Columbia University Press, 1985), 11.

50. Eva Kittay, *Metaphor: Its Cognitive Force and Linguistic Structure* (New York: Oxford University Press, 1987).

51. Emile Durkheim, *The Division of Labor in Society*, trans. George Simpson (New York: Free Press, 1964), 101.

52. Ibid., 85, 88, 100.

53. For more recent discussions of the punitive and the symbolic, see Joel Feinberg, "The Expressive Function of Punishment," *The Monist* 49 (1965): 397–408; Joseph Gusfield, "Moral Passage: The Symbolic Process in Public Designation of Deviance," *Social Problems* 15 (1968): 175–188. For an interesting argument in favor of "blaming" as a mode of communal signification, see James Boyd White, "Criminal Law as a System of Meaning," in *Heracles' Bow:*

Essays on the Rhetoric and Poetry of Law (Madison: University of Wisconsin Press, 1985), 192–214.

54. Jeremy Bentham, *An Introduction to the Principles of Morals and Legislation* (1789; rpt. Oxford: Clarendon Press, 1907), 178.

55. Ibid., 171, 194, italics in original text.

56. Ibid., 194–195.

57. For the relation between Holmes and Bentham, see H. L. Pohlman, *Justice Oliver Wendell Holmes and Utilitarian Jurisprudence* (Cambridge: Harvard University Press, 1984).

58. Mark Kelman, "Interpretive Construction in the Substantive Criminal Law," *Stanford Law Review* 33 (1981): 591–673. Kelman's essay is part of a larger effort, associated with Critical Legal Studies, to deconstruct the putative neutrality of legal reasoning. His argument has implications outside the criminal law as well. See, for example, the responses to him in the "Symposium on Causation in the Law of Torts," *Chicago-Kent Law Review* 63 (1987): 397–680.

59. Stanley Fish, for example, has objected to Kelman on the grounds that "what Kelman is really complaining about is that there is a criminal law at all." But that seems to me to be precisely Kelman's point. See Fish, *Doing What Comes Naturally: Change, Rhetoric, and the Practice of Theory in Literary and Legal Studies* (Durham, N.C.: Duke University Press, 1989), 392–398. For a more sustained, if implicit, response to Kelman, see Michael S. Moore, "The Moral and Metaphysical Sources of the Criminal Law," in *Criminal Justice*, vol. 27 of *Nomos: Yearbook of the American Society for Political and Legal Philosophy*, ed. J. Roland Pennock and John W. Chapman (New York: New York University Press, 1985), 11–51.

60. E. P. Thompson, "The Crime of Anonymity," in *Albion's Fatal Tree*, 255–308, quotations from 272.

61. Jan Lewis, "The Republican Wife: Virtue and Seduction in the Early Republic," *William and Mary Quarterly*, 3rd ser., 44 (1987): 689–721, esp. 707–713.

62. Rosemarie Zagarri, "Morals, Manners, and the Republican Mother," *American Quarterly* 44 (1992): 192–216, quotation from 207.

63. John Witherspoon, "On Conjugal Affection," *Ladies Magazine* (Philadelphia), September 1792, 176, quoted in Lewis, "Republican Wife," 710 n. 79.

64. For a discussion of marriage in the context of race, see Philip Fisher, *Hard Facts* (New York: Oxford University Press, 1987), 22–86.

65. James Fenimore Cooper, *The American Democrat: Or, Hints on the Social and Civic Relations of the United States of America* (1838; rpt., New York: Knopf, 1931), 110.

66. Victor Turner, "Betwixt and Between: The Liminal Period in *Rites de Passage*," in *The Forest of Symbols* (Ithaca: Cornell University Press, 1967), 93–111, quotations from 96–97. Turner draws on Arnold van Gennep, *The Rites of Passage* (Chicago: University of Chicago Press, 1960).

67. Turner, "Betwixt and Between," 110.

68. Turner himself has suggested that, in contrast to the localized and terminal liminality of tribal society, liminality in modern societies might be universal and permanent: "What appears to have happened is that with the increasing specialization of society and culture, with progressive complexity in the social division of labor, what was in tribal society principally a set of transitional qualities . . . has become itself an institutionalized state." See *The Ritual Process: Structure and Anti-Structure* (Ithaca: Cornell University Press, 1969), 107.

69. Karen Halttunen uses the word "liminality" specifically and extensively. See her *Confidence Men and Painted Women: A Study of Middle-Class Culture of America, 1830–1870* (New Haven: Yale University Press, 1982), 1–32. See also Jean-Christophe Agnew, *Worlds Apart: The Market and the Theater in Anglo-American Thought, 1550–1750* (New York: Cambridge University Press, 1986), 195–203.

70. Gordon Wood, *The Creation of the American Republic, 1776–1787* (Chapel Hill: University of North Carolina Press, 1969), 606–607.

71. J. G. A. Pocock, *The Machiavellian Moment: Florentine Political Thought and the Atlantic Republican Tradition* (Princeton: Princeton University Press, 1975), 516.

72. Pocock, *Machiavellian Moment,* 469; Pocock, "Virtues, Rights, and Manners: A Model for Historians of Political Thought," *Political Theory* 9 (1981): 353–368, reprinted in his *Virtue, Commerce, and History* (New York: Cambridge University Press, 1985), 37–50, quotation from 42–43.

73. J. R. Pole, *The Pursuit of Equality in American History* (Berkeley: University of California Press, 1978), 13.

74. James Madison, *The Federalist Papers,* ed. Clinton Rossiter (New York: New American Library, 1961), no. 10 (79, 81).

75. Alexander Hamilton, *The Federalist Papers,* no. 6, (56, 59).

76. Ibid., 56, 59.

77. Madison to Jefferson, April 23, 1787, quoted in Wood, *Creation of the American Republic,* 413.

78. Theodore Sedgwick to Governor Bowdoin, April 8, 1787, quoted in Wood, *Creation of the American Republic,* 467.

79. Some historians take Shays's Rebellion to be the cause (or at least the pretext) of the 1787 Constitutional Convention in Philadelphia. For more qualified views, see Robert A. Feer, "Shays's Rebellion and the Constitution: A Study in Causation," *New England Quarterly* 42 (1969): 388–410; Gordon Wood, "Interests and Disinterestedness in the Making of the Constitution," in *Beyond Confederation: Origins of the Constitution and American National Identity,* ed. Richard Beeman et al. (Chapel Hill: University of North Carolina Press, 1987), 69–109.

80. For a meditation on the political institutions of republicanism now lost to us, see Hannah Arendt, *On Revolution* (New York: Viking, 1965).

81. Aside from already cited works by Wood and Pocock, see Bernard Bailyn, *The Ideological Origins of the American Revolution* (Cambridge: Harvard

University Press, 1967), and *The Origins of American Politics* (New York: Knopf, 1968). Bailyn, Wood, and Pocock all argue, implicitly or explicitly, against the "liberal tradition" posited by Louis Hartz, *The Liberal Tradition in America* (New York: Harcourt Brace Jovanovich, 1955). For summaries of the debate, see Robert Shalhope, "Toward a Republican Synthesis: The Emergence of an Understanding of Republicanism in Early American Historiography," *William and Mary Quarterly*, 3rd ser., 29 (1972): 49–80; Dorothy Ross, "The Liberal Tradition Revisited and the Republican Tradition Addressed," in *New Directions in American Intellectual History*, ed. John Higham and Paul K. Conkin (Baltimore: Johns Hopkins University Press, 1979), 116–131; Isaac Kramnick, "Republican Revisionism Revisited," *American Historical Review* 87 (1982): 629–664; Lance Banning, "Jeffersonian Ideology Revisited: Liberal and Classical Ideas in the American Republic," *William and Mary Quarterly*, 3rd ser., 43 (1986): 3–19; Joyce Appleby, *Liberalism and Republicanism in the Historical Imagination* (Cambridge: Harvard University Press, 1992). Appleby and Kramnick, I should point out, continue to argue for the centrality of liberalism in American political thought. For a debate about the contemporary usefulness of classical republicanism, see "Symposium: The Republican Civic Tradition," *Yale Law Journal* 97 (1988): 1493–1723.

82. Rawls, *A Theory of Justice*, 29.

83. See, for example, Bernard Williams, "The Idea of Equality," in *Problems of the Self* (Cambridge: Cambridge University Press, 1973), 230–249.

84. Samuel Williams, *The Natural and Civil History of Vermont* (Walpole, N.H.: Isaiah Thomas and David Carlisle, 1794), 330, quoted in Wood, *Creation*, 607.

85. Lance Banning, "Jeffersonian Ideology Revisited," 12. In this context, we must also entertain the possibility that liberalism and republicanism had *always* been a hybrid formation. See, for example, Thomas Pangle's discussion of Montesquieu's "liberal republicanism."

86. Cooper, *The American Democrat*, 41.

87. Ibid., 41.

88. For the centrality of consensus to American culture, see Sacvan Bercovitch, *The American Jeremiad* (Madison: University of Wisconsin Press, 1978), and *The Office of "The Scarlet Letter"* (Baltimore: Johns Hopkins University Press, 1991).

89. Indeed, as Michael McKeon points out, the emergence of the very category of "class" already signaled a destabilized traditional order. See his *The Origins of the English Novel, 1600–1740* (Baltimore: Johns Hopkins University Press, 1987), 162–167, 255–265.

90. Raymond Williams, *Marxism and Literature* (Oxford: Oxford University Press, 1977), 121–127.

91. Mary Douglas, *Purity and Danger* (Harmondsworth: Penguin, 1970), 137–195.

92. See especially Linda K. Kerber, *Women of the Republic: Intellect and Ideology in Revolutionary America* (Chapel Hill: University of North Carolina Press, 1980), and Mary Beth Norton, *Liberty's Daughters: The Revolutionary*

Experience of American Women, 1750–1800 (Boston: Little, Brown, 1980). Important exceptions are Cathy Davidson and Carroll Smith-Rosenberg, both of whom have written on the rhetoricity of gender in the early republic. See, for example, Davidson, *Revolution and the Word* (New York: Oxford University Press, 1986); Smith-Rosenberg, "Dis-covering the Subject of the 'Great Constitutional Discussion,' 1786–1789," *Journal of American History* 79 (1992): 841–873.

93. Hanna Fenichel Pitkin, *Fortune Is a Woman: Gender and Politics in the Thought of Niccolò Machiavelli* (Berkeley: University of California Press, 1984), 25, 144.

94. Montesquieu, *The Spirit of the Laws*, trans. Anne Cohler, Basia Miller, and Harold Stone (New York: Cambridge University Press, 1989), 104.

95. Gordon Wood and J. G. A. Pocock have done much to elevate "virtue" into the key term of Revolutionary thinking. See Wood, *Creation of the American Republic*, 65–70; Pocock, *Machiavellian Moment*, 462–552. Numerous other accounts have followed. See especially John T. Agresto, "Liberty, Virtue, and Republicanism, 1776–1787," *Review of Politics* 39 (1977): 473–504; John P. Diggins, *The Lost Soul of American Politics: Virtue, Self-Interest, and the Foundations of Liberalism* (Chicago: University of Chicago Press, 1984); James T. Kloppenberg, "The Virtues of Liberalism: Christianity, Republicanism, and Ethics in Early American Political Discourse," *Journal of American History* 74 (1987): 9–33; Lance Banning, "Some Second Thoughts on Virtue and the Course of Revolutionary Thinking," in *Conceptual Change and the Constitution*, ed. Terence Ball and J. G. A. Pocock (Lawrence: University Press of Kansas, 1988), 194–212.

96. *The Debates in the Several State Conventions*, ed. Jonathan Elliot (Washington, D.C.: Taylor and Maury, 1854), 3:536–537, quoted in Banning, "Second Thoughts on Virtue," 194.

97. Watt, *The Rise of the Novel*, 157.

98. Ruth Bloch, "The Gendered Meanings of Virtue in Revolutionary America," *Signs* 13 (1987): 37–58; Carroll Smith-Rosenberg, "Domesticating 'Virtue': Coquettes and Revolutionaries in Young America," in *Literature and the Body*, ed. Elaine Scarry (Baltimore: Johns Hopkins University Press, 1988), 160–183. This is also Ann Douglas's more general point in *The Feminization of American Culture* (New York: Avon, 1977). But see also Jan Lewis, who argues that the emphasis on chastity was already pervasive in classical republicanism ("Republican Wife," 716–721), and Nancy Cott, who sees chastity as an ideal consciously advocated by women as a means of empowerment. See her "Passionlessness: An Interpretation of Victorian Sexual Ideology, 1790–1850," *Signs* 4 (1978): 219–236.

99. For the emergence of political parties and partisan maneuverings as a feature of modern liberalism, see Lee Benson, *The Concept of Jacksonian Democracy* (Princeton: Princeton University Press, 1961); and Joel Silbey, *The Partisan Imperative: The Dynamics of American Politics Before the Civil War* (New York: Oxford University Press, 1985). For the separation of spheres, see Al-

asdair MacIntyre, *After Virtue* (Notre Dame: University of Notre Dame Press, 1981), 38–39.

100. See, for example, John P. McWilliams, *Political Justice in a Republic: James Fenimore Cooper's America* (Berkeley: University of California Press, 1972), 237–297. In *The Pioneers* Natty is put on trial for violating the civil law.

101. Prominently featured in *The Pathfinder* is Lieutenant Muir, the quartermaster, whose unseemly desire for Mabel Duncan and treacherous alliance with the French make him doubly objectionable.

102. Gordon Wood, "Conspiracy and the Paranoid Style: Causality and Deceit in the Eighteenth Century," *William and Mary Quarterly*, 3rd ser., 39 (1982): 402–441, quotations from 409, 430, 411, 409.

103. For a history of the changing status of promises (especially in relation to contractual obligations), see P. S. Atiyah, *The Rise and Fall of Freedom of Contract* (Oxford: Clarendon Press, 1979), 139–218, 652–659. For a contemporary statement, see Charles Fried, *Contract as Promise: A Theory of Contractual Obligation* (Cambridge: Harvard University Press, 1981). For one of the most eloquent defences of promise keeping, see Hannah Arendt, *The Human Condition* (Chicago: University of Chicago Press, 1958), 243–247.

104. David Hume, *A Treatise of Human Nature*, ed. Ernest C. Mossner (London: Penguin, 1984), 568, 574, 571, 568, italics in original.

105. Ibid., 530–531.

2. PART AND WHOLE

1. Michael Walzer, *The Spheres of Justice* (New York: Basic Books, 1983), 3, 5, 3.

2. Plato, *The Republic*, trans. Benjamin Jowett (New York: Vintage, 1991), Book 4 (129).

3. In recent years, a lively debate has sprung up on just this point. The most influential position to date, the Tucker-Wood thesis (proposed by Richard Tucker and Allen Wood), maintains that in Marx's critique of capitalism, injustice is *not* adduced as the ground of critique. This view has been further refined and elaborated by Richard Miller and Allen Buchanan, both of whom emphasize Marx's critique of justice. See R. C. Tucker, *The Marxian Revolutionary Idea* (New York: Norton, 1969), 37–53; Allen Wood, "The Marxian Critique of Justice," *Philosophy and Public Affairs*, 1 (1972): 244–282; Allen Buchanan, *Marx and Justice: The Radical Critique of Liberalism* (Totowa, N.J.: Rowman and Littlefield, 1982); Richard Miller, *Analyzing Marx* (Princeton: Princeton University Press, 1984).

4. Emerson, "The American Scholar," in *Selections from Ralph Waldo Emerson*, ed. Stephen E. Whicher (Boston: Houghton Mifflin, 1957), 64.

5. Henry David Thoreau, *Walden and Other Writings*, ed. Brooks Atkinson (New York: Modern Library, 1950), 41.

6. Chapters 1–3 of Adam Smith's *Wealth of Nations* (1776) bear the respective titles, "Of the Division of Labour," "Of the Principle which gives occa-

sion to the Division of Labour," and "That the Division of Labour is limited by the Extent of the Market." See *An Inquiry into the Nature and Causes of the Wealth of Nations*, ed. R. H. Campbell and A. S. Skinner (Oxford: Clarendon Press, 1976). Smith was not the first one to hit upon the concept. Sir William Petty, in *Political Arithmetic* (1690), and Bernard Mandeville, in *The Fable of the Bees* (1714), also wrote approvingly of the division of labor.

7. Smith, *Wealth of Nations*, 1:15.

8. Ralph Waldo Emerson, "Doctrine of the Hands," lecture given on December 13, 1837, at the Masonic Temple, Boston, reprinted in *Early Lectures of Ralph Waldo Emerson*, ed. Stephen E. Whicher, Robert E. Spiller, and Wallace E. Williams (Cambridge: Belknap, 1964), 2:230.

9. John Ruskin, *The Stones of Venice*, vol. 10 of *The Complete Works of John Ruskin*, ed. E. T. Cook and Alexander Wedderburn (London: George Allen, 1904), 196.

10. Karl Marx, *Capital*, trans. Samuel Moore and Edward Aveling (New York: International Publishers, 1967), 1:339, 345.

11. Ibid., 360.

12. Jakobson sees metonymy as a principle of contiguity and contrasts it with metaphor as a principle of equivalence. He associates the former with Realist narrative and the latter with Romantic poetry. See his "Linguistics and Poetics," in *The Structuralists: From Marx to Lévi-Strauss*, ed. Richard T. DeGeorge and Fernande M. DeGeorge (Garden City, N.Y.: Doubleday, 1972), 85–122. See also Roman Jakobson and Morris Halle, *Fundamentals of Language* (The Hague: Mouton, 1956).

13. Kenneth Burke, *A Grammar of Motives* (Berkeley: University of California Press, 1969), 503–511. I should point out that Burke distinguishes between metonymy and synecdoche, associating the former with reduction and the latter with relations between part and whole. However, as he readily allows, the tropes "do shade into one another," and "metonymy may be treated as a special application of synecdoche." In short, even though Burke's "metonymy" is narrower than Lakoff's, the former can nonetheless be assimilated to the latter.

14. For instance, as Lakoff points out, the subcategory *working mother* is actually defined against a silent normative category, *housewife-mother*, comprising those who presumably do not "work." For Lakoff's interesting "culturization" of metonymy, see his *Women, Fire, and Dangerous Things: What Categories Reveal about the Mind* (Chicago: University of Chicago Press, 1987), 77–90.

15. Hayden White, *Metahistory: The Historical Imagination in Nineteenth-Century Europe* (Baltimore: Johns Hopkins University Press, 1973), 281–330.

16. Charles Taylor, *Sources of the Self: The Making of the Modern Identity* (Cambridge: Harvard University Press, 1989), 159–207, quotations from 176, 177.

17. Karl Marx, *A Contribution to the Critique of Political Economy*, ed. Maurice Dodd (New York: International Publishers, 1970), 20.

18. Sandel, for example, has critiqued Rawls for assuming that "the

bounds of the subject unproblematically correspond to the bodily bounds between human beings." See Michael Sandel, *Liberalism and the Limits of Justice* (New York: Cambridge University Press, 1982), 80.

19. Aristotle, *Nicomachean Ethics*, trans. Martin Ostwald (Indianapolis: Bobbs-Merrill, 1962), 125–127.

20. Charles Taylor, *Sources of the Self*, 186–192. Actually, in his respect for the concrete particular, Aristotle is much less committed to ontic logos than Plato is, a point noted by Taylor and Martha Nussbaum, among others. So, in citing Aristotle, we are already encountering the lowest common denominator of the tradition of ontic logos.

21. Adelmannus of Brescia, *Epistle to Berengar; Sentences of Florian*, 66; Alger of Liege, *On the Sacraments*, I.17; William of Saint-Thierry, *On the Sacrament of the Altar*, 12. All quoted in Jaroslav Pelikan, *The Growth of Medieval Theology (600–1300)*, vol. 3 of *The Christian Tradition* (Chicago: University of Chicago Press, 1978), 191.

22. 1 Corinthians 10:16–17.

23. Augustine, *Exposition of the Gospel of John*, 26.15, quoted in Pelikan, *The Growth of Medieval Theology*, 191.

24. Hugh of Breteuil, *On the Body and Blood of Christ*, quoted in Pelikan, *The Growth of Medieval Theology*, 199.

25. Berengar of Tours, *On the Holy Supper*, quoted in Pelikan, *The Growth of Medieval Theology*, 192, 194.

26. Guitmond of Aversa, *On the Reality of the Body and Blood of Christ in the Eucharist*, quoted in Pelikan, *The Growth of Medieval Theology*, 197.

27. Berengar of Tours, *Fragments*, quoted in Pelikan, *The Growth of Medieval Theology*, 198.

28. Ibid., 203.

29. In the Thomistic formula, the effects of the Fall chiefly involved the disordering of the faculties and the rebellion of the senses against reason. See Barbara Kiefer Lewalski, *Protestant Poetics and the Seventeenth-Century Religious Lyric* (Princeton: Princeton University Press, 1979), 15.

30. Galileo, *Dialogue Concerning the Two Chief World Systems* (1632), quoted in Ian Hacking, *The Emergence of Probability* (Cambridge: Cambridge University Press, 1975), 26.

31. Pelikan, *The Growth of Medieval Theology*, 185, 201.

32. Kantorowicz, of course, sees this as an instance of "political theology": the transposition of a religious faith into an ideology of the state. Ernest H. Kantorowicz, *The King's Two Bodies: A Study in Medieval Political Theology* (Princeton: Princeton University Press, 1957).

33. Edmund Plowden, *Commentaries or Reports*, quoted in Kantorowicz, *The King's Two Bodies*, 9.

34. Bacon, *Post-nati*, 651, quoted in Kantorowicz, *The King's Two Bodies*, 448.

35. Frederic W. Maitland, "The Crown as Corporation" (1901), in *Collected Papers*, ed. H. A. C. Fisher (Cambridge: Cambridge University Press, 1911), 3:249.

36. See Christopher Lawrence, "The Nervous System and Society in the Scottish Enlightenment," and Steven Shapin, "Homo Phrenologicus," both in *Natural Order: Historical Studies of Scientific Culture*, ed. Barry Barnes and Steven Shapin (Beverly Hills: Sage, 1979), 19–40, 41–71; Simon Schaffer, "States of Mind: Enlightenment and Natural Philosophy," in *Languages of Psyche: Mind and Body in Enlightenment Thought*, ed. G. S. Rousseau (Berkeley: University of California Press, 1990), 233–290; John W. Yolton, *Thinking Matter: Materialism in Eighteenth-Century Britain* (Oxford: Basil Blackwell, 1984).

37. See especially the chapter on "The Evidence of the Senses: Secularization and Epistemological Crisis," in Michael McKeon, *The Origins of the English Novel, 1600–1740* (Baltimore: Johns Hopkins University Press, 1987), 65–89.

38. On this point, see Alasdair MacIntyre, *After Virtue* (Notre Dame: University of Notre Dame Press, 1981), esp. 79–108.

39. Indeed, from a certain perspective, materialism and dualism might turn out to be the same thing. For this stunning point, see Richard Rorty, *Philosophy and the Mirror of Nature* (Princeton: Princeton University Press, 1979).

40. This "Enlightenment" Marx is currently embraced by some Marxists. See especially, Sebastiano Timpanaro, *On Materialism*, trans. Lawrence Garner (London: Verso, 1980).

41. Michel Foucault, *The Order of Things: An Archaeology of the Human Sciences* (New York: Vintage, 1973), 251.

42. Karl Marx and Frederic Engels, *The Holy Family* (Moscow: Foreign Languages Publishing House, 1956), 172. This particular chapter was written by Marx.

43. Ibid., 173.

44. Karl Marx, *The Economic and Philosophic Manuscripts of 1844*, ed. Dirk J. Struik (New York: International Publishers, 1964), 180, italics in original. This "corporeal" aspect of materialism has been largely overlooked. For a notable exception, see Elaine Scarry's brilliant reading of materialism as corporealism in *The Body in Pain: The Making and Unmaking of the World* (New York: Oxford University Press, 1985), 242–277.

45. Marx and Engels, *The Holy Family*, 173, italics in original.

46. MacIntyre, *After Virtue*, x.

47. Karl Marx, *Grundrisse: Introduction to the Critique of Political Economy*, trans. Martin Nicolaus (New York: Vintage, 1973), 83.

48. Marx, *Grundrisse*, 472–473, italics in original.

49. Ibid., 474, 483, italics in original.

50. Raymond Williams, "Problems of Materialism," *New Left Review* 109 (1978): 3–17, quotation from 3–4.

51. The critique of Bruno Bauer is developed in *The Holy Family* (1844), the critique of Ludwig Feuerbach in *The German Ideology* (1845) and in "Theses on Feuerbach," where Marx observes that Feuerbach reduces all historical process to the "abstract individual," an "inward dumb generality which naturally unites the many individuals." Against this view, Marx argues that "the

essence of man is no abstraction inherent in each separate individual. In its reality it is the *ensemble* (aggregate) of social relations." See "Theses on Feuerbach," appendix to *The German Ideology*, ed. R. Pascal (New York: International Publishers, 1947), 198–199.

52. Marx and Engels, *The Holy Family*, 52–53, italics in original.

53. In the last chapter of *Capital*, Marx seemed to be moving away from his longstanding conception of an "objective" class identity. He wrote, "What constitutes a class?—and the reply to this follows naturally from the reply to another question, namely: What makes wage-labourers, capitalists, and landlords, constitute the three great social classes?" And he went on to say, "*At first glance*—the identity of revenues and sources of revenue," which would seem to suggest that he was about to change his mind (or at least to offer an amendment). However, since the manuscript broke off at just this point, the amendment was never developed. See *Capital* 3:886, italics mine.

54. Marx and Engels, *The Holy Family*, 52, 53.

55. Marx further clarifies this point in his preface to *A Contribution to the Critique of Political Economy* (1859), where he suggests that "the bourgeois mode of production is the *last* antagonistic form of the social process of production, . . . but the productive forces developing within bourgeois society create also the material conditions for a *solution* of this antagonism" (21, italics mine).

56. Karl Marx, *Critique of the Gotha Programme* (New York: International Publishers, 1966), 10.

57. Louis Althusser, *For Marx*, trans. Ben Brewster (New York: Vintage, 1970), 127, 197.

58. See, for example, Althusser's "Contradiction and Overdetermination," and "On the Materialist Dialectic," in *For Marx*, 87–128, 161–218; see also Louis Althusser and Etienne Balibar, "Marxism Is Not a Historicism," in *Reading Capital*, trans. Ben Brewster (London: NLB, 1975), 119–144.

59. Althusser, *For Marx*, 203, italics in original.

60. For example, in all his writings, and especially in "On the Materialist Dialectic," Althusser refers routinely to a "pre-given complex structured whole."

61. For an illuminating discussion, along the axis of gender, of this individualist deployment of difference in the service of identity, see Mary Poovey, *Uneven Developments: The Ideological Work of Gender in Mid-Victorian England* (Chicago: University of Chicago Press, 1988).

62. Marx, *Capital*, 1:354, 351, 356, 351.

63. In this sense, Marx's position in *Capital* actually represents a retreat from (and a simplifying of) his earlier position, articulated for example in *The German Ideology*, where he concedes the involuntary character of the social division of labor and at least entertains the possibility of a parallel between it and the industrial division of labor. See *The German Ideology*, 22.

64. Emile Durkheim, *The Division of Labor in Society*, trans. George Simpson (New York: Free Press, 1964), 41.

65. Marx's economism is qualified, of course, by his observation, in his

unfinished 1857 "Introduction" to the *Critique* (subsequently published as the "Introduction" to the *Grundrisse*), about the "uneven development of material production relative to e.g. artistic development" and (he further adds) "legal relations" (*Grundrisse*, 109). The phrase "uneven development" has been a major inspiration for political theorists and literary critics, though it remains asserted rather than elaborated in Marx. And, in any case, since the 1857 "Introduction" was not published until 1903 in *Die Neue Zeit*, and the *Grundrisse* not published until 1939 in Moscow, Durkheim certainly would not have known about it when he published *The Division of Labor in Society* in 1893.

66. Anthony Giddens has since revised Durkheim into an impressive nonfunctionalist theory of structuration. See, for example, his *Central Problems in Social Theory* (Berkeley: University of California Press, 1979).

67. This is Durkheim's central argument in *The Division of Labor in Society*. See especially 70–173, 256–282, 329–352.

68. Ernesto Laclau and Chantal Mouffe, *Hegemony and Socialist Strategy: Towards a Radical Democratic Politics* (London: Verso, 1985), esp. 93–148; quotation from 95.

69. Charles Taylor, *Sources of the Self*, 186.

70. The scholarship on this point is voluminous. For a standard account, see Anthony Kenny, *Descartes* (New York: Random House, 1968), 96–125.

71. My previous book, *Empire for Liberty: Melville and the Poetics of Individualism* (Princeton: Princeton University Press, 1989) was certainly one example of this practice. But then, that book was among distinguished company.

72. Herman Melville, "The Paradise of Bachelors and the Tartarus of Maids," in *The Piazza Tales and Other Prose Pieces*, ed. Harrison Hayford et al. (Evanston and Chicago: Northwestern University Press and the Newberry Library, 1987), 316. All subsequent citations to this edition will appear in the text.

73. Eve Kosofsky Sedgwick, *Between Men: English Literature and Male Homosocial Desire* (New York: Columbia University Press, 1985), esp. 83–96.

74. Francis J. Grund, *The Americans in Their Moral, Social, and Political Relations* (London: Longman, Rees, Orme, Brown, Green, and Longman, 1837), 2:1–2, italics in original.

75. Henry Ward Beecher, *Lectures to Young Men* (1844; rpt. New York: J. C. Derby, 1856), 35–36.

76. Henry Ward Beecher, *Norwood: or, Village Life in New England* (New York: Charles Scribner, 1868), 23, 24.

77. Henry Ward Beecher, "Dream-Culture," in *Star Papers: Experiences of Art and Nature* (New York: J. C. Derby, 1855), 263, 268, 263, 269.

78. Nor was this the only occasion he was known to do so. William C. McLoughlin, for example, has compared Beecher's "massive inconsistency" to Whitman's. See *The Meaning of Henry Ward Beecher: An Essay on the Shifting Values of Mid-Victorian America, 1840–1870* (New York: Knopf, 1970), 30.

79. This was true not just of America, but also of industrial England. See, for example, E. P. Thompson's seminal essay, "Time, Work-Discipline, and Industrial Capitalism," *Past and Present* 38 (December 1967): 56–97.

80. James Leonard Corning, *The Christian Law of Amusement* (Buffalo: Phinney and Co., 1859), 7.

81. The historian Daniel T. Rodgers, puzzling over these seeming contradictions, has come up with what seems to be a crucial organizing principle: "The sermons explicitly directed at the young, the poor, or the working class tended also to be those in which the gospel of work was most prominent; in thinking of the prosperous, overtaxed businessmen in his congregation he often chose the counsel of leisure." See Rodgers, *The Work Ethic in Industrial America, 1850–1920* (Chicago: University of Chicago Press, 1978), 98.

82. Beecher, *Norwood*, 16. The idea that leisure is properly enjoyed only by those entitled to it is not unique to Beecher, of course. Joseph Addison, for example, in *The Spectator* 411 (June 21, 1712), had long ago suggested that "there are, indeed, but very few who know how to be idle and innocent, or have a relish of any pleasures that are not criminal." I am indebted to John Buck for bringing this citation to my attention.

83. Henry Ward Beecher, "Popular Amusements," in *Lectures to Young Men*, 215–251, quotations from 249, 250, 251. As Lawrence Levine has persuasively demonstrated, the theater was popular entertainment in the nineteenth century, quite different from the exclusive pastime it has become today. See "William Shakespeare in America," in his *Highbrow/Lowbrow: The Emergence of Cultural Hierarchy in America* (Cambridge: Harvard University Press, 1988), 11–82.

84. Beecher, preface to *Star Papers*.

85. See Richard H. Brodhead, *Culture of Letters* (Chicago: University of Chicago Press, 1993).

86. The allure of such a world as found in "The Paradise of Bachelors" was personally experienced by Melville himself during his visit to London in December 1849, when he was wined and dined by the literary and legal community.

87. Robert K. Martin has argued for an affirmative view of male friendship in Melville. See his *Hero, Captain, and Stranger: Male Friendship, Social Critique, and Literary Form in the Sea Novels of Herman Melville* (Chapel Hill: University of North Carolina Press, 1986). For a contrary account (emphasizing Melville's complex relation to homophobia), see Eve Kosofsky Sedgwick, *Epistemology of the Closet* (Berkeley: University of California Press, 1990), 91–130.

88. Judith A. McGaw, *Most Wonderful Machine: Mechanization and Social Change in Berkshire Paper Making, 1801–1885* (Princeton: Princeton University Press, 1987), 335.

89. Joan Wallach Scott, " 'L'ouvrière! Mot impie, sordide . . .': Women Workers in the Discourse of French Political Economy," in her *Gender and the Politics of History* (New York: Columbia University Press, 1988), 139–163, quotations from 158, 155.

90. The pioneering and still useful account of the doctrine is Barbara Welter, "The Cult of True Womanhood, 1820–1860," *American Quarterly* 18 (1966): 151–174. Since then, a vast body of scholarship has sprung up on the subject.

For a good summary of the now diverse positions, see Linda Kerber, "Separate Spheres, Female Worlds, Woman's Place: The Rhetoric of Women's History," *Journal of American History* 75 (1988): 9–39.

91. "Scribbling women" is Hawthorne's phrase, not Melville's. For Melville's anxieties about authorship, see Michael Newbury, "Figurations of Authorship in Antebellum America" (Ph.D. diss., Yale University, 1992). See also Michael T. Gilmore, *American Romanticism and the Marketplace* (Chicago: University of Chicago Press, 1985).

92. For extensive discussions of this point, see Thomas Bender, *Toward an Urban Vision: Ideas and Institutions in Nineteenth Century America* (Baltimore: Johns Hopkins University Press, 1975), 21–93; John F. Kasson, *Civilizing the Machine: Technology and Republican Values in America, 1776–1900* (New York: Penguin, 1977), 53–106.

93. Charles Dickens, *American Notes* (1842; rpt. New York: St. Martin's Press, 1985), 60–61.

94. William Scoresby, *American Factories and Their Female Operatives* (1845; rpt. New York: Burt Franklin, 1968), 54, 55, 69, 82, 88, 51.

95. Christine Stansell, for example, has emphasized the benefits of factory work, as opposed to the take-home "outwork," which not only paid less but also "bolstered up older forms of partriarchal supervision and curtailed the ways in which single women could turn manufacturing work to the uses of independence." See her *City of Women: Sex and Class in New York, 1789–1860* (Urbana: University of Illinois Press, 1987). The upbeat conclusions of Stansell (and Thomas Dublin, discussed below) need to be supplemented, however, by the work of other historians, who call attention to the persistent low pay, the job segregation, and the failure of women workers to break free from traditional families. See, for example, Mary Blewett, *Men, Women, and Work: A Study of Class, Gender, and Protest in the Nineteenth-Century Shoe Industry* (Urbana: University of Illinois Press, 1988), and McGaw, *Most Wonderful Machine.* For critiques of mainstream labor history as insufficiently attentive to questions of gender, see Sally Alexander, Anna Davin, and Eve Hostettler, "Labouring Women: A Reply to Eric Hobsbawm," *History Workshop* 8 (Autumn 1979): 174–182; Joan Wallach Scott, "Women in *The Making of the English Working Class*," in her *Gender and the Politics of History,* 68–92; Susan Levine, "Class and Gender: Herbert Gutman and the Women of 'Shoe City,' " *Labor History* 29 (1988): 344–355; Alice Kessler-Harris, "Gender Ideology in Historical Reconstruction," *Gender and History* 1 (1989): 31–49, esp. 31–37. For a useful survey of the vast scholarship on this subject, see Ava Baron, "Gender and Labor History," in *Work Engendered,* ed. Ava Baron (Ithaca: Cornell University Press, 1991), 1–46. For a more general discussion of the methodological entanglements between Marxism and feminism, see Heidi Hartmann, "The Unhappy Marriage of Marxism and Feminism: Towards a More Progressive Union," in *Women and Revolution: A Discussion of the Unhappy Marriage of Marxism and Feminism,* ed. Lydia Sargent (Boston: South End Press, 1981), 1–42.

96. Thomas Dublin, *Women at Work: The Transformation of Work and Community in Lowell, Massachusetts, 1826–1860* (New York: Columbia University Press, 1979), quotation from 89. I should point out that in his recent work, Dublin has somewhat qualified this enthusiastic account. See his *Transformation of Women's Work: New England Lives in the Industrial Revolution* (Ithaca: Cornell University Press, 1994).

97. This is, in fact, something of a convention in their writings. Harriet Hanson Robinson insists, for example, "When I look back into the factory life of fifty or sixty years ago, I do not see what is called 'a class' of young men and women going to and from their daily work, like so many ants that cannot be distinguished one from another" (*Loom and Spindle, or Life among the Early Mill Girls* [1898; rpt. Kailua, Hawaii: Press Pacifica, 1976], 37). In the same vein, Lucy Larcom suggests that every woman should "ask herself whether she would like to hear herself or her sister spoken of as a shop-girl, or a factory-girl, or a servant-girl," and "if she would shrink from it a little, then she is a little inhuman when she puts her unknown human sisters who are so occupied into a class" (*A New England Girlhood* [1899; rpt. Gloucester, Mass.: Peter Smith, 1973], 200). For a parallel argument about the nonintegral "multiple consciousness" of black women in the twentieth century, see Angela P. Harris, "Race and Essentialism in Feminist Legal Theory," *Stanford Law Review* 42 (1990): 581–616.

98. *The Lowell Offering: Writings by New England Mill Women (1840–1845)*, ed. Benita Eisler (Philadelphia: J. B. Lippincott, 1977), 52.

99. Ibid., 53.

100. Robinson, *Loom and Spindle*, 43.

101. Here, I am giving voice to a position well articulated by women historians. See, for example, Sally Alexander, "Women, Class, and Sexual Difference," *History Workshop* 17 (Autumn 1984): 125–149; Ava Baron, "Women and the Making of the American Working Class: A Study of the Proletarianization of Printers," *Review of Radical Political Economics* 14 (Fall 1982): 23–42; Emily Hicks, "Cultural Marxism: Nonsynchrony and Feminist Practice," in *Women and Revolution*, ed. Sargent, 219–238; Sonya Rose, "Gender at Work: Sex, Class, and Industrial Capitalism," *History Workshop* 21 (Spring 1986): 113–121; Joan Wallach Scott, "Work Identities for Men and Women," in her *Gender and the Politics of History*, 93–112.

102. Larcom, *A New England Girlhood*, 178–179.

103. Ibid., 223.

104. Nell Kull, " 'I Can Never Be So Happy There among All Those Mountains': The Letters of Sally Rice," *Vermont History* 38 (1970): 49–57, quoted in Dublin, *Women at Work*, 37.

105. For an important collection of letters by the factory women, see *Farm to Factory: Women's Letters, 1830–1860*, ed. Thomas Dublin (New York: Columbia University Press, 1981). Also valuable is the Harriet Hanson Robinson Collection at the Schlesinger Library, Radcliffe College, which includes letters from the Currier sisters.

106. Rebecca Harding Davis, *Life in the Iron Mills* (Old Westbury, N.Y.: Feminist Press, 1972), 22. All subsequent citations to this edition will appear in the text.

3. LUCK AND LOVE

1. Jorge Luis Borges, "The Lottery in Babylon," in his *Labyrinths*, ed. Donald A. Yates and James E. Irby (New York: New Directions, 1964), 30, 34.

2. Barbara Goodwin, *Justice by Lottery* (Chicago: University of Chicago Press, 1992).

3. James Wycliffe Headlam-Morley, *Election by Lot at Athens* (Cambridge: Cambridge University Press, 1933), 2.

4. E. S. Staveley, *Greek and Roman Voting and Elections* (Ithaca: Cornell University Press, 1972), 61–72.

5. Calabresi and Bobbitt took this phrase from William Arrowsmith, who speaks of "a nightmare of justice in which the assertion of any right involves a further wrong, in which fate is set against fate in an intolerable necessary sequence of violence." See his *Tragedy: Vision and Form*, ed. William Corrigan (San Francisco: Chandler Publishing, 1965), 332.

6. Guido Calabresi and Philip Bobbitt, *Tragic Choices* (New York: Norton, 1978), 18, 41, 44.

7. Bernard Williams, *Moral Luck* (Cambridge: Cambridge University Press, 1981), 18.

8. Robert Nozick (a philosopher I never expect to agree with!) has recently argued that "many of philosophy's traditional problems have turned out to be intractable and resistant to rational resolution [because] these problems may result from attempts to extend rationality beyond its delimited evolutionary function." Among those problems he includes the problem of "justifying goals." See his *The Nature of Rationality* (Princeton: Princeton University Press, 1993), esp. 133–139.

9. Bernard Williams, *Moral Luck*, and *Ethics and the Limits of Philosophy* (Cambridge: Harvard University Press, 1985). See also the important essay by Thomas Nagel, "Moral Luck" (in which he discusses our "fractional" contribution to the effects of our action), in *Mortal Questions* (New York: Cambridge University Press, 1979). For a collection of essays on this subject, see *Moral Luck*, ed. Daniel Statman (Albany: SUNY Press, 1993). Relatedly, also see Judith Shklar's brilliant analysis of the unstable distinction between "misfortune" and "injustice" in *The Faces of Injustice* (New Haven: Yale University Press, 1990).

10. Williams's example (after Charles Fried's) is the absurdity of justification when a man saves his wife rather than a stranger when those two are in equal peril.

11. This is, I think, a fairly standard summary of Kant's *Groundwork of the Metaphysics of Morals* (1785) and *Critique of Practical Reason* (1788).

12. See Jon Elster, *Ulysses and the Sirens: Studies in Rationality and Irrationality* (Cambridge: Cambridge University Press, 1984), and *Solomonic Judge-*

ments: Studies in the Limitations of Rationality (Cambridge: Cambridge University Press, 1989). Quotation from *Solomonic Judgements,* 121.

13. It might seem odd to speak of Christian theology in terms of luck, but here I claim the precedent of Bernard Williams, who writes, "the idea that one's whole life can in some such way be rendered immune to luck has perhaps rarely prevailed (it did not prevail, for instance, in mainstream Christianity)." See *Moral Luck,* 20. Also, we might want to consider the intimate ties between Christianity and magic, analyzed by Keith Thomas and David Hall, among others. See Keith Thomas, *Religion and the Decline of Magic* (New York: Scribners, 1971); David D. Hall, *Worlds of Wonder, Days of Judgment: Popular Religious Belief in Early New England* (Cambridge: Harvard University Press, 1989).

14. Jonathan Edwards, "God Glorified in Man's Dependence," in *The Works of President Edwards,* vol. 4, *Containing Forty Sermons on Various Subjects* (New York: Leavitt and Allen, 1858), 172. This sermon, delivered before an expectant Boston audience in 1731, was the first sermon published by Edwards.

15. Immanuel Kant, *Groundwork of the Metaphysics of Morals,* trans. H. J. Paton (New York: Harper, 1964), 57.

16. For a classic statement, see David Ross, *The Right and the Good* (Oxford: Clarendon Press, 1930). For a vigorous defense of desert and a response to Rawls, see George Sher, *Desert* (Princeton: Princeton University Press, 1987). Robert Nozick, in the face of Rawls's argument against desert, has retreated however to the weaker claim of "entitlement" as the ground of distributive justice. See Nozick, *Anarchy, State, and Utopia* (New York: Basic Books, 1974), 185–231.

17. John Rawls, *A Theory of Justice* (Cambridge: Harvard University Press, 1971), 310–315, quotation from 314.

18. Ibid., 75.

19. Ibid., 74.

20. Nozick, *Anarchy, State, and Utopia,* 219.

21. Rawls, *A Theory of Justice,* 3.

22. Ibid., 12.

23. In his most recent work, *Political Liberalism* (New York: Columbia University Press, 1993), Rawls has put considerable distance between himself and Kant. He insists, for example, that justice as fairness is "political constructivism," as opposed to Kant's "moral constructivism." However, the difference here is a difference in scope, not a difference in their commitment to the categorical.

24. In *Political Liberalism,* Rawls argues that much of the criticism directed at his abstract conception of the person comes from not seeing the veil of ignorance as a hypothetical construct. To my mind, however, this abstractness governs not only the specific device of the veil of ignorance but also his general conception of political personhood.

25. Rawls, *A Theory of Justice,* 15.

26. Ibid., 47. See also 491, where Rawls once again compares ethical understanding to grammatical knowledge.

27. Noam Chomsky, *Syntactic Structures* (The Hague: Mouton, 1957), 5.

28. A cursory list of semantic theorists would include Rudolf Carnap, Donald Davidson, Michael Dummett, Hilary Putnam, W. V. Quine, Alfred Tarski, the later Wittgenstein, and Paul Ziff. Some of these, needless to say, themselves have complicated arguments about the analyzability of semantics. (Quine, for example, argues against the factuality of semantics in favor of its indeterminacy.)

29. Chomsky, *Syntactic Structures*, 100, 101, 106.

30. Chomsky's own impatience with semantics, of course, has not prevented other Chomskian linguists from trying to work out a generative semantic theory. See, for example, Jerrold J. Katz and Jerry A. Fodor, "The Structure of a Semantic Theory," in *The Structure of Language: Readings in the Philosophy of Language*, ed. Jerry A. Fodor and Jerrold J. Katz (Englewood Cliffs, N.J.: Prentice-Hall, 1964), 479–518.

31. For that reason, poetry, a linguistic *performance* if ever there is one, would also make no analytic sense to Chomsky. John Hollander seems to have this in mind when he incorporates a sentence Chomsky finds nonsensical ("Colorless green ideas sleep furiously") into his poem "Coiled Alizarine," his playful tribute and gentle rebuke to Chomsky.

32. This point emerges most clearly in Chomsky's critique of Paul Grice, Peter Strawson, and especially John Searle. See Chomsky, "The Object of Inquiry," in his *Reflections on Language* (New York: Pantheon, 1975), esp. 53–77. For a useful (and complexly qualifying) account of this debate, see Michael Dummett, "Language and Communication," in *Reflections on Chomsky*, ed. Alexander George (Oxford: Basil Blackwell, 1989), 192–212.

33. Noam Chomsky, *Cartesian Linguistics: A Chapter in the History of Rationalist Thought* (New York: Harper and Row, 1966), and *Language and Mind*, enlarged ed. (New York: Harcourt Brace Jovanovich, 1972), 1–23.

34. Chomsky, *Language and Mind*, 12.

35. Noam Chomsky, *Aspects of the Theory of Syntax* (Cambridge: MIT Press, 1965), 58.

36. Ludwig Wittgenstein, *Philosophical Investigations*, trans. G. E. M. Anscombe, 3rd ed. (New York: Basil Blackwell, 1958), §373.

37. Ludwig Wittgenstein, *Philosophical Grammar*, ed. Rush Rhees, trans. Anthony Kenny (Oxford: Basil Blackwell, 1974), part 1, §§104, 23.

38. Ibid., part 1, §133.

39. Wittgenstein, *Philosophical Investigations*, §19.

40. J. S. Thompson, "The Reactionary Idealist Foundation of Noam Chomsky's Linguistics," *Literature and Ideology* 4 (1969): 1–20.

41. "Linguistics and Politics: Interview with Noam Chomsky," *New Left Review* 57 (September–October 1969): 21–34, quotation from 31–32.

42. Chomsky, "On Cognitive Capacity," in *Reflections on Language*, 4.

43. On the whole, Chomsky is much more impressed by Descartes than he is by Kant, whom he tends to assimilate into the Cartesian tradition, noting that Kant's ideas are "rather similar" to the "rich and varied work of seventeenth-century rationalists." See *Reflections on Language*, 7, also 131.

44. Chomsky's commitment to civil disobedience is well known. For Rawls's detailed discussion of this subject, see *A Theory of Justice*, 363–391.

45. Ludwig Wittgenstein, *Tractatus Logico-Philosophicus*, trans. D. F. Pears and B. F. McGuinness (London: Routledge and Kegan Paul, 1961), 6.341.

46. Rawls himself has now come to concede this point. In *Political Liberalism*, acknowledging that his theory of justice is not and cannot be a comprehensive doctrine, he forthrightly says, "The idea of political justice does not cover everything, nor should we expect it to." And he goes on, "Political justice needs always to be complemented by other virtues" (21).

47. Rawls, *A Theory of Justice*, 494–495.

48. Gregory Vlastos, "The Individual as Object of Love in Plato's Dialogues," in his *Platonic Studies* (Princeton: Princeton University Press, 1973), 1–34, quotation from 32.

49. Michael Sandel, *Liberalism and the Limits of Justice* (Cambridge: Cambridge University Press, 1982), 181.

50. Rawls, *A Theory of Justice*, 191. Susan Moller Okin has critiqued this neglect of feeling in Rawls as part of his Kantian heritage. See Okin, "Reason and Feeling in Thinking about Justice," *Ethics* 99 (1989): 229–249. See also her *Justice, Gender, and the Family* (New York: Basic Books, 1989). Okin's critique, however, does not extend to the ideal of justice, which remains for her a foundational ideal.

51. Kant, *Groundwork of the Metaphysics of Morals*, passim, quotation from 66.

52. Ibid., 66.

53. Walt Whitman, "Song of Myself," in *Leaves of Grass: The First (1855) Edition*, ed. Malcolm Cowley (New York: Viking, 1959), 28, ellipses in original. All subsequent citations to this edition will appear in the text.

54. My argument here parallels Philip Fisher's, in his discussion of Whitman's democratic poetics as an "aesthetics of the social space." See Fisher, "Democratic Social Space: Whitman, Melville, and the Promise of American Transparency," *Representations*, no. 24 (1988): 60–101.

55. Allen Grossman has written that Whitman's is "a world composed of a limitless series of brilliant finite events each of which imposed closure at the grammatical end of its account." See his "The Poetics of Union in Whitman and Lincoln," in *The American Renaissance Reconsidered: Selected Papers from the English Institute, 1982–83*, ed. Walter Benn Michaels and Donald E. Pease (Baltimore: Johns Hopkins University Press, 1985), 183–208, quotation from 189.

56. Allen Grossman is exactly right, I think, when he writes that "the fullness of articulation of Whitman's poem" depends "on the failed predecessor system of which all that survives is love without an object" (ibid., 199).

57. For a fine reading of this detail, see Karen Sanchez-Eppler, *Touching Liberty: Abolition, Feminism, and the Politics of the Body* (Berkeley: University of California Press, 1993), 77.

58. Michael Sandel, "The Procedural Republic and the Unencumbered Self," *Political Theory* 12 (1984): 81–96.

59. Kant, *Groundwork of the Metaphysics of Morals*, 105.

60. The literature on this subject is formidable. See, for example, Paul Ziff, *Semantic Analysis* (Ithaca: Cornell University Press, 1960); Jerry A. Fodor and Jerrold J. Katz, "The Structure of a Semantic Theory," *Language* 39 (1963): 170–210; reprinted in *The Structure of Language*, ed. Fodor and Katz, 479–518. For more recent discussions, see Norbert Hornstein, "Meaning and the Mental: The Problem of Semantics after Chomsky," in *Reflections on Chomsky*, ed. George, 23–40, and Dummett, "Language and Communication."

61. John Searle, "Chomsky's Revolution in Linguistics," *The New York Review of Books* June 29, 1972, 16–24, reprinted in *On Noam Chomsky*, ed. Gilbert Harman (Garden City, N.Y.: Anchor Press, 1974), 2–33.

62. J. L. Austin, "A Plea for Excuses," *Philosophical Papers*, 3rd ed. (Oxford: Clarendon Press, 1979), 201.

63. Mikhail Bakhtin, *The Dialogic Imagination*, ed. Michael Holquist, trans. Caryl Emerson and Michael Holquist (Austin: University of Texas Press, 1981), 293.

64. Quoted by Horace Traubel in his foreword to *The American Primer* (1904; rpt. Stevens Point, Wis.: Holy Cow! Press, 1987), viii–ix.

65. Martha C. Nussbaum, *The Fragility of Goodness: Luck and Ethics in Greek Tragedy and Philosophy* (New York: Cambridge University Press, 1986).

66. The charge of sentimentalism, influentially leveled by Ann Douglas in her *The Feminization of American Culture* (New York: Knopf, 1977), has actually not been disputed by Jane Tompkins in her equally influential defense of the women writers in *Sensational Designs: The Cultural Work of American Fiction* (New York: Oxford University Press, 1985).

67. Susan Warner, *The Wide, Wide World* (1850; rpt. New York: Feminist Press, 1987), 208. All subsequent citations to this edition will appear in the text.

68. Warner's father was ruined in the panic of 1837, and the family had to move from New York to Constitution Island, where Warner began writing novels to support her family and where she and her sister Anna remained for the rest of their lives.

69. The Catholic Church refers to Augustine as *Doctor Gratiae*. As Albert C. Outler notes in his introduction to Augustine, "The central theme in all of Augustine's writings is the sovereign God of grace and the sovereign grace of God." See *Confessions and Enchiridion*, ed. and trans. Albert C. Outler (Philadelphia: Westminster Press, 1955), 14. See also Jaroslav Pelikan's excellent discussion of Augustine's "paradox of grace" in *The Emergence of the Catholic Tradition (100–600)*, vol. 1 of *The Christian Tradition* (Chicago: University of Chicago Press, 1971), 292–307.

70. Augustine, *Enchiridion*, in *Confessions and Enchiridion*, §107 (404).

71. Augustine, *On Christian Doctrine*, trans. D. W. Robertson (Indianapolis: Bobbs-Merrill, 1958), 23.

72. Augustine, *Enchiridion*, §§99, 107 (pp. 398, 404). The quotation "God maketh one vessel for honorable, another for ignoble use" is from Proverbs 8:35.

73. Jaroslav Pelikan, *The Growth of Medieval Theology (600–1300)*, vol. 2 of *The Christian Tradition* (Chicago: University of Chicago Press, 1978), 81. My discussion of Augustine and of Luther (to follow) is heavily indebted to this magisterial study.

74. Martin Luther, *Lectures on the First Epistle of St. John* (1527), trans. Walter A. Hansen, *Luther's Works* (St. Louis: Concordia Publishing House, 1956), 30:300.

75. The phrase, "I, Martin Luther, Augustinian," appeared in the letter to Mayor Muhlphordt, appended to *The Freedom of a Christian* (1520), trans. W. A. Lambert, rev. Harold J. Grimm, *Luther's Works*, 31:333.

76. Martin Luther, *Lectures on Galatians, Chapters 1–4* (1535), trans. Jaroslav Pelikan, *Luther's Works*, 26:377.

77. The verse is "And because you are sons, God has sent the Spirit of His Son into your hearts" (Galatians 4:6).

78. Luther, *Lectures on Galatians, Chapters 1–4*, 386–387, 380, 386, 387.

79. Ibid., 375.

80. *The Bondage of the Will*, a polemic against Erasmus, was considered by Luther himself to be one of his two or three best works.

81. Martin Luther, *The Bondage of the Will* (1525), trans. Philip S. Watson, *Luther's Works*, 33:37, 38, 43, 291.

82. John Calvin, *The Institutes of the Christian Religion*, ed. John T. McNeill, trans. Ford Lewis Battles (Philadelphia: Westminster Press, 1960), 205–212.

83. As Philip S. Watson points out in his notes to *The Bondage of the Will*, Luther is actually using the word "contingent" rather imprecisely, since he interprets "contingency" as virtually equivalent to "chance," as the Schoolmen did not. In Scholastic theology a distinction is made between *necessitas consequentiae* ("necessity of consequence") and *necessitas consequentis* ("necessity of the thing consequent"). The latter is absolute, but the former is conditional and includes contingency as part of its workings. Luther's imprecision has been noted by Erasmus as well, who, in his reply, said that most Christian theologians "define 'contingent' rather more accurately than you do."

84. Luther, *Lectures on Galatians, Chapters 1–4*, 226–227.

85. Luther, *Lectures on the First Epistle of St. John*, 311.

86. Ibid.

87. Luther, *Lectures on Galatians, Chapters 1–4*, 231, 226.

88. Against Max Weber's emphasis on the connection between Reformation theology and economic discipline (in *The Protestant Ethic and the Spirit of Capitalism*), Michael Walzer emphasizes the connection between Reformation theology and political discipline. See Walzer, *The Revolution of the Saints* (Cambridge: Harvard University Press, 1965), quotation from 25–26.

89. Since much of my discussion will appear as a critique of Luther, I want to take this opportunity to acknowledge an aspect of Luther not emphasized in this chapter. In the same commentary on Galatians 4:6 in which Luther so frequently used the word "certainty," he also wrote movingly about the "sigh" uttered by the Holy Spirit when Moses, pursued by the

Egyptians, "saw the very presence of death in the water and wherever he turned his gaze," and became "thoroughly terrified." Then the Holy Spirit

> emits what seems to us to be some sort of sob and sigh of the heart; but in the sight of God this is a loud cry and a sigh too deep for words. . . . Then the Father says: "I do not hear anything in the whole world except this single sigh, which is such a loud cry in My ears that it fills heaven and earth and drowns out all the cries of everything else." You will notice that Paul does not say that the Spirit intercedes for us in temptation with a long prayer, but that He intercedes with a sigh.

See *Lectures on Galatians, Chapters 1–4*, 384–385.

90. Sacvan Bercovitch, *The American Jeremiad* (Madison: University of Wisconsin Press, 1978).

91. Luther, *Lectures on Galatians, Chapters 1–4*, 124, 127, 128.

92. Augustine, *Confessions*, in *Confessions and Enchiridion*, Book 10, §6 (pp. 205–206).

93. Augustine, *On Christian Doctrine*, 9, 18, 10. Augustine here also distinguishes between two kinds of love, the love that uses and the love that enjoys, our relation to God being inimitably a case of the latter but also supremely a case of the latter.

94. Interestingly, Luther did critique Augustine for giving too little attention to faith: "In Augustine one finds too little faith, in Jerome none at all. No one among the ancient teachers is sincere to the extent that he teaches the pure faith" (*Lectures on the First Epistle of St. John*, 313).

95. Luther, *Lectures on Galatians, Chapters 1–4*, 127, 129.

96. Ibid., 129.

97. Luther, *The Freedom of a Christian*, 367.

98. Edward Taylor, *Preparatory Meditations*, First Series, no. 12, in *The Poems of Edward Taylor*, ed. Donald E. Stanford (New Haven: Yale University Press, 1960), 25.

99. Of course, Taylor also wrote (and perhaps is better known for) many other poems, not about the delights of loving God but about a debilitating sense of personal unworthiness.

100. Stanley Fish argues for the importance of Augustine to Donne and Herbert; Louis Martz argues for the importance of the medieval heritage to metaphysical poetry in general; Barbara Kiefer Lewalski argues against both Fish and Martz in presenting the metaphysical poets not as the tag-ends of medieval or Counter Reformation spirituality, but as pioneers of a Protestant poetics. However, since this Protestant poetics owes its vitality to the continuing presence of Augustine and to the poetic genres of the Bible, Lewalski's work actually supports my point here about the "historical memory" of Protestantism. See Fish, *Self-Consuming Artifacts* (Berkeley: University of California Press, 1972); Martz, *The Poetry of Meditation* (New Haven: Yale University Press, 1954); Lewalski, *Protestant Poetics and the Seventeenth-Century Religious Lyric* (Princeton: Princeton University Press, 1979).

101. David Hall, *Worlds of Wonder, Days of Judgment*, 11, and "The World

of Print and Collective Mentality in Seventeenth-Century New England," in *New Directions in American Intellectual History*, ed. John Higham and Paul Conkin (Baltimore: Johns Hopkins University Press, 1979), 169.

102. Sydney E. Ahlstrom, introduction to *Theology in America* (Indianapolis: Bobbs-Merrill, 1967), 24.

103. Perry Miller, *The New England Mind: The Seventeenth Century* (New York: Macmillan, 1939), 3–34.

104. For an account of the "multivocal" religious culture in Massachusetts, see Janice Knight, *Orthodoxies in Massachusetts* (Cambridge: Harvard University Press, 1994). For an account of the heterogeneity of popular religion, see Jon Butler, *Awash in a Sea of Faith: Christianizing the American People* (Cambridge: Harvard University Press, 1990).

105. Ahlstrom, introduction to *Theology in America*, 23.

106. Douglas, *The Feminization of American Culture*, 74–75.

107. For a suggestive reading of Edwards along these lines, see Sandra Gustafson, "Jonathan Edwards and the Reconstruction of 'Feminine' Speech," *American Literary History* 6 (1994): 185–212.

108. Jonathan Edwards, *A Treatise Concerning Religious Affections*, ed. John E. Smith, vol. 2 of *Works of Jonathan Edwards* (New Haven: Yale University Press, 1959), 107, 108.

109. Ibid., 100.

110. Ibid., 96.

111. To a modern reader, Locke uses the word "preference" in a rather peculiar way. A typical construction is: a man "prefers his not falling to falling," or "a Man would preferr flying to walking." In other words, the phenomenon of preference is related to the question of free agency. But Locke is also careful to distinguish between preference and volition ("Preference, which seems perhaps best to express the Act of Volition, does it not precisely"). See *An Essay Concerning Human Understanding*, ed. Peter H. Nidditch (1690; rpt. Oxford: Clarendon Press, 1979), II.xxi.5–15 (236–241). Edwards, on the other hand, uses the word "preference" in a way much closer to our modern usage, relating it, that is, to our likes and dislikes. Perry Miller has presented Locke as the "central and decisive event" in Edwards's intellectual life. This view has now been challenged, especially by Norman Fiering. See Miller, *Jonathan Edwards* (New York: William Sloane, 1949), 52; Fiering, *Jonathan Edwards's Moral Thought and Its British Context* (Chapel Hill: University of North Carolina Press, 1981), 35–40.

112. Edwards, *A Treatise Concerning Religious Affections*, 97.

113. In this sense, Edwards's position is actually surprisingly close to Hobbes's. Hobbes writes, "Every man, for his own part, calleth that which pleaseth, and is delightful to himself, good; and that evil which displeaseth him. . . . And as we call good and evil the things that please and displease; so call we goodness and badness, the qualities or powers whereby they do it." See Hobbes, *The English Works of Thomas Hobbes of Malmesbury*, ed. Sir William Molesworth (Aalen, Germany: Scientia, 1962), 4:32.

114. Jonathan Edwards, *Concerning the End for Which God Created the World*, in *Ethical Writings*, ed. Paul Ramsey, vol 8. of *Works of Jonathan Edwards* (New Haven: Yale University Press, 1989), 422.

115. Ibid., 446.

116. Jonathan Edwards, "Love More Excellent than Extraordinary Gifts of the Spirit" (sermon), in *Ethical Writings*, 160.

117. Edwards, *Concerning the End*, 419.

118. Alan Heimert, *Religion and the American Mind: From the Great Awakening to the Revolution* (Cambridge: Harvard University Press, 1966), 108–112; Fiering, *Jonathan Edwards's Moral Thought*, 126.

119. Edwards, *The Nature of True Virtue*, in *Ethical Writings*, 568.

120. Ibid., 569, italics in original.

121. Edwards defines "a sense of *desert*" as "that sense of *justice*, before spoken of, consisting in an apprehension of that secondary beauty that lies in uniformity and proportion. . . . Which is indeed a kind of moral sense, or sense of a beauty in moral things. But, as was before shown, it is a moral sense of a *secondary* kind, and is entirely different from a sense or relish of the original essential beauty of true virtue" (ibid., 582, italics in original).

122. Ibid., 573. I should point out, of course, that Edwards is not unguilty of aestheticism himself, since he defines "true virtue" as that which "is beautiful by a general beauty" (540).

123. Ibid., 540.

4. PAIN AND COMPENSATION

1. Richard A. Posner, *The Economics of Justice* (Cambridge: Harvard University Press, 1981), 1.

2. This movement, especially powerful in the field of torts, is usually understood to have begun in the 1960s with Guido Calabresi and Ronald Coase. See Calabresi, "Some Thoughts on Risk Distribution and the Law of Torts," *Yale Law Journal* 70 (1961): 499–553; Coase, "The Problem of Social Cost," *Journal of Law and Economics* 1 (1960): 3–7.

3. Beginning with his 1957 dissertation on the economics of racial discrimination, Gary Becker has argued forcefully for the centrality of economic reasoning even in supposedly nonmarket domains (including the utilization of time, crime and prosecution, choice of marriage partners, reproduction, adultery, and suicide). For a classic statement of this economic fundamentalism, see Becker, *The Economic Approach to Human Behavior* (Chicago: University of Chicago Press, 1976).

4. Posner, *The Economics of Justice*, 1, 2, 3, 60, 87.

5. Howells, *The Rise of Silas Lapham*, ed. Walter J. Meserve and David J. Nordloh (Bloomington: Indiana University Press, 1977), 241. All subsequent citations to this edition will appear in the text.

6. Jeremy Bentham, *A Fragment on Government*, ed. F. C. Montague (Oxford: Oxford University Press, 1951), 93.

7. John Stuart Mill, *Utilitarianism,* in *Essential Works of John Stuart Mill,* ed. Max Lerner (New York: Bantam, 1961), 194.

8. Jeremy Bentham, *Works,* ed. John Bowring (New York: Russell and Russell, 1962), 1:31, italics in the original.

9. For one example of such critique, see George Fletcher, "Why Kant," *Columbia Law Review* 87 (1987): 421–432. Interestingly, Fletcher sees not only Law and Economics but also Critical Legal Studies as descendants of utilitarianism.

10. Posner, *The Economics of Justice,* 48, 33, 2.

11. On this point, see my introduction. Posner mentions Aristotle in passing, although oddly enough he seems to associate Aristotle only with corrective justice, whereas the discussion of justice in the *Nicomachean Ethics* is actually much broader in scope. See Posner, *The Economics of Justice,* 73.

12. Theodor W. Adorno and Max Horkheimer, *Dialectic of Enlightenment,* trans. John Cumming (New York: Continuum, 1989), 7, 6, 10, 7, 13, 10. The quotation from Bacon is from *Advancement of Learning,* in *The Works of Francis Bacon,* ed. Basil Montagu (London: W. Pickering, 1825), 2:126.

13. Descartes's influence on the Enlightenment is a much debated matter. An authoritative account is Ernst Cassirer, *Philosophy of the Enlightenment,* trans. Fritz C. A. Koelln and James P. Pettegrove (Boston: Beacon Press, 1955). For a valuable summary and partisan statement, see Aram Vartanian, *Diderot and Descartes: A Study of Scientific Naturalism in the Enlightenment* (Princeton: Princeton University Press, 1963). For the influence of Descartes in England, see Rosalie Colie, *Light and Enlightenment: A Study of the Cambridge Platonists and the Dutch Arminians* (Cambridge: Cambridge University Press, 1957). See also the excellent bibliographical essay appended to Peter Gay, *The Enlightenment: The Science of Freedom* (New York: Norton, 1977), 617–620.

14. Thomas Hobbes, *De Cive,* in *Man and Citizen,* ed. Bernard Gert (Indianapolis: Hackett, 1991), 91.

15. But see also Richard McKeon, *The Philosophy of Spinoza* (New York: Longmans, Green and Co., 1928), 153–157, 161–165, for an account of Spinoza's reservations about the mathematical model.

16. Quoted in John Grier Hibben, *The Philosophy of the Enlightenment* (New York: Scribner's, 1910), 165. It is fair to say, however, that this was a youthful remark; later in his life, Leibniz was not so confident. See, for example, his letter to Remond, in Ernst Cassirer, *The Platonic Renaissance in England,* trans. James P. Pettegrove (Austin: University of Texas Press, 1953), 152.

17. Locke, *An Essay Concerning Human Understanding,* ed. Peter H. Nidditch (Oxford: Clarendon Press, 1979), II.xvi.1 (205), italics in original.

18. Ibid., III.xi.16 (516), italics in original.

19. Garry Wills, *Inventing America: Jefferson's Declaration of Independence* (New York: Vintage, 1979), 151.

20. Bentham, *Works,* 3:286–287. For Bentham's indebtedness to (and divergence from) Beccaria, see H. L. A. Hart, "Bentham and Beccaria," in his *Essays on Bentham* (Oxford: Clarendon Press, 1982), 40–52.

21. The authoritative accounts remain Leslie Stephen, *English Utilitarians* (1900; rpt. New York: P. Smith, 1950), and *History of English Thought in the Eighteenth Century*, 3rd ed., vol. 2 (1876; rpt. New York: P. Smith, 1949). See also Ernest Albee, *A History of English Utilitarianism* (New York: Macmillan, 1902), 1–190; John Plamenatz, *The English Utilitarians* (Oxford: Basil Blackwell, 1949), 22–58; Anthony Quinton, *Utilitarian Ethics* (London: Macmillan, 1973), 11–26.

22. William Wollaston, for example, in his influential *Religion of Nature Delineated* (London: S. Palmer, 1724), had done much the same thing, and with the same degree of obsessiveness. A representative passage from Wollaston reads as follows (35–36):

> When pleasures and pains are equal, they mutually destroy each other; when the one exceeds, the excess gives the true quantity of pleasure or pain. For nine degrees of pleasure, less by nine degrees of pain, are equal to nothing; but nine degrees of one, less by three degrees of the other, give six of the former net and true. . . . [T]he man who enjoys three degrees of such pleasure as will bring upon him nine degrees of pain, when three degrees of pain are set off to balance and sink the three of pleasure, can have remaining to him only six degrees of pain[.]

23. Robert Shackleton, "The Greatest Happiness of the Greatest Number: The History of Bentham's Phrase," first published in *Studies in Voltaire and the Eighteenth Century* (1972), reprinted in *Essays on Montesquieu and on the Enlightenment*, ed. David Gilson and Martin Smith (Oxford: Voltaire Foundation, 1988), 375–89.

24. Francis Hutcheson, *Inquiry into the Original of Our Ideas of Beauty and Virtue* (1725; rpt. Hildesheim: Olms, 1971), 1:163–164.

25. For Bentham's *lack* of influence, see P. A. Palmer, "Benthamism in England and America," *American Political Science Review* 35 (1941): 855–871; C. W. Everett, "Bentham in the United States of America," in *Jeremy Bentham and the Law*, ed. George W. Keeton and Georg Schwarzenberger (London: Stevens, 1948), 185–201. However, as I have been arguing, we should perhaps look at Bentham not as an isolated figure but as part of a broad intellectual tradition. For Bentham's influence on American legal thought, see Peter J. King, *Utilitarian Jurisprudence in America: The Influence of Bentham and Austin on American Legal Thought in the Nineteenth Century* (New York: Garland, 1986). For Bentham's influence on William Paley's "theological utilitarianism" as well as Paley's influence in America, see Wilson Smith, *Professors and Public Ethics: Studies of Northern Moral Philosophers before the Civil War* (Ithaca: Cornell University Press, 1956), 44–73; Herbert Schneider, *A History of American Philosophy* (New York: Columbia University Press, 1946), 37–42.

26. For an excellent account of the interchangeability of the moral and the economic in Adam Smith, see Istvan Hont and Michael Ignatieff, "Needs and Justice in the *Wealth of Nations*," in *Wealth and Virtue: The Shaping of Political Economy in the Scottish Enlightenment*, ed. Istvan Hont and Michael Ignatieff (Cambridge: Cambridge University Press, 1983), 1–44. The literature on the subject is voluminous. See also Glenn Morrow, *The Ethical and Economic Theo-*

ries of Adam Smith (New York: A. M. Kelley, 1969); Hiroshi Mizuta, "Moral Philosophy and Civil Society," in *Essays on Adam Smith*, ed. Andrew S. Skinner and Thomas Wilson (Oxford: Clarendon Press, 1975); Ralph Anspach, "The Implications of *The Theory of Moral Sentiments* for Adam Smith's Economic Thought," *History of Political Economy* 4 (1972): 176–194; Nathan Rosenberg, "Adam Smith and the Stock of Moral Capital," *History of Political Economy* 22 (1990): 1–17. I don't mean to suggest, of course, that the discipline of economics is exclusively traceable only to moral philosophy. For alternative genealogies, see William Letwin, *The Origins of Scientific Economics* (Garden City, N.Y.: Doubleday, 1964). For a complex account of the relations between "political arithmetic," moral philosophy, and political economy, see Mary Poovey, "Toward a History of Classificatory Thinking," in *Rethinking Class*, ed. Wai Chee Dimock and Michael Gilmore (New York: Columbia University Press, 1994), 15–56.

27. Terence Martin, *The Instructed Vision: Scottish Common Sense Philosophy and the Origins of American Fiction* (Bloomington: Indiana University Press, 1961).

28. Henry F. May, *The Enlightenment in America* (New York: Oxford University Press, 1976), 346.

29. Oddly, the seminal essay undermining the centrality of Locke is by a leading Locke scholar. See John Dunn, "The Politics of Locke in England and America in the Eighteenth Century," in *John Locke: Problems and Perspectives*, ed. John Yolton (London: Cambridge University Press, 1969), 45–80. On classical republicanism, see above, chapter 2. Garry Wills has argued most strenuously for the centrality of the Scottish Enlightenment. See his *Inventing America*, and *Explaining America: The Federalist* (Garden City, N.Y.: Doubleday, 1981). For a critique, see Ronald Hamowy, "Jefferson and the Scottish Enlightenment: A Critique of Garry Wills' *Inventing America*," *William and Mary Quarterly*, 3rd ser., 36 (1979): 503–523. For connections between classical republicanism and the Scottish Enlightenment, see John Robertson, "The Scottish Enlightenment at the Limits of the Civic Tradition"; Nicholas Phillipson, "Adam Smith as Civic Moralist"; J. G. A. Pocock, "Cambridge Paradigms and Scotch Philosophers," all in *Wealth and Virtue*, ed. Hont and Ignatieff, 137–178, 179–202, 235–252.

30. Donald Meyer, *The Instructed Conscience: The Shaping of the American National Ethic* (Philadelphia: University of Pennsylvania Press, 1972); Wilson Smith, *Professors and Public Ethics*, 3–43; Douglas Sloan, *The Scottish Enlightenment and the American College Ideal* (New York: Teachers College Press, 1971), 73–184; David Fate Norton, "Francis Hutcheson in America," *Studies on Voltaire and the Eighteenth Century* 154 (1976): 1547–1568; Norman S. Fiering, "President Samuel Johnson and the Circle of Knowledge," *William and Mary Quarterly*, 3rd ser., 28 (1971): 199–236.

31. The other three divisions were natural theology, ethics, and jurisprudence. See Dugald Stewart, "Account of the Life and Writings of Adam Smith," in Adam Smith, *Essays on Philosophical Subjects*, ed. W. P. D. Wightman and J. C. Bryce (Oxford: Clarendon Press, 1980), 273–275.

32. For an account of Wayland, see Joseph Blau, *Men and Movements in American Philosophy* (Westport, Conn.: Greenwood Press, 1977), 82–92. See also Joseph Dorfman, *The Economic Mind in American Civilization, 1606–1865* (New York: Viking, 1946), 2:758–767.

33. For an amusing account of the "overworked" Alford Professor, see Bruce Kuklick, *The Rise of American Philosophy* (New Haven: Yale University Press, 1977), xv–xvi, 28–45.

34. Francis Wayland, *The Elements of Political Economy* (New York: Leavitt, Lord and Co., 1837), vi.

35. Albert O. Hirschman, *The Passions and the Interests* (Princeton: Princeton University Press, 1977). I should point out that for Hirschman, "passions" are associated primarily with the political sphere and not with the moral. The relation he examines is thus between the economy and the polity (in a sustained disagreement with Joseph Cropsey's *Polity and Economy*). However, as his own discussions of Hume and Adam Smith suggest, the economic would seem to be a moral instrumentality as well. See especially 48–66, 108–110.

36. John McVickar, *Outlines of Political Economy* (New York: Wilder and Campbell, 1825), 186–187. Quoted in Gladys Bryson, "Emergence of the Social Sciences from Moral Philosophy," *International Journal of Ethics* 42 (1931–1932): 304–323, quotation from 311.

37. A nineteenth-century descendent of utilitarianism, "marginal utility analysis" was developed by William Stanley Jevons in England and Karl Menger in Austria.

38. These arguments were developed by Patten in *The Stability of Prices* (Baltimore: American Economic Association, 1889); in an essay entitled "The Effect of the Consumption of Wealth on the Economic Welfare of Society," in *Science Economic Discussion*, ed. Richard T. Ely (New York: The Science Company, 1886), 123–135; and in *The Consumption of Wealth* (Philadelphia: T. and J. W. Johnson, 1889). For a useful discussion of Patten, see Daniel M. Fox, *The Discovery of Abundance: Simon N. Patten and the Transformation of Social Theory* (Ithaca: Cornell University Press, 1967).

39. Simon Nelson Patten, *The Theory of Social Forces* (1896; rpt. New York: Kraus Reprint, 1970), 75–108, quotation from 76.

40. Morton White, *Social Thought in America: The Revolt against Formalism* (Boston: Beacon Press, 1957), 14.

41. In particular, I would disagree with White's characterization of Holmes, who, far from recoiling from utilitarianism, was on record stating just the opposite. Holmes wrote, "For the philosophy of law, the *Fragment on Government* and Austin's lecture are worth the whole corpus [of Roman law]" from "Value of Precedent," *American Law Review* 7 (1873): 579, reprinted in *Justice Oliver Wendell Holmes—His Book Notices, Uncollected Letters, and Papers*, ed. Harry C. Shriver (New York: Central Book Co., 1936), 34–35. For a detailed discussion, see H. L. Pohlman, *Justice Oliver Wendell Holmes and Utilitarian Jurisprudence* (Cambridge: Harvard University Press, 1984).

42. Simon Nelson Patten, *The New Basis of Civilization*, ed. Daniel M. Fox

(1907; rpt. Cambridge: Harvard University Press, 1968), 145–164, quotation from 149.

43. Patten, *The Theory of Social Forces*, 77, 122.

44. G. Edward White, *Tort Law in America: An Intellectual History* (New York: Oxford University Press, 1980), xvi.

45. For a fuller discussion of penal reform, see chapter 1.

46. For a parallel argument about the persisting vitality of utilitarianism in late-nineteenth-century England, see Ellen Frankel Paul, *Moral Revolution and Economic Science* (Westport, Conn.: Greenwood Press, 1979).

47. David Rothman, *The Discovery of the Asylum: Social Order and Disorder in the New Republic* (Boston: Little, Brown, 1971), 155–179; Paul Boyer, *Urban Masses and Moral Order in America, 1820–1920* (Cambridge: Harvard University Press, 1978); Alan Trachtenberg, *The Incorporation of America: Culture and Society in the Gilded Age* (New York: Hill and Wang, 1982), 101–139. For a parallel account of humanitarianism in England, see Gertrude Himmelfarb, *Poverty and Compassion: The Moral Imagination of the Late Victorians* (New York: Vintage, 1992).

48. Quoted in Asa Briggs, "The Human Aggregate," in *The Victorian City: Images and Realities*, ed. H. J. Dyos and Michael Wolff (London: Routledge, 1973), 1:87.

49. Stuart Blumin, "Explaining the New Metropolis: Perception, Depiction, and Analysis in Mid-Nineteenth-Century New York City," *Journal of Urban History* 11 (1984): 9.

50. Boyer, *Urban Masses and Moral Order in America*, 123–124.

51. Ibid., 146.

52. My argument here about "rational benevolence" in organized charities parallels Lori Ginzberg's argument about the "passion for efficiency" in civil war relief. See Ginzberg, *Women and the Work of Benevolence: Morality, Politics, and Class in the Nineteenth-Century United States* (New Haven: Yale University Press, 1990).

53. Josephine Shaw Lowell, *Public Relief and Private Charity* (1884; rpt. New York: Arno Press, 1971), 90.

54. Ibid., 89, 111.

55. Ibid., 58, italics mine.

56. Ibid., 89, 90, 66, 103.

57. Herbert Spencer, *Social Statics* (1850; rpt. New York: Appleton, 1882), 353, 355.

58. Lowell, *Public Relief and Private Charity*, 104–105, 94, italics in original.

59. Thomas Haskell, "Capitalism and the Origins of the Humanitarian Sensibility," parts 1 and 2, *American Historical Review* 90 (1985): 339–361, 547–566. See also the AHR Forum on Haskell's essay, with responses to Haskell from David Brion Davis and John Ashworth and a further response from Haskell himself, in *American Historical Review* 92 (1987): 797–878. For the ongoing debate, see *The Antislavery Debate: Capitalism and Abolitionism as a Problem in Historical Interpretation*, ed. Thomas Bender (Berkeley: University of California Press, 1992).

60. I am indebted to Richard Brodhead for suggesting this important qualification to the Haskell thesis.

61. Lowell, *Public Relief and Private Charity*, 69.

62. S. Humphreys Gurteen, *A Handbook of Charity Organization* (Buffalo: The Courier Company, 1882), 205.

63. William Graham Sumner, "The Shifting of Responsibility," *The Independent*, March 24, 1887, collected in *Essays of William Graham Sumner*, ed. Albert Galloway Keller and Maurice R. Davie (New Haven: Yale University Press, 1934), 1:260–265.

64. William Graham Sumner, *What Social Classes Owe to Each Other* (1883; rpt. Los Angeles: Caldwell, Idaho, Caxton Printers, 1952), 11.

65. William Graham Sumner, "The Forgotten Man," in *Essays*, 1:483, 479, 477, 486, 481, 483.

66. Sumner, *What Social Classes Owe to Each Other*, 98.

67. Francis Wayland, *The Limitations of Human Responsibility* (Boston: Gould, Kendall and Lincoln, 1838), 19.

68. Ibid., 162, 181–182.

69. *The Elements of Moral Science*, for example, sold more than two hundred thousand copies in the sixty years after its publication. See Blau, *Men and Movements*, 86.

70. See Lawrence M. Friedman and Jack Ladinsky, "Social Change and the Law of Industrial Accidents," *Columbia Law Review* 67 (1967): 53.

71. Lawrence M. Friedman, *A History of American Law*, 2nd ed. (New York: Simon and Schuster, 1985), 468.

72. Another interesting juncture is the rise of life insurance. For an account of that development, see Viviana Zelizer, *Morals and Markets: The Rise of Life Insurance* (New York: Columbia University Press, 1979).

73. Friedman, *History of American Law*, 299–302, 467–487; Morton J. Horwitz, *The Transformation of American Law, 1780–1860* (Cambridge: Harvard University Press, 1977), 63–108, 201–210. See also Charles O. Gregory, "Trespass to Negligence to Absolute Liability," *Virginia Law Review* 37 (1951): 359–397. For a dissent from the Horwitz-Friedman position, see Gary Schwartz, "Tort Law and the Economy in Nineteenth-Century America: A Reinterpretation," *Yale Law Journal* 90 (1981): 1717–1775.

74. For a discussion of Holmes and liability, see Grant Gilmore, *The Death of Contract* (Columbus: Ohio State University Press, 1974).

75. Oliver Wendell Holmes, *The Common Law* (1881; rpt. Boston: Little Brown, 1946), 17, 90, 96, 79, 94.

76. See the preface to *Towards a Jurisprudence of Injury*, a 1984 report to the American Bar Association.

77. Oliver Wendell Holmes, "The Path of the Law," *Harvard Law Review* 10 (1897): 459–460.

78. See Richard A. Posner, "A Theory of Negligence," *Journal of Legal Studies* 1 (1972): 27–96. See also *Law, Economics, and Philosophy*, ed. Mark Kuperberg and Charles Beitz (Totowa, N.J.: Rowman and Allenheld, 1983); William Landes and Richard Posner, *Economic Structure of Tort Law* (Cambridge:

Harvard University Press, 1987); Steven Shavell, *Economic Analysis of Accident Law* (Cambridge: Harvard University Press, 1987). For contemporary approaches to torts different from the above, see George P. Fletcher, "Fairness and Utility in Tort Theory," *Harvard Law Review* 85 (1972): 537–573; Robert Epstein, "A Theory of Strict Liability," *Journal of Legal Studies* 2 (1973): 151–204; E. Weinrib, "Toward a Moral Theory of Negligence Law," *Law and Philosophy* 2 (1983): 37–62.

79. For the relation between Holmes and Peirce, see Note, "Holmes, Peirce, and Legal Pragmatism," *Yale Law Journal* 84 (1975): 1123; Herbert Hovenkamp, "Pragmatic Realism and Proximate Cause in America," *Journal of Legal History* 3 (1982): 3–30. For the relation between Holmes and Green, see Philip Wiener's chapter on "The Pragmatic Legal Philosophy of Nicholas St. John Green," in his *Evolution and the Founders of Pragmatism* (Cambridge: Harvard University Press, 1949), 152–171.

80. Morton J. Horwitz, "The Doctrine of Objective Causation," in *The Politics of Law*, ed. David Kairys (New York: Pantheon, 1982), 201–213. For a more general discussion of the legal significance of causation, see H. L. A. Hart and A. M. Honore, *Causation in the Law* (Oxford: Clarendon Press, 1985); Robert E. Keeton, *Legal Cause in the Law of Torts* (Columbus: Ohio State University Press, 1963).

81. *Stone v. Boston and Albany Railroad Co.* 51 N.E. 1 (Mass., 1898); *Central of Georgia Railway Co. v. Price*, 32 S.E. 77 (Ga., 1898). Discussed in Hovenkamp, "Pragmatic Realism," 4.

82. Francis Wharton, "The Liability of Railway Companies for Remote Fires," *Southern Law Review* 1 (1876), 729.

83. Ibid., 745, 730, 746.

84. Francis Wharton, *A Suggestion as to Causation* (Cambridge, Mass.: Riverside Press, 1874), 8; also published as appendix to *Treatise on the Law of Negligence* (Philadelphia: Kay and Brother, 1874).

85. Wharton, "Liability of Railroad Companies," 732, 744.

86. Ibid., 739, 733.

87. Herbert Spencer, *The Data of Ethics* (New York: A. L. Burt, 1879), subsequently published as part 1 of *The Principles of Ethics* (New York: Appleton, 1892), quotations from 1:186, 183, 176, 175. As Spencer notes in his 1893 General Preface, the ideas assembled here "date back to 1851," and "it yields me no small satisfaction to find that these ideas which fell dead in 1850, have now become generally diffused" and "have met with so wide an acceptance that the majority of recent works on Ethics take cognizance of them."

88. Martin Pernick, *A Calculus of Suffering: Pain, Professionalism, and Anesthesia in Nineteenth-Century America* (New York: Columbia University Press, 1985).

89. Thomas Trotter, *A View of the Nervous Temperament; Being a Practical Inquiry into the Increasing Prevalence, Prevention, and Treatment of Those Diseases Commonly Called Nervous, Bilious, Stomach and Liver Complaints* (1808; rpt. New York: Arno Press, 1976), 21–22.

90. Pernick, *A Calculus of Suffering*, 148–157.

91. S. Weir Mitchell, "Civilization and Pain," originally published in *Annals of Hygiene*, summarized in *Journal of the American Medical Association* 18 (1892): 108. This is the same Dr. S. Weir Mitchell who prescribed the rest cure to Charlotte Perkins Gilman, a treatment she attacked in *The Yellow Wallpaper*.

92. Benjamin Rush, "Medicine among the Indians of North America: A Discussion" (1774), in his *Selected Writings*, ed. Dagobert D. Runes (New York: Philosophical Library, 1947), 259.

93. A. P. Merrill, "An Essay on Some of the Distinctive Peculiarities of the Negro Race," *Memphis Medical Recorder* 4 (1855): 67, quoted in Pernick, *A Calculus of Suffering*, 155. Blacks were understood to have a hereditary disease called "dyaesthesia Aethiopsis," which induced in them an "obtuse sensibility of body."

94. Horace Mann, "Twelfth Annual Report" (1848), in his *Annual Reports on Education* (Boston: Lee and Shepard, 1872), 676.

95. Letter of John William De Forest to his brother, November 27, 1863, De Forest Papers, Yale University Library. Quoted in George M. Fredrickson, *The Inner Civil War: Northern Intellectuals and the Crisis of the Union* (New York: Harper and Row, 1965), 87.

96. Lydia Maria Child, *An Appeal in Favor of That Class of Americans Called Africans* (Boston: Allen and Ticknor, 1833), 189.

97. Spencer, *Principles of Ethics*, 1:vii, 186.

98. Herbert Spencer, *First Principles*, 3rd ed. (London: Williams and Norgate, 1870), 489–490.

99. Spencer, *Principles of Ethics*, 1:x, 373, 372, 369.

100. I have taken this phrase from Bernard Williams, who calls attention to the "imperfect rationalisation" in any ethical theory that aspires to be a "model of theoretical rationality and adequacy." See Williams, *Moral Luck* (New York: Cambridge University Press, 1981), 81.

101. Here, I want both to acknowledge my indebtedness to Fredric Jameson and to distinguish my usage from his. For Jameson, "cognitive mapping" is a gesture toward some unrepresentable social totality; for me, "cognitive mapping" unsettles the very notion of totality. See Jameson, "Cognitive Mapping," in *Marxism and the Interpretation of Culture*, ed. Laurence Grossberg and Cary Nelson (Urbana: University of Illinois Press, 1988), 347–357.

102. William Dean Howells, *The Minister's Charge*, ed. Howard Munford, David Nordloh, and David Kleinman (Bloomington: Indiana University Press, 1978), 139. For an interesting discussion of this novel (focusing on the relation between language and complicity), see Elsa Nettels, *Language, Race, and Social Class in Howells' America* (Lexington: University Press of Kentucky, 1988), 153–162.

103. The classic statement on the "incommensurability of paradigms" is, of course, Thomas Kuhn, *The Structures of Scientific Revolution* (Chicago: University of Chicago Press, 1962).

104. Thomas Laqueur also commented on the linkage between humanitarianism and the novel. See his "Bodies, Details, and the Humanitarian Nar-

rative," in *The New Cultural History*, ed. Lynn Hunt (Berkeley: University of California Press, 1989).

105. Here, I would simply like to acknowledge my indebtedness to Anthony Giddens's important "antifunctionalist" theory of society, especially his emphasis on time and space. See, for example, his *Central Problems in Social Theory* (Berkeley: University of California Press, 1979), and *A Contemporary Critique of Historical Materialism* (Berkeley: University of California Press, 1981).

106. In this context, it is interesting to speculate on the "superfluous" in other literary forms as well. See, for example, Richard Poirier, "Superfluous Emerson," in his *Poetry and Pragmatism* (Cambridge: Harvard University Press, 1992), 37–75. For an implicit argument against using engineering as a model for literary analysis, see Martha Banta, *Taylored Lives: Narrative Productions in the Age of Taylor, Veblen, and Ford* (Chicago: University of Chicago Press, 1993).

107. In this sense, my book is a sustained argument with Walter Benn Michaels, *The Gold Standard and the Logic of Naturalism* (Berkeley: University of California Press, 1987).

108. William Dean Howells, "Editor's Study," *Harper's* 72 (May 1886): 973.

109. William Dean Howells, "Concerning a Counsel of Imperfection," *Literature* 1 (April 7, 1899): 290.

110. William Dean Howells, "The Man of Letters as a Man of Business," in his *Literature and Life* (New York: Harper and Brothers, 1902), 33–34.

111. Howells, letter to Roger A. Pryor, chief counsel of the anarchists, November 4, 1887, published in the *New York Tribune*, November 6, 1887, under the headline "Clemency for the Anarchists. A letter from Mr. W. D. Howells." William Dean Howells Papers, Houghton Library, Harvard University.

112. Howells to Francis Fisher Browne, November 4, 1887. Howells had written the letter with the understanding that it would be published, as indeed it was—in the *Chicago Tribune*, November 8, 1887. William Dean Howells Papers, Houghton Library, Harvard University.

113. See, for instance, Donald Pizer, *Realism and Naturalism in Nineteenth-Century American Literature* (Carbondale: Southern Illinois University Press, 1966); Harold Kolb, *The Illusion of Life: American Realism as a Literary Form* (Charlottesville: University of North Carolina Press, 1969); Edwin H. Cady, *The Light of Common Day: Realism in American Fiction* (Bloomington: Indiana University Press, 1971). For qualifying views, see Kermit Vanderbilt, *The Achievement of William Dean Howells* (Princeton: Princeton University Press, 1968); Henry Nash Smith, "Fiction and the American Ideology: The Genesis of Howells' Early Realism," in *The American Self*, ed. San Girgus (Albuquerque: University of New Mexico Press, 1981), 43–57.

114. In fact, as Patrick Dooley points out, contemporary readers of Howells "often focused on the love plot [and] all but ignored the bankruptcy plot." See "Nineteenth-Century Business Ethics and *The Rise of Silas Lapham*," *American Studies* 21 (1980): 79–93.

115. William Dean Howells, "Equality as the Basis of Good Society," *Century* 51 (November 1895): 64, 63, 64, 63.

116. Henry James, *The Bostonians* (Harmondsworth: Penguin, 1966), 390.

117. Alfred Habegger has also noted the less than happy endings in Howells and James. He sees those endings, however, as a protest by male authors against the "fantasy" endings of "women's fiction." See his *Gender, Fantasy, and Realism in American Literature* (New York: Columbia University Press, 1982), 109–110.

5. RIGHTS AND REASON

1. Mary Ann Glendon, *Rights Talk: The Impoverishment of Political Discourse* (New York: Free Press, 1991), x–xii.

2. See, for example, Roberto Unger, *Knowledge and Politics* (New York: Free Press, 1975); Duncan Kennedy, "The Structure of Blackstone's Commentaries," *Buffalo Law Review* 28 (1979): 205–382. See also a special issue of the *Texas Law Review*, "Symposium: A Critique of Rights," *Texas Law Review* 62 (1984): 1363–1617, especially Mark Tushnet, "An Essay on Rights," 1363–1403, and Allan C. Hutchinson and Patrick J. Monahan, "The 'Rights' Stuff: Roberto Unger and Beyond," 1477–1539.

3. The prime example here is J. G. A. Pocock. See, for example, his "Virtues, Rights, and Manners: A Model for Historians of Political Thought," *Political Theory* 9 (1981): 353–368; reprinted in Pocock, *Virtue, Commerce, and History* (New York: Cambridge University Press, 1985), 37–50. Pocock's advocacy of classical republicanism is, of course, more fully articulated in *The Machiavellian Moment: Florentine Political Thought and the Atlantic Republican Tradition* (Princeton: Princeton University Press, 1975).

4. Glendon herself is a communitarian. See also Alasdair MacIntyre, *After Virtue* (Notre Dame: University of Notre Dame Press, 1981); Michael Sandel, *Liberalism and the Limits of Justice* (Cambridge: Cambridge University Press, 1982).

5. Glendon, *Rights Talk*, passim, quotation from xii.

6. Ibid., 9.

7. I might mention, in this context, that Lani Guinier's advocacy of "cumulative voting" represents one of the most imaginative efforts to circumvent this "winner takes all" philosophy.

8. Ronald Dworkin, "Justice and Rights," in his *Taking Rights Seriously* (Cambridge: Harvard University Press, 1977), 177.

9. Ibid., 176, italics in original; Dworkin, "Taking Rights Seriously," in his *Taking Rights Seriously*, 199.

10. Joel Feinberg, "Nature and Value of Rights," *Journal of Value Inquiry* 4 (1970): 243–257; reprinted in his *Rights, Justice, and the Bounds of Liberty* (Princeton: Princeton University Press, 1980), 151.

11. Thomas Hobbes, *De Homine*, in *Man and Citizen*, ed. Bernard Gert (Indianapolis: Hackett, 1991), 47, italics in original.

12. Ian Shapiro, *The Evolution of Rights in Liberal Theory* (New York: Cambridge University Press, 1986), 48, 47.

13. It is worth pointing out that *A Letter Concerning Toleration, An Essay Concerning Human Understanding*, and the *Two Treatises of Government* were all published in the space of two years: the *Letter* in 1689, the *Essay* and the *Two Treatises* in 1690. James Tully has been especially persuasive in challenging Peter Laslett's view that the *Essay* is irrelevant to the *Two Treatises*. See Tully, *A Discourse on Property: John Locke and His Adversaries* (Cambridge: Cambridge University Press, 1980).

14. As John Dunn long ago pointed out, the starting point for Locke is the "necessary autonomy of individual religious judgment," and the "transposition of this theme from theology and epistemology to sociology and politics made each individual man the final judge" of "the society in which he lived." See Dunn, *The Political Thought of John Locke* (Cambridge: Cambridge University Press, 1969), 39.

15. John Locke, *An Essay Concerning Human Understanding*, ed. Peter H. Nidditch (Oxford: Clarendon Press, 1979), II.xxi.47 (263–264).

16. Ibid., II.xxi.48 (264).

17. John Locke, *A Letter Concerning Toleration*, ed. James H. Tully (Indianapolis: Hackett, 1983), 26, 27, 28, 31.

18. The relative priority of rights or duties in Locke is a much debated matter, one that I do not wish to take up here. For a full discussion, see A. John Simmons, *The Lockean Theory of Rights* (Princeton: Princeton University Press, 1992).

19. John Locke, *Second Treatise of Government*, ed. Thomas Peardon (Indianapolis: Bobbs-Merrill, 1952), 55.

20. John Rawls, *A Theory of Justice* (Cambridge: Harvard University Press, 1971), especially 22–33, 310–315. The commentaries on Rawls are staggering in number. Ronald Dworkin, in particular, has emphasized the importance of rights to Rawls. See Dworkin, "Justice and Rights," 150–183. Also relevant here are *Reading Rawls: Critical Studies of "A Theory of Justice,"* ed. Norman Daniels (New York: 1974); Robert Paul Wolff, *Understanding Rawls: A Reconstruction and Critique of "A Theory of Justice"* (Princeton: Princeton University Press, 1977); James Fishkin, *Tyranny and Legitimacy* (Baltimore: Johns Hopkins University Press, 1979); Sandel, *Liberalism and the Limits of Justice*; Rex Martin, *Rawls and Rights* (Lawrence: University of Kansas Press, 1985); George Sher, *Desert* (Princeton: Princeton University Press, 1987). For my own sustained discussion of Rawls, see chapter 3 of this book.

21. This is the opening statement in Robert Nozick's *Anarchy, State, and Utopia* (New York: Basic Books, 1974). The commentaries on Nozick are likewise voluminous. In fact, most of the aforementioned discussions of Rawls discuss Nozick as well. In addition, see *Reading Nozick: Essays on "Anarchy, State, and Utopia,"* ed. Jeffrey Paul (Oxford: Basil Blackwell, 1982).

22. MacIntyre, *After Virtue*, 69. But also see Richard Tuck, *Natural Rights Theories* (Cambridge: Cambridge University Press, 1979), which, in locating

the origins of natural rights in antiquity, somewhat qualifies MacIntyre's assertion. Also relevant here is Leo Strauss's spirited discussion of "classic natural rights" in *Natural Rights and History* (Chicago: University of Chicago Press, 1953).

23. Robert Filmer, *Patriarcha and Other Political Works*, ed. Peter Laslett (Oxford: Oxford University Press, 1949), 185–231, 241–251.

24. Emile Durkheim, *The Division of Labor in Society*, trans. George Simpson (New York: Free Press, 1933), 116–117.

25. Pocock, "Virtues, Rights, and Manners," 37, 43, 44.

26. Unger, *Knowledge and Politics*, 7.

27. I take this phrase from Lawrence Freidman. See Friedman, *Total Justice* (New York: Russell Sage, 1985).

28. Patricia J. Williams, *The Alchemy of Race and Rights* (Cambridge: Harvard University Press, 1991), 153. See also an earlier essay by Williams, "Alchemical Notes: Reconstructing Ideals from Deconstructed Rights," in *A Less Than Perfect Union: Alternative Perspectives on the U.S. Constitution*, ed. Jules Lobel (New York: Monthly Review Press, 1988), 56–70.

29. Since my reading of *The Awakening* is at odds with most mainstream accounts, I want here simply to acknowledge my disagreement with three influential essays, all of which emphasize the "emancipatory" character of the novel: Elaine Showalter, "Tradition and Female Talent: *The Awakening* as a Solitary Book," in *New Essays on "The Awakening,"* ed. Wendy Martin (New York: Cambridge University Press, 1988), 33–58; Sandra M. Gilbert, "The Second Coming of Aphrodite: Kate Chopin's Fantasy of Desire," *Kenyon Review* 5 (Summer 1983): 42–66; Patricia Yaeger, " 'A Language Which Nobody Understood': Emancipatory Strategies in *The Awakening*," *Novel* 20 (1987): 197–219.

30. Samuel D. Warren and Louis D. Brandeis, "The Right to Privacy," *Harvard Law Review* 4 (1890): 193.

31. Kate Chopin, *The Awakening* (New York: Bantam, 1981), 1. All subsequent citations to this edition will appear in the text.

32. These denials of rights persisted into the twentieth century. See *How Louisiana Laws Discriminated against Women* (Washington, D.C.: National Women's Party, 1922).

33. Warren and Brandeis, "The Right to Privacy," 207, 193, 205, 204, 195, 205, 193.

34. Ibid., 211.

35. Privacy did not become a general unified right in tort law (as articulated by Warren and Brandeis); its crucial importance began only some thirty years later, when it migrated into constitutional law.

36. Locke, *Second Treatise of Government*, 79.

37. Ibid., 17. This image of Locke is, of course, the one that Macpherson wants to perpetuate. For discussions that qualify that image, see Tully, *A Discourse on Property*, 1–94; Alan Ryan, *Property and Political Theory* (Oxford: Basil Blackwell, 1984), 14–48; Richard Ashcraft, *Revolutionary Politics and Locke's Two Treatises of Government* (Princeton: Princeton University Press, 1986), 257–281.

38. This "possessive" aspect of liberal theory is the central emphasis in C. B. Macpherson's *The Political Theory of Possessive Individualism* (Oxford: Oxford University Press, 1962), a book that, not surprisingly, has generated (and continues to generate) a good deal of response, including Ian Shapiro's recent and persuasive objection that Macpherson's "anachronistic" market model fails to provide any *historical* understanding of the political writings of seventeenth-century England. See Shapiro, *The Evolution of Rights in Liberal Theory,* 69–79.

39. Feinberg, "Nature and Value of Rights," 151.

40. Ibid.

41. Richard Flathman, *The Practice of Rights* (New York: Cambridge University Press, 1976), 71.

42. Bentham writes, "It is by imposing obligations, or by abstaining from imposing them, that rights are established or granted. . . . All rights rest therefore upon the idea of obligation as their necessary foundation." See *Works,* ed. John Bowring (New York: Russell and Russell, 1962), 3:181. Wesley Newcomb Hohfeld, while classifying rights into four well-known categories—liberty rights, claim rights, power rights, and immunity rights—also argues that only claim rights can be discussed in a manner that is not "nebulous" and so commits himself to a positivist notion of rights that resembles Bentham's. See his influential *Fundamental Legal Conceptions* (New Haven: Yale University Press, 1919), 38–39. For the relation between Bentham and Hohfeld, see H. L. A. Hart, "Bentham on Legal Rights," in *Oxford Essays in Jurisprudence,* 2nd ser., ed. A. W. B. Simpson (Oxford: Oxford University Press, 1973), 171–201, and Joseph Singer, "The Legal Rights Debate in Analytical Jurisprudence from Bentham to Hohfeld," *Wisconsin Law Review* 6 (1982): 975–1060. Many political theorists, I should also point out, have vigorously disagreed with the notion of "correlativity." For them, rights and duties are neither substantively nor even structurally symmetrical. See, for example, David Lyons, "The Correlativity of Rights and Duties," *Nous* 4 (1970): 45–55.

43. Thomas Hobbes, *Leviathan,* ed. C. B. Macpherson (Harmondsworth: Penguin, 1968), 189–190.

44. Warren and Brandeis, "The Right to Privacy," 213, italics mine.

45. Alan R. White calls attention to this unidiomatic usage: see "Rights and Claims," in *Law, Morality, and Rights,* ed. M. A. Stewart, Royal Institute of Philosophy Conferences, vol. 79 (Dordrecht and Boston: Reidel, 1983), 154. One thinker who is clearly worried about this "against" aspect of rights is H. J. McCloskey, who has tried to theorize about rights simply as abstract entitlement, independent of actual (and potentially coercive) enforcement. See McCloskey, "Rights," *Philosophical Quarterly* 15 (1965): 115–127.

46. Dworkin, "Taking Rights Seriously," 184. As already noted, Dworkin is an outspoken advocate of rights, so it is especially noteworthy that this statement is coming from him.

47. Carl Wellman, "Upholding Legal Rights," *Ethics* 86 (1975): 52.

48. Glendon, *Rights Talk,* 18–46.

49. H. L. A. Hart, "Are There Any Natural Rights?" *Philosophical Review*

64 (1955): 151–191, reprinted in *Rights*, ed. David Lyons (Belmont, Calif.: Wadsworth, 1979), 16.

50. Laurence H. Tribe, "The Abortion Funding Conundrum: Inalienable Rights, Affirmative Duties, and the Dilemma of Dependence," *Harvard Law Review* 99 (1985): 342. For a related argument, see also Tribe, "Foreword: Toward a Model of Roles in the Due Process of Life and Law," *Harvard Law Review* 87 (1973): 1–53, in which he links *Roe v. Wade* to *Lochner*.

51. Catherine MacKinnon, "Privacy v. Equality: Beyond Roe v. Wade," in her *Feminism Unmodified: Discourses on Life and Law* (Cambridge: Harvard University Press, 1987), 94, italics mine.

52. Feinberg, "Nature and Value of Rights," 149.

53. Hart, "Are There Any Natural Rights?" 19.

54. Roberto Unger, *Law in Modern Society* (New York: Free Press, 1976), 85. See also Hendrik Hartog, "The Constitution of Aspiration and 'The Rights that Belong to Us All,'" *Journal of American History* 74 (1987): 1013–1034, esp. 1024–1028.

55. Herbert Morris, "Persons and Punishment," *The Monist* 52 (1968): 499.

56. Joel Feinberg, *Social Philosophy* (Englewood Cliffs, N.J.: Prentice-Hall, 1973), 75.

57. Martha Minow advocates an "interpretive" approach to rights, which, in effect, constitutes all rights as *prima facie* rights. See her "Interpreting Rights: An Essay for Robert Cover," *Yale Law Journal* 96 (1987): 1860–1915. In this context, see also her critique of "Reason" as an abstract norm in *Making All the Difference: Inclusion, Exclusion, and American Law* (Ithaca: Cornell University Press, 1990). For a "moderate historicist" position that not only argues that rights are conventional but defends them as such, see Thomas Haskell, "The Curious Persistence of Rights Talk in the 'Age of Interpretation,'" *Journal of American History* 74 (1987): 984–1012. For an advocacy of *prima facie* rights in an international context, see James W. Nickel, *Making Sense of Human Rights* (Berkeley: University of California Press, 1987).

58. MacIntyre, *After Virtue*, 33.

59. Ralph Waldo Emerson, "Self-Reliance," in *Selections from Ralph Waldo Emerson*, ed. Stephen E. Whicher (Boston: Houghton Mifflin, 1957), 150, italics in original.

60. Ibid., 147.

61. In his important study of evidence and narrative, Alexander Welsh emphasizes the rise of circumstantial evidence as the ground for drawing inferences. See his *Strong Representations: Narrative and Circumstantial Evidence in England* (Baltimore: Johns Hopkins University Press, 1992). Here, I emphasize subjective evidence as the ground for justifying claims.

62. Morton J. Horwitz, *The Transformation of American Law, 1780–1860* (Cambridge: Harvard University Press, 1977), 160–210. But see also A. W. B. Simpson, "The Horwitz Thesis and the History of Contracts," *University of Chicago Law Review* 46 (1979): 542–601, which challenges the sharp distinction Horwitz draws between the eighteenth and the nineteenth centuries.

63. What I am describing here parallels the shift Horwitz himself sug-

gests, namely, from an antebellum "instrumental" conception of the law to a postbellum "formalist" conception. See *The Transformation of American Law*, 253–266.

64. See Eric Foner, *Free Soil, Free Labor, Free Men: The Ideology of the Republican Party before the Civil War* (New York: Oxford University Press, 1970), and *Politics and Ideology in the Age of the Civil War* (New York: Oxford University Press, 1980).

65. Arnold M. Paul, *Conservative Crisis and the Rule of Law: Attitudes of Bar and Bench, 1887–1895* (Ithaca: Cornell University Press, 1960), 235.

66. For a standard account, see Charles W. McCurdy, "Justice Field and the Jurisprudence of Government-Business Relations: Some Parameters of Laissez Faire Constitutionalism, 1863–1897," *Journal of American History* 61 (1975): 970–1005.

67. The first critique of substantive due process is Edward S. Corwin, "The Supreme Court and the Fourteenth Amendment," *Michigan Law Review* 7 (1909): 643–672. Since then, constitutional scholars have united in condemning the doctrine. Indeed, the bad reputation of *Lochner* is such that Morton Horwitz is moved to offer a revisionist reading. See his "History and Theory," *Yale Law Journal* 96 (1987): 1825–1835. For discussions about the expanded role of the Supreme Court, see Raoul Berger, *Government by Judiciary: The Transformation of the Fourteenth Amendment* (Cambridge: Harvard University Press, 1977); Christopher Wolfe, *The Rise of Modern Judicial Review: From Constitutional Interpretation to Judge-Made Law* (New York: Basic Books, 1986), 144–163; William E. Nelson, *The Fourteenth Amendment: From Political Principle to Judicial Doctrine* (Cambridge: Harvard University Press, 1988), 148–200.

68. In *Slaughterhouse*, 16 Wall.36 (1873), the Court upheld a Louisiana legislation creating a monopoly in the New Orleans slaughtering business. However, as legal historians have noted, it is the minority opinion there (put forth by Justice Stephen J. Field) that prevailed as a judicial doctrine in the decades to come.

69. *Lochner v. New York*, 198 U.S. 45, 56, 64 (1905), quoted in Laurence Tribe, *American Constitutional Law* (Mineola, N.Y.: Foundation Press, 1988), 568. The other phrases are quoted in William Nelson, "The Impact of the Antislavery Movement upon Styles of Judicial Reasoning," *Harvard Law Review* 87 (1974): 513–566. Nelson argues for a direct link between the philosophy of natural rights and the doctrine of substantive due process.

70. For the centrality of the substantive in late-nineteenth-century and early-twentieth-century jurisprudence, see Tribe's excellent discussion in *American Constitutional Law*, 560–586.

71. *Lochner* was overturned in 1937, with *West Coast Hotel v. Parrish*, 300 U.S. 379 (1937).

72. *Lochner v. New York*, 198 U.S. 45 (1905).

73. *Adkins v. Children's Hospital*, 261 U.S. 525, 559 (1923). The quotation is from Herbert Hovenkamp, "The Political Economy of Substantive Due Process," *Stanford Law Review* 40 (1988): 380.

74. An even more chilling example is the *Dred Scott* case (1857), also decided by appealing to the "Doctrine of Vested Rights." See Jennifer Nedelsky, *Private Property and the Limits of American Constitutionalism* (Chicago: University of Chicago Press, 1990), 225.

75. The quotation is from Unger, *Knowledge and Politics*, 90, in the context of a larger and more complex argument about liberal psychology and liberal political theory, 29–144.

76. Lafcadio Hearn, "Creole Servant Girls," *New Orleans Item*, December 20, 1880, collected in *Creole Sketches*, ed. Charles Woodward Hutson (Boston: Houghton Mifflin, 1924), 160–162.

77. George Washington Cable, *The Grandissimes* (1879; rpt. New York: Hill and Wang, 1957), 60.

78. As a further point of contrast, it is helpful to compare Chopin's portrait of Désirée in "Désirée's Baby" and Cable's portrait of Madame Delphine in *Old Creole Days*. Désirée is, of course, actually *not* a quadroon, even though she is made to suffer the fate of one. The injustice in Chopin's story is the injustice of a *mistaken* racial identity. Cable's Madame Delphine, by contrast, both suffers the fate of a quadroon and is actually a quadroon. The injustice in his story is the injustice of racial identity itself.

79. For the centrality of composition in *The Awakening*, see Michael T. Gilmore, "Revolt against Nature: The Problematic Modernism of *The Awakening*," in *New Essays on "The Awakening*," 59–87; for other examples of such "compositional" uses of human figures, see Jean-Christophe Agnew, "The House of Fiction," in *Consuming Visions: Accumulation and Display of Goods in America, 1880–1920*, ed. Simon Bronner (New York: Norton, 1989), 133–156.

80. Pertinent to my discussion here is Gayatri Chakravorty Spivak's discussion of the "subaltern subject-effect." See her "Subaltern Studies: Deconstructing Historiography," in her *In Other Worlds: Essays in Cultural Politics* (New York: Methuen, 1988), 204. For two different efforts to reorient the marginality of black women, see Angela P. Harris, "Race and Essentialism in Feminist Legal Theory," *Stanford Law Review* 42 (1990): 581–616, and Kimberle Crenshaw, "Mapping the Margins: Intersectionality, Identity Politics, and Violence against Women of Color," *Stanford Law Review* 43 (1991): 1241–1299.

81. See, for instance, John W. Blassingame, *Black New Orleans* (Chicago: University of Chicago Press, 1973); Dale A. Somers, "Black and White in New Orleans: A Study in Urban Race Relations, 1865–1900," *Journal of Southern History* 40 (1974): 19–42.

82. C. Vann Woodward, *Origins of the New South* (Baton Rouge: Louisiana State University Press, 1971), 211–212; Eric Foner, *Reconstruction* (New York: Harper and Row, 1988), 200–201, 550–551. The White League (formed in 1874) was a group openly advocating the use of violence to restore white supremacy. On Oscar Chopin's membership in this group, see Per Seyersted, *Kate Chopin: A Critical Biography* (Baton Rouge: Louisiana State University Press, 1969), 42, 45, 95.

83. Eric Sundquist, "Mark Twain and Homer Plessy," *Representations*, no.

24 (1988): 102–127; Walter Benn Michaels, "The Souls of White Folks," in *Literature and the Body,* ed. Elaine Scarry (Baltimore: Johns Hopkins University Press, 1988), esp. 188–190; Brook Thomas, "Tragedies of Race, Training, Birth, and Communities of Competent Pudd'nhead," *American Literary History* 1 (1989): 754–785.

84. *Plessy v. Ferguson,* 163 U.S. 537; decision by Justice Henry Billings Brown, May 18, 1896, reprinted in *The Thin Disguise: Turning Point in Negro History. Plessy v. Ferguson: A Documentary Presentation (1864–1896),* ed. Otto H. Olsen (New York: Humanities Press, 1967), 111. For a discussion of this "reasonableness" argument, see also Charles Lofgren, *The Plessy Case* (New York: Oxford University Press, 1987), 183–184.

85. *People v. Gallagher,* 93 N.Y. 438, 448 (1883); cited in the *Plessy* decision by Justice Henry Billings Brown, reprinted in *The Thin Disguise,* 112.

86. Editorial, *New Orleans Times-Democrat,* July 9, 1890, reprinted in *The Thin Disguise,* 53.

87. *The Thin Disguise,* 111–112.

88. Editorial, *New Orleans Times,* May 7, 1867, reprinted in *The Thin Disguise,* 35.

89. Editorial, *New Orleans Times-Democrat,* November 19, 1892, reprinted in *The Thin Disguise,* 70–71.

90. The gravamen of relator's plea, cited by Justice Charles E. Fenner, *Ex parte Homer A. Plessy,* 45 La. Ann. 80; decision by Justice Charles E. Fenner, December 19, 1892, reprinted in *The Thin Disguise,* 71.

91. The analogy between marriage and slavery, I should add, was a standard trope in nineteenth-century feminist rhetoric. See Amy Dru Stanley, "Conjugal Bonds and Wage Labor: Rights of Contract in the Age of Emancipation," *Journal of American History* 75 (1988): 471–500.

92. See William Ivy Hair, *Carnival of Fury: Robert Charles and the New Orleans Race Riot of 1900* (Baton Rouge: Louisiana State University Press, 1976).

93. Richard Wright, "How 'Bigger' Was Born," in *Native Son* (New York: Harper, 1940), xi.

94. *New Orleans Daily Picayune,* June 29, August 1, 1900; *New Orleans Times-Democrat,* August 6, 1900; *New Orleans Southwestern Presbyterian,* August 9, 1900. All quoted in *Carnival of Fury,* 2.

95. *Carnival of Fury,* xiii.

96. *New Orleans Times-Democrat,* July 29, 1900, epigraph to *Carnival of Fury.*

Index of Names

Subject Index

Abortion, 198
Adaptation: to pain, 163–166
Anesthesia: selective, 152, 164, 166
Athenian democracy: and election by
lot, 97

Bachelors: as degenerate aristocrats, 80–
81, 83, 84
Bodily subject, 60–61, 69–74
Body: of Christ, 63–65; and industrial labor, 59–60, 89–92; as legal fiction, 66–
67; materialist, 69–74; and metonymic
thinking, 60–62, 69, 71, 85

Capitalism: and causation, 154–155,
161–162; and humanitarianism, 154–
156. *See also* Economic rationality
Categorical thinking: and justice, 13, 99;
and rights, 183, 188, 190, 197–198, 211,
214–218; and syntax, 105–106, 109,
110, 113
Causation: and capitalism, 154–155,
161–162; and the novel, 167–168, 172–
173; and tort law, 160–163
Charities Organization Movement, 153–
154
Choice: rational, 97–100. *See also* Deliberative rationality; Economic Rationality
Civil war, 157–158; as epistemological
crisis, 208. *See also* Slavery
Classical Republicanism, 13, 36, 42, 48–
49, 147, 182; and political rationality,
42–46, 48. *See also* Liberalism
Cognition: and economic rationality, 12–
13, 140; and the novel, 167–172, 180–
181; and syntax, 107–110. *See also*
Reason
Commensurability, 144; materialist, 60–
62, 67–68, 73–74, 89; moral and economic, 147, 149–150, 155–156, 162,
172; political, 42–48; punitive, 11–19,
53–54; rational, 187, 200–201, 202, 203,
207, 223; reflexive, 50–54, 162–163,
165–166; syntactic, 111, 116–119,
220
Compensatory equilibrium: and evolu-

tionary theory, 163–166; and the
novel, 166–167, 175, 177; and tort law,
159, 161–163
Constitutional law, 193, 195, 207, 209–
210; and racial segregation, 214–217;
and substantive due process, 209–211
Communitarianism, 182
Crime: of anonymity, 30, 35; prevention
of, 15–19; and retribution, 11–12, 19,
54, 55; as signifying field, 25, 26, 31–
34, 37–38, 55; and sin, 20–24, 28
Criminal law, 8; and evolving taxono-
mies, 20–24; and shifting jurisdictions,
20–23; strict construction in, 23–25, 33.
See also Punishment; Punitive rationality
Critical Legal Studies Movement, 182,
189, 199

Death penalty: and Beccaria, 15; and
Kant, 11–12
Deliberative rationality, 97–100, 104–
105, 109
Democracy, 43–44; and affective preferences, 113, 115, 117–118, 123–124; as
epistemology, 104–105; as syntax, 108–
110. *See also* Liberalism; Substitutability; Syntactic equivalents
Desert, 101, 103, 127, 135, 138. *See also*
Justice, distributive

Economic rationality: and humanitarianism, 153–156; and justice, 12–13, 140–
142, 180–181; and morality, 140–142,
147, 149–150, 155–156, 162, 173; and
the novel, 173–177, 180–181; and pain,
141, 142, 151–154, 158, 162–163; and
tort law, 158–163
Enlightenment: and materialism, 67–69;
and punitive rationality, 11–19, 53;
and quantification, 144–149
Evidence: physical, 67–69, 75–76; selective accrediting of, 197, 205–206, 209–
217. *See also* Materialism; Moral subjectivism
Evolution, 163–166

Compositor: Keystone Typesetting, Inc.
Text: 10 / 12 Palatino
Display: Palatino
Printer: Thomson-Shore, Inc.
Binder: Thomson-Shore, Inc.

lit as the residue. the
memives.

vs. Jameson + williams = the
ideological structure